Building Confidence FOR DUMMIES

by Kate Burton and Brinley Platts

JOHN WILEY & SONS, LTD

Building Confidence For Dummies®

Published by
John Wiley & Sons, Ltd
The Atrium
Southern Gate
Chichester
West Sussex
PO19 8SQ
England

E-mail (for orders and customer service enquires): cs-books@wiley.co.uk

Visit our Home Page on www.wileyeurope.com

Copyright © 2006 John Wiley & Sons, Ltd, Chichester, West Sussex, England

Published by John Wiley & Sons, Ltd, Chichester, West Sussex

Wiley also publishes its books in a variety of electronic formats. Some content that appears in print may not be available in electronic books.

British Library Cataloguing in Publication Data: A catalogue record for this book is available from the British Library

ISBN-13: 978-0-470-01669-5

ISBN-10: 0-470-01669-8

Printed and bound in Great Britain by TJ International, Padstow, Cornwall

10 9 8 7 6 5 4 3 2 1

WILEY

About the Authors

Kate Burton is an independent executive coach, author, and trainer who enables individuals and organisations to focus their energy with confidence. She is co-author of the best selling *Neuro-linguistic Programming For Dummies* with Romilla Ready. Her business career began in corporate advertising and marketing with Hewlett-Packard. Since then she has worked with varied businesses across industries and cultures on how they can be great and confident communicators. What she loves most is delivering custom-built coaching and training programmes. She thrives on supporting people in boosting their motivation, self-awareness, and confidence. Her belief is that people all have unique talents, abilities, and core values. The skill is about honouring them to the full.

Brinley Platts is a leading executive coach, researcher, and consultant to FTSE 100 companies. He is one of the UK's leading authorities on CIO and IT executive careers and works with international companies on the integration of senior executive life and career goals. He is a behavioural scientist by training, and his passion is to enable large organisations to become places where ordinary decent people can grow and express their talents freely to the benefit of all stakeholders. He is a co-founder of the Bring YourSELF To Work campaign, which aims to release the pent-up talent and passion of today's global workforce to create the better world we all desire and want our children to inherit.

Authors' Acknowledgments

From Kate: The seeds for this book were sown long ago, so I'd like to acknowledge my teachers who got me curious about this elusive concept of confidence and Margaret who asked the powerful question I wanted to answer: 'So where do you keep your confidence?'

Writing another book is like having another baby. It seems like a great idea until you are giving birth and then a joy when it's safely delivered. My special thanks go to my writing partner Brinley who adopted this concept with me. To all my family and friends I appreciate your continual love and support. Bob – you're a star.

To my clients, colleagues and coaches, thank you for the stories, inspiration and support. To Dan, Kathleen, Sam, and Jason plus all at Wiley, thank you for your cool, calm confidence over the hurdles.

Now it's over to you the reader to make this book really work for you. Please take the baby now and run with it!

From Brinley: After a long and relatively conventional business career it is an amazing thing to reconnect with the passions and drivers of my youth and find them all as fresh as they were in the 1970s and bursting for their opportunity to be fully expressed in the world. This has been my experience over the last 4–5 years and I am grateful to everyone who has played a part in my awakening.

My mission now is to be an awakener to anyone who feels there should be the opportunity for a full and rich life that integrates home and work and which doesn't 'cost the earth'.

My special thanks go to Kate for this opportunity to work with her, the Wiley publishing team, and to my wife Nicola, mother of our two young children. I also want to acknowledge my older children Loretta and Oliver for their wonderful inspiration and love over the last 20 years, and to my parents who raised me to think for myself.

I encourage you, the reader, to take on your work in the world with a renewed confidence and sense of purpose. The world is changing and it needs to change further and faster. With your commitment we can make it happen.

Publisher's Acknowledgments

We're proud of this book; please send us your comments through our Dummies online registration form located at www.dummies.com/register/.

Some of the people who helped bring this book to market include the following:

Acquisitions, Editorial, and Media Development

Project Editor: Daniel Mersey

Commissioning Editor: Samantha Clapp

Content Editor: Simon Bell

Copy Editor: Sally Lansdell

Proofreader: Sue Gilad

Technical Editor: Brenda Pugh, Achieve Greatness

Executive Editor: Jason Dunne

Executive Project Editor: Amie Jackowski Tibble

Cover Photos: © Aflo Foto Agency / Alamy

Cartoons: Rich Tennant, www.the5thwave.com

Composition Services

Project Coordinator: Maridee Ennis

Layout and Graphics: Karl Brandt, Carl Byers, Andrea Dahl, Mary J. Gillot, Lauren Goddard, Stephanie D. Jumper, Barry Offringa, Julie Trippetti

Proofreaders: Susan Moritz, Brian H. Walls

Indexer: TECHBOOKS Production Services

Publishing and Editorial for Consumer Dummies

> **Diane Graves Steele,** Vice President and Publisher, Consumer Dummies
>
> **Joyce Pepple,** Acquisitions Director, Consumer Dummies
>
> **Kristin A. Cocks,** Product Development Director, Consumer Dummies
>
> **Michael Spring,** Vice President and Publisher, Travel
>
> **Kelly Regan,** Editorial Director, Travel

Publishing for Technology Dummies

> **Andy Cummings,** Vice President and Publisher, Dummies Technology/General User

Composition Services

> **Gerry Fahey,** Vice President of Production Services
>
> **Debbie Stailey,** Director of Composition Services

Contents at a Glance

Introduction..*1*

Part 1: Considering the Basics............................*7*

Chapter 1: Assessing Your Confidence 9
Chapter 2: Identifying Your Sticking Points 25
Chapter 3: Charting Your Course Ahead 39

Part 11: Gathering the Elements...............................*49*

Chapter 4: Finding Your Motivation...51
Chapter 5: Sticking to Your Principles...63
Chapter 6: Making Friends with Your Emotions.................................75
Chapter 7: Unleashing Your Passion...87

Part 111: Building Your Confident Self...............*101*

Chapter 8: Using What You Already Know 103
Chapter 9: Moving beyond Perfection 111
Chapter 10: Stretching Yourself Mentally..125
Chapter 11: Developing Your Physical Confidence............................143

Part 1V: Communicating Your Confidence.........*151*

Chapter 12: Raising Your Voice 153
Chapter 13: Looking the Part..163
Chapter 14: Acting with Confidence in Your Daily Life 173

Part V: Engaging Others *181*

Chapter 15: Demonstrating Confidence in the Workplace................183
Chapter 16: Approaching Romantic Relationships with
    Confidence 205
Chapter 17: Raising Confident Children 219

Part V1: The Part of Tens....................................*229*

Chapter 18: Ten Great Questions to Spur You into Action 231
Chapter 19: Ten Daily Habits to Raise Your Confidence....................237
Chapter 20: Ten Keys to Effective Affirmations 243

Appendix: Resource List.................................*247*

Index...*251*

Table of Contents

Introduction *1*

    About This Book 1

    Conventions Used in This Book 2

    What You're Not to Read..2

    Foolish Assumptions 3

    How This Book Is Organised...3

        Part I: Considering the Basics 3

        Part II: Gathering the Elements 3

        Part III: Building Your Confident Self 4

        Part IV: Communicating Your Confidence 4

        Part V: Engaging Others...4

        Part VI: The Part of Tens...4

    Icons Used in This Book...5

    Where to Go from Here 5

Part 1: Considering the Basics................................*7*

    Chapter 1: Assessing Your Confidence **9**

    Defining Confidence...9

        What it is in practice 10

        How it feels 11

    Determining Where You Stand Now 12

        Looking at indicators of confidence..........................12

        Finding your place on the scale.................................13

    Recognising Your Strengths...17

        Celebrating your own talents first..............................18

        Gathering feedback 20

    Picturing the Life You'd Like to Lead 21

        Paying attention to what matters 21

        Uncovering your confidence 22

    Preparing for Action 23

        Setting your intentions..23

        Acknowledging the perils and perks of change..........24

    Chapter 2: Identifying Your Sticking Points **25**

    Digging Down to Root Issues.......................................26

        Forgetting the blame mindset 27

        Rewriting your role in your family...............................27

        Benefiting from your life experiences 29

Cleaning Out the Negatives 30
Tackling unhelpful assumptions 31
Staying busy but not overwhelmed 32
Redirecting those inner voices 33
Discovering What Drains Your Batteries 34
Counting the cost of toleration................................35
Trying to meet everyone's needs except your own...37

Chapter 3: Charting Your Course Ahead 39

Knowing Where You Want to Go 39
Determining your areas of focus...............................40
Mapping your own journey 41
Choosing Role Models 44
Finding reliable guides 44
Becoming your own coach 46
Becoming the hero in your own life 46

Part II: Gathering the Elements...........................49

Chapter 4: Finding Your Motivation 51

Driving Forward in Your Life 51
Rising through Maslow's hierarchy of needs 52
Greeting the world with grace 53
Taking Charge at Work 55
Looking at usable theory 55
Recognizing the importance of achievement.............61
Going for the next promotion 61

Chapter 5: Sticking to Your Principles 63

Understanding Your Values 63
Discovering your values 63
Uncovering your ends values....................................65
Resolving values conflicts 66
Living Your Values Every Day...69
Focusing on what's important 70
Sprinkling your values through your day...................70
Reviewing your day 71
Living Authentically..71
Developing your identity 72
Facing up to your demons...74

Chapter 6: Making Friends with Your Emotions 75

Getting a Grip on Your Emotions 75
Accessing your emotional intelligence 76
Pitting rational thought against emotion 77

Connecting creativity and confidence 78
Finding courage to voice your emotions 79
Tracking Your Moods 79
Staying in touch with your mood patterns 79
Becoming more aware of your natural state..............80
Trusting Your Intuition...81
Tuning in to the gifts of intuition 81
Listening to your inner self 82
Harnessing Your Darker Emotions................................83
Turning your anger into energy....................................83
Letting go of unhelpful emotions................................84
Allowing yourself to forgive and move on.................85

Chapter 7: Unleashing Your Passion 87

Discovering Your Passionate Self................................87
Becoming more passionate 88
Exploring your neurological levels with Dilts 89
Tapping into your natural passion 94
Realising your dreams...94
Putting Your Passion into Action.................................95
Starting your journey...96
Using your passion to lead 99

Part III: Building Your Confident Self...............101

Chapter 8: Using What You Already Know. 103

Accentuating Your Positives..103
Expecting the best...104
Distilling the essence of positive outcomes..............105
Going with the flow..105
Managing Your Fears 106
Avoiding the trap of fear..107
Transforming your fears into confidence..................108

Chapter 9: Moving beyond Perfection. 111

Letting Go of Unreal Expectations 111
Admitting that you can't be perfect (and that
you don't want to be)..112
Focusing on perfection distracts you from
excellence 113
Being Generous to Yourself First 113
Acknowledging your successes 114
Accepting help and delegating 115
Overcoming Procrastination 116
Breaking the gridlock...117
Biting off smaller chunks 118

Taking Time Off – for You 119
    Slowing down 119
    Adopting the 80/20 principle..120
Generating Realistic Standards of Behaviour.....................122
    Adjusting your goals to the circumstances 122
    Staying positive while keeping it real........................123
    Increasing your flexibility...123

Chapter 10: Stretching Yourself Mentally **125**

Expanding Your Comfort Zone...126
    Understanding the limits of your zone 126
    Stretching your boundaries: Expanding your zone...128
Driving Safely in the Fast Lane 131
    Creating a haven for yourself......................................131
    Preparing for the future 135
Attracting More of What You Want......................................138
    Getting back what you give out 139
    Finding what you're looking for 140
Feeling Your Power 140
    Appreciating a new way of being................................140
    Trusting it will be okay 141
    Listening to the voice of reason..................................142

Chapter 11: Developing Your Physical Confidence ... **143**

Connecting Your Mind and Body 144
Considering What Makes You Healthy 145
    Releasing stress, staying healthy................................145
    Following the golden rules for a healthy diet 148
    Believing in your health..149
Looking Forward to Your Healthy Future Self 150

Part 1V: Communicating Your Confidence.......... 151

Chapter 12: Raising Your Voice **153**

Speaking Out with Confidence 153
    Listening to yourself 154
    Breathing to improve your speaking..........................155
Saying What You Mean and Meaning What You Say..........158
    Holding onto your integrity..158
    Having difficult conversations 159
Recognising that the Message Is More than Words............160
    Experiencing the natural school..................................161
    Acting out the theatrical school 161
    Finding your authentic approach 161

Chapter 13: Looking the Part........................ 163

Being Judged by Appearances 163
Appearing confident................................164
Making the best first impression 165
Conveying the right attitude with your dress 166
Finding Your Own Style...167
Assessing your wardrobe 169
Shopping smart...................................170

Chapter 14: Acting with Confidence in Your Daily Life 173

Dealing with Resistance to the New, Confident You...........173
Being firm with loved ones who want the
old you 174
Finding the confidence to rise above.......................175
Reinforcing the Assertive You..............................176
Coping with external pressures 177
Staying on top of your confidence game 178
Living Powerfully 179

Part V: Engaging Others 181

Chapter 15: Demonstrating Confidence in the Workplace 183

Developing Confidence in Your Professional Life..............183
Realising that your job isn't you...................184
Defining your professional identity...........................185
Uncovering what you want to do..........................186
Finding value in what you do 188
Becoming Assertive...188
Showing Confidence in Specific Work Situations..............189
Demonstrating power and presence in meetings.....190
Shining during presentations 191
Rejecting manipulation and bullying 192
Managing Your Boss 194
Dealing with feedback...195
Getting your boss to keep her promises 197
Telling your boss she's wrong...............................199
Casting Off Your Cloak of Invisibility....................200
Dealing Confidently with Corporate Change 201
Getting through rejection 202
Taming the threat of redundancy...........................204

Chapter 16: Approaching Romantic Relationships with Confidence 205

Relating with Romance...206
Checking in on cultural notions of romance............206
Choosing your own view of romance........................207
Realising What Really Matters 208
Looking at Relationships with Open Eyes 210
Making that first move 210
Filling your partner's needs without running
dry yourself 212
Getting by with some help from your friends...........213
Eliciting Your Love Strategy 214
Facing Up to Changing Relationships....................216
Making decisions 216
Redesigning the way you are together.....................217

Chapter 17: Raising Confident Children 219

Securing the Foundations 219
Being fast to praise.......................................221
Setting safe boundaries....................................222
Helping Children Develop Curiosity 224
Providing a helpful environment 224
Encouraging a space to play 225
Championing Your Children 226
Accepting the Differences Between You 227

Part VI: The Part of Tens *229*

Chapter 18: Ten Great Questions to Spur You into Action 231

How Does Your Inner Voice Speak to You? 231
Are You Proud of Your Name? 232
Who Do You Hang Out With?....................................232
What's Your Confident Thought for the Day? 232
Where Are the Tensions in Your Life? 233
What's Your Sticking Point?....................................233
Who Are You Going to Be When You Grow Up? 234
How Do You Experience Failures and Mistakes? 234
How Do You Balance Time Alone and Time with
Others? 235
What's Your 120 per cent Dream?....................................235

Chapter 19: Ten Daily Habits to Raise Your Confidence................................237

Start Each Day Alert and Ready for Action 237
Concentrate Your Mind on the Page....................................238
Put Your Best Sunglasses On 238
Track Your Moods and Emotions..239
Exercise Your Body..239
Take Quiet Moments Alone...240
Go Outside and Wonder at the Beauty of the Sky...............240
Operate from a Position of Generosity.................................240
Review Today and Create Your Tomorrow...........................241
Connect with Your Life Purpose 241

Chapter 20: Ten Keys to Effective Affirmations 243

Building from the Right Structure..243
Using Affirmations Every Day 246

Appendix: Resource List 247

Contact the Authors 247
Books 247
Training and Coaching Web Sites 248
Professional Bodies 249

Index 251

Introduction

● ●

Confidence is one of those odd things in life that turn out to be surprisingly difficult to tie down (beauty and quality belong to this strange group too). You may think you know what it is, and you may feel certain that you can recognise it when you see it, but you may struggle to define exactly what 'it' is. Confidence is an everyday experience, something you have quite often, except on those all important occasions when it seems to leave you and you could really use more of it – whatever 'it' is.

In this book, you can clear up the confusion around confidence, and particularly what you may refer to as self-confidence. You dispel a lot of the mystique around how you can develop and build your self-confidence; perhaps to an extent you feared would never be possible for you.

Every chapter of this book is designed to help you understand: where your personal confidence comes from, how you can generate an incredibly powerful type of confidence in your life on demand, and how you can do it more reliably with less stress. You will make the fastest progress by immediately putting what you learn into action, by trying out the advice and exercises as you go along, and achieving the deep and lasting personal confidence you were born to enjoy.

Are you up for this? Let's go.

About This Book

Type the word 'confidence' into an Internet search engine and you can expect over 50 million hits. That's a lot of published material about something so natural. It is also an indication of the breadth of the subject so, as you want to get straight to the heart of your confidence, we have been selective in *Building Confidence For Dummies*.

The task ahead of you is to build your confidence so that you can be more powerful, more engaging, and more at ease in every aspect of your life. These areas include your work and your private life (friends and family, romance, community, and so on). We steer clear of more complex explorations of personal development and except where they translate into immediate practical guidance.

You should be able to dip into this book for practical and rapid support on such everyday confidence problems as:

- ✔ Preparing for an important presentation or job interview
- ✔ Asking the man or woman of your dreams to marry you
- ✔ Picking up the phone to make that difficult call to an important new customer
- ✔ Asking for the order, if you're in sales
- ✔ Picking yourself up quickly and appropriately after any setback

Conventions Used in This Book

To help you navigate through this book, we set up a few conventions:

- ✔ *Italics* are used for emphasis and to highlight new words or defined terms.
- ✔ **Bold faced** text indicates the key concept in a list.
- ✔ Monofont is used for web and e-mail addresses.

What You're Not to Read

This book is primarily an action guide to building your confidence. In many places, this requires us to set the context you need to grasp the situation. In other places, we include material useful for your full understanding, but not essential for you to be able to take the action and get the benefit. Much as we want you to take all of it on board in time, we make it easy for you to identify those parts that you can leave for later.

- ✔ **The text in the sidebars:** The shaded boxes that appear here and there share personal stories and anecdotes, but they're not integral to your taking action, and you can safely skip reading them if you're not interested.
- ✔ **The stuff on the copyright page:** You'll find nothing here of value unless you're looking for legal notices and reprint information. If you are, then this is the place to look.

Foolish Assumptions

We make a few other assumptions about you. We assume you're a normal human being who wants to be happy and confident. You're probably interested in becoming more effective in various parts of your life and in becoming more comfortable when you face demanding situations and people. Although you're probably already acting confidently in many areas, you may lack the power and skills to perform the way you want to in some others. This book is for you if you want to:

- Grow in the areas where you currently feel stuck
- Become better at your job and get acknowledged for it
- Feel less anxious and stressed about things you have to do
- Step up to become a powerful leader in your work or community
- Feel confident that no matter what life throws at you, you can find a way to deal with it

How This Book Is Organised

The book is divided into seven main sections, with each of these broken into chapters. The table of contents gives you details on each chapter.

Part 1: Considering the Basics

In the chapters in this part, we explain exactly what we mean by confidence and how it feels. You can evaluate how much confidence you have currently. You discover how to spot where your confidence is waxing or waning, in what areas of your life you need more confidence right now, and what is keeping you stuck.

Armed with all this insight, you can create your personal programme to the new super confident version of you that you want to present to the world.

Part 11: Gathering the Elements

Everyone would like to be more confident on occasion, but to take action, whether at work or socially, when you're feeling anything but confident requires motivation. In this part, you're invited to connect with your main drivers in life, gain a better understanding of your deepest values, and leverage this information to get what you want.

You venture into the sometimes messy world of emotions and mood swings – including the extremes of ecstasy, anger, and despair. This part guides you to safe connection with your personal motivation.

Part III: Building Your Confident Self

In this part, you pull up your most confident self and reconnect with how you do it. You let go of perfectionism in pursuit of effectiveness, let go of unreal expectations to enjoy your experiences. You find out how to extend your comfort zone and become relaxed and focused in achieving whatever you want. Finally, in this part, you forge a link between your mind and body and realise that taking better care of yourself helps you maintain your self confidence.

Part IV: Communicating Your Confidence

You naturally want to use your increasing self-confidence to influence others. In this part, you discover how to project your confident self out into the world through your powerful voice and personal appearance. We help you prioritise to get more done in the world and deal with blockers and resistance. This part helps you make the most confident you the permanent you.

Part V: Engaging Others

In this part, of your journey to self-confidence, you get tips on putting your increased personal power to use at work and in your private life. You use what you know about building confidence to ensure that your children grow up with a natural awareness of what it is to be and to act confidently as they face their new challenges every day.

Part VI: The Part of Tens

When you want a quick fix of inspiration or a reminder of what is important every day, you can find it here. This part takes you straight to some top-ten tips and lists on daily habits, affirmations to plant deep in your unconscious, and questions to spur you into action.

Icons Used in This Book

Within each chapter you find the following icons pointing you to particular types of information that you may find immediately useful. Here is an explanation of what each icon stands for:

This icon brings your attention to a personal story you may find inspiring or useful.

The bull's-eye highlights practical advice you can use to boost your confidence immediately.

This icon indicates an exercise you can use to broaden your understanding of yourself and your own confidence issues.

Information to take note of and keep in mind as you apply your boosted confidence in the world is indicated with the finger and string.

Text next to the Warning icon urges you to take special care of yourself in dealing with specific issues.

Where to Go from Here

Although all the material in this book is relevant to building your most confident version of yourself, you don't have to read it cover to cover over any set period. You benefit most if you address first those sections that are most relevant to the areas of your life where you feel the need for more self-confidence most keenly. For example, if you are feeling nervous about changes happening at work, or going to a party, say, go first to the chapters that deal with this; feel free to dip in where you need guidance and support right now.

After you read the book and are keen to take your levels of confidence and achievement to even higher levels, we recommend more personalised forms of development training and coaching. Take a look at the further guidance and resources we recommend at www.yourmostconfidentself.com.

Part I
Considering the Basics

"I'm tired of letting everyone pull my strings."

In this part...

*F*rom understanding what confidence is and how it feels to tackling unhelpful assumptions you make about yourself, the chapters in this part help you lay the foundations for your new, confident self. Armed with all kinds of insights into what you want for yourself, you can use these chapters to design your own journey and set the milestones along the way.

Chapter 1

Assessing Your Confidence

In This Chapter

▶ Identifying the key ingredients of confidence

▶ Rating yourself on the confidence indicators

▶ Celebrating your good points

▶ Visualising the super-confident new you

▶ Getting started on changing

*W*elcome to the start of your confidence-building programme. It's great to have you on board for what we promise will be a wonderful and transformational journey. With confidence comes more fun, freedom, and opportunities to do what really works for you.

In this chapter, we lay the foundations for our travels together, starting with some definitions of confidence and a practical, nuts-and-bolts assessment of where you are today.

Here you start flexing your confidence muscles – and we know from experience that you're probably in a much more confident shape than you may give yourself credit for. You can also celebrate what you're already good at and imagine the new super-confident you on the horizon as your confidence-building work progresses.

Then, it's about getting tooled up ready for action. After all, what's the point of hiding your talents when there's so much important work to be done in this world?

Defining Confidence

When asked to think what confidence means, most people have a feel for it but find it quite difficult to tie down precisely. After all, confidence is not some miracle pill or wonder food you can buy in a shop.

Before you dive into this book on how to be more confident, we invite you to explore the definition of confidence. A good dictionary provides at least three definitions for *confidence,* and it's important to understand each aspect as it is easy to muddle them:

- ✔ **Self-assuredness:** This relates to your confidence in your ability to perform to a certain standard.

- ✔ **Belief in the ability of other people:** This definition focuses on how you expect others to behave in a trustworthy or competent way.

- ✔ **Keeping certain information secret or restricted to a few people:** This definition concerns the idea of keeping a confidence.

We think an even better definition exists. One that's more useful to you in everyday life. One that's true no matter how tough a situation you face, or how comfortable you feel about it. Our definition:

At its heart, *confidence* is the ability to take appropriate and effective action in any situation, however challenging it appears to you or others.

Confidence is not about feeling good inside, although it's a bonus if you do.

What it is in practice

Now, how does confidence show up in daily life? Well, have you ever started something – perhaps an exercise session or presentation at work – even though you didn't feel like doing it at that moment, only to find that once you got going, you started to feel okay about it and even glad you tackled it? This kind of shift in how you experience a situation gives you a taste of what confidence is in practice. It is your ability to reach beyond how you are feeling in the moment in order to take action that leads to the outcome you want.

Anish is an accountant turned management consultant who has travelled the world on international assignments for large corporations. Now running his own partnership, he leads complex projects and presents a calm, rational, and focused image in business meetings. When deadlines are pressing and tempers rise in project teams, he is the one who patiently exudes confidence that delivery can and will happen on time.

How does he do this under pressure? 'I experience the situation as a series of hoops that I just need to get through – like a tunnel,' he says. 'Sometimes there will just be two or three. At other times, as many as twenty in a row. I can feel as anxious inside about what needs to be done as the next person, but I experience it as a sequence to go through patiently one by one, and it gets easier as I see the light beckoning at the end.'

Approaching challenges with confidence in Anish's style brings clear benefits. For example:

✔ You believe that it is possible to tackle and achieve things that others consider difficult.

✔ You inspire others around you and stop them panicking.

✔ You break down a large project into smaller parts that you can tackle one by one.

How it feels

Don't worry about whether you feel comfortable performing a challenging activity or are fully relaxed about the action you are taking. Confident people are okay with the feeling of not knowing all the answers. Phew, what a relief. Confidence is just the feeling that it'll be okay.

The sense of feeling confident inside comes with increased practice and familiarity with what you do. You can also create it from your life experiences and bring it out when you need it. This doesn't mean that you won't ever feel scared. You will, but the good news is that you'll be able to live with the fear.

Here are some ways that you can recognise confidence in yourself:

✔ You feel poised and balanced.

✔ You are breathing easily.

✔ You are moving towards a goal or action with a sense of purpose.

✔ You are being proactive rather than defensive.

✔ You know that you'll be able to deal with whatever life throws at you, even if you can't control it.

✔ You can laugh at yourself.

✔ You know everything will be alright in the end, however long it takes.

So, we're going to support you as you find your inner confidence to take the first step to wherever you want to go, however scary or difficult it seems just now.

Determining Where You Stand Now

Any measure of confidence is by its nature pretty subjective. Other people may form an opinion about how confident you are based on your outside appearance and actions, but only you can know for sure what you feel like on the inside – what you believe to be true, and what it's like to be you.

In this section, we invite you to make your own assessment of where your confidence level is today.

Your confidence level is different according to the time and place. If you think back ten years to a younger you, you probably realise that your confidence has grown since then according to the experiences you have faced, knowing that you have lived to tell the tale. How confident you feel differs in various situations, and may well fluctuate from day to day and week to week according to what's happening at work and at home. There may be areas where you've taken a risk, or suffered a loss, for example, and your confidence has dropped.

If you've been unwell and have taken on too much work, your confidence level may dip and wobble. Yet when you're well and have a sense of completing your work, you may feel as if you can conquer the world. Think of your confidence as a pair of old-fashioned scales – it's a delicate balancing mechanism and anything, even something feather light, may tip it either way unexpectedly.

Make change easy on yourself. Rome wasn't built in a day. We're not going to suggest you go hang gliding off a mountain top today if standing on a stepladder gives you the collywobbles in your stomach. Allow yourself time and space to improve. Lots of smaller steps are often more realistic and maintainable compared to giant leaps for mankind.

Looking at indicators of confidence

We pinpoint ten core indicators of confidence that we explore in depth throughout this book. When you act with confidence, you are likely to have a good selection of these ten qualities:

> ✔ **Direction and values:** You know what you want, where you want to go, and what's really important to you.

✔ **Motivation:** You are motivated by and enjoy what you do. In fact, you're likely to get so engrossed in what you're doing that nothing distracts you.

✔ **Emotional stability:** You have a calm and focused approach to how you are yourself and how you are with other people as you tackle challenges. You notice difficult emotions such as anger and anxiety, but you work with them rather than letting them overcome you.

✔ **A positive mind-set:** You have the ability to stay optimistic and see the bright side even when you encounter setbacks. You hold positive regard for yourself as well as other people.

✔ **Self-awareness:** You know what you are good at, how capable you feel, and how you look and sound to others. You also acknowledge that you are a human being, and you don't expect to be perfect.

✔ **Flexibility in behaviour:** You adapt your behaviour according to circumstance. You can see the bigger picture as well as paying attention to details. You take other people's views on board in making decisions.

✔ **Eagerness to develop:** You enjoy stretching yourself, treating each day as a learning experience, rather than acting as if you are already an expert with nothing new to find out. You take your discoveries to new experiences.

✔ **Health and energy:** You're in touch with your body, respect it, and have a sense that your energy is flowing freely. You manage stressful situations without becoming ill.

✔ **A willingness to take risks:** You have the ability to act in the face of uncertainty – and put yourself on the line even when you don't have the answers or all the skills to get things right.

✔ **A sense of purpose:** You have an increasing sense of the coherence of the different parts of your life. You have chosen a theme or purpose for your life.

You can use these indicators to help figure out where you are stuck in life because you lack the confidence to move on. Moving out of that feels like escaping from treading in treacle.

Finding your place on the scale

The 20 statements in Table 1-1 relate to the indicators of confidence we laid out in the preceding section. Consider each and decide on the extent to which you agree or disagree using the five-point scale provided. Take the test as often as you like and keep a note of your developing profile.

Frankl's search for meaning

Viktor E. Frankl, the founder of Logotherapy, was one of the 20th century's great therapists. He formulated his revolutionary approach to psychotherapy in four Nazi death camps, including Auschwitz, where he was captive from 1942 to 1945.

At the heart of his theory is the belief that, whatever our personal circumstance, what keeps us going most surely is the meaning we find in living. This belief helped him survive the camps against all odds when millions of others perished, and after the war it enabled him to treat many of its victims.

Frankl agreed with the philosopher Nietzsche that 'he who has a *why* to live for can bear with almost any *how*.' In the camps, Frankl saw that people who had hope of being reunited with loved ones, who had projects they felt a need to complete, or who had great faith tended to have a better chance at survival than those who had little to keep them going through the difficulties.

When one of Frankl's patients faced a collapse of confidence through the loss of meaning in his or her life, Frankl would seek to bring relief through three routes:

1. To broaden the patient's appreciation of life by making conscious the fuller value of all that person was achieving, creating, and accomplishing (and yet dismissing).

2. To recover and re-live powerful if transient experiences of feeling most alive: the view from a mountain top, the love for another, the perfect athletic performance (what Maslow might have called 'Peak Experiences' see Chapter 4).

3. To find a powerful positive meaning by the reframing of apparently meaningless situations. For example, a man surviving his wife after a long and happy union had saved her from the trauma he was having to bear of living alone.

Frankl's experience and his thinking are beautifully set out in his book: Man's Search for Meaning.

Do the evaluation now and make a note in your diary to come back and review it in, say, six months' time and notice what you've learnt.

Completing this questionnaire provides you with a very simple stock take of some of the main areas of your life affecting your confidence right now. If you answer the questions accurately, you can use specific chapters of this book to target the areas that merit your immediate attention.

There are no right or wrong answers. If you answer as honestly as you can, you get a rounded view of how your confidence indicators stack up as you begin building your confidence through this book.

Table 1-1	Evaluating Your Confidence				
Statement	**Strongly Agree**	**Agree**	**Neutral**	**Disagree**	**Strongly Disagree**
I have a clear sense of what is important to me.					
I know what I want in life.					
I never beat myself up about my failings.					
I can stand back and think clearly when things get emotional.					
A lot of my work involves things I enjoy doing.					
I sometimes become totally engrossed in an activity.					
I am known for being optimistic.					
I respect myself and many of those around me.					
I have a realistic view of my strengths and weaknesses.					
I know what others consider to be my strengths.					
I consult others, where appropriate, before taking decisions.					
I am comfortable with both the big picture and the important details of a situation.					
I enjoy doing new things and taking on fresh challenges.					
I relish the opportunity to learn and to grow.					

(continued)

Table 1-1 *(continued)*

Statement	Strongly Agree	Agree	Neutral	Disagree	Strongly Disagree
I take care of my body.					
I feel able to handle any stress in my life.					
I have a healthy attitude to risk taking.					
I don't always have to have every 't' crossed and 'i' dotted before taking action.					
I sometimes meditate or think deeply about the connectedness of different parts of my life.					
I know what I am here to do. I have a chosen mission or purpose.					

Now, give yourself 5 points for every tick in the *strongly agree* column, 4 for every one in the *agree* column, 3 for *neutral*, 2 for *disagree*, and finally 1 for *strongly disagree*. Add up your points and check the next section for advice related to your total score. The second stage of the scoring process – in the 'Personal profile' section – encourages you to determine which areas of your life and this book are worthy of your immediate attention.

Overall rating

Find your total score in one of the following categories:

✔ **80–100: Congratulations!** By any standards, you are what most people consider to be a confident person. You are clear on your priorities and are in positive pursuit of the life you want.

Take note of any areas where you scored below par and consider the advice in the 'Personal profile' section below.

✔ **60–80: Well done!** You are already pretty confident in most situations. Just a few areas bring you down in the test and in your life. You can find plenty of guidance for dealing with these trouble spots in this book. Look at the advice in next section to make the most rapid progress.

✔ **40–60: You are in the right place!** You may be experiencing some confusion or uncertainty in your life right now, and you may wonder whether there is anything you can do about it. Give yourself time to work on the areas that need attention and you will be amazed by the progress you can make.

✔ **20–40: Full marks for honesty and courage!** Your confidence may be at low ebb right now, but it doesn't have to stay that way. You can find good advice that you can put to use on almost every page of this book. If you take our advice, and act upon it, you face the possibility of life transformation.

Personal profile

After you score your questionnaire and read the relevant advice in the preceding section, take another look at your scoring and note the areas that brought your overall score down. Look at statements you most strongly disagreed with. If you scored high on most questions, look at the statements with which you find yourself unable to strongly agree.

You can use your individual scores to create your personal confidence profile. This now gives you something specific to think about. Let's say you are unclear about what is most important to you in life, or you beat yourself up over every little mistake. Perhaps you fail to consult others, or you feel alone and isolated. All of these things affect how confident you feel, and how prepared you are to take action.

You can find advice and action guidance on all these issues in the chapters that follow. Use the contents pages and chapter summaries to find those areas that can give your confidence the quickest and biggest boosts.

 This is a simple exercise, designed to give you a quick start and an immediate agenda for improvement. You can use the test to monitor your growing confidence. However, if you want a more detailed analysis, go to our Web site at www.yourmostconfidentself.com.

Recognising Your Strengths

Mark Twain said that each one of us has the substance within to achieve whatever our goals and dreams define. What we are missing are the wisdom and insight to use what we already have.

A key aspect of confident people is that they have high self-esteem – they hold themselves in positive self-regard. This means that they know how to love themselves and that they acknowledge what they're good at. These realisations boost their resilience and ability to take on greater challenges.

Your ability to take appropriate, effective action is affected by various things in your life that may seem to have little direct relation to the task at hand. Your values are a good example of this. Your self-confidence is likely to waver if you don't value what you excel at doing. Research shows that if you value what you're good at, you're likely to be highly confident in that area. If you value what you're not so good at, then you will not feel so confident, even though your friends may reassure you that this is not much of a problem at all.

Building confidence begins with going with your strengths. If you're great at music, don't beat yourself up because you're not going to play international rugby. Pat yourself on the back, practise accepting compliments for everything you do well, and enjoy the positive reinforcement from others. Respect and honour yourself, and you'll find that you get respect and honour from those around you.

For confidence to thrive and grow, you must concentrate your attention on what you're good at, rather than trying to turn yourself into something that you're not.

You also need to free yourself from unhelpful negative thoughts about your shortcomings or negative incidents in your life – more about that in Chapter 2.

Celebrating your own talents first

Everybody has different interests and skills. (Thank goodness for that!) So, your first step in developing confidence is to decide what you're really good at, and build on it. It's time to recognise your qualities and build up your talent store. Use the worksheet in Table 1-3 to list some of the things you think you're good at both at work and in your home life. Record during what period of your life you best put those skills and talents to use.

We want you to become consciously aware of what you are good at. It's too easy to take your talents for granted and assume everyone else is good at what you're good at. Well, they're not. You have your own special skills – attributes that make you stand out. When you notice what you do well, and when, in what context, then you can choose to repeat these to build your confidence.

The sample worksheet in Table 1-2 gives you some ideas for the kinds of strengths you can include in your own worksheet.

Table 1-2	Sample Strengths Worksheet	
Things I Am Good At	*When I Was At My Best*	*Actions I Can Put in Place to Encourage This Talent*
At work		
Strong, decisive manager at the power plant.	Put myself forward for next promotion board.	
Good, creative contributor in team meetings.	Suggested the new shift rota, which was adopted.	Follow through other suggestions with my boss.
At home		
Telling jokes that people find funny.	Speech at my brother's wedding.	Get more funny material to do Comic Relief spot at the Arts Centre.
House improvements – I'm constantly repairing or upgrading something in the house.	New bathroom – installed all by myself in six weekends.	Agree on list of creative DIY projects with my wife.
Football coaching for John's school team.	Best results in ten sessions. Strong competition for places.	Get school team to enter for higher league.

Now, fill out Table 1-3 with your own strengths and talents.

Table 1-3	Strengths Worksheet	
Things I Am Good At	*When I Was At My Best*	*Actions I Can Put in Place to Encourage This Talent*
At work		
At home		

Decide which of these talents you'd like to make more of and what action you can take to sponsor and encourage each of your useful talents.

Once you're with your list of actions, don't file them away in a drawer and forget about them until next year. Instead, set a timescale for things you'll do in the shorter term – next week or month – and for those to do in the longer term. Chapter 3 offers advice on setting steps to achieve your goals.

Gathering feedback

Getting feedback from others is a powerful shortcut to building your confidence. Apart from performance reviews at work, you may not be in the habit of asking people to give you feedback on how you're doing, and you may be amazed at what you learn about yourself by doing so. Quite often people don't recognise what they do well. 'Isn't everyone good at that?' they ask. Most people are their own worst critic, and it can be a wonderful experience to receive positive feedback from your nearest and dearest. Having that outside view from another person may help you notice what you excel at and uncover some hidden talents.

Ask six people who have known you a while if they'd be prepared to give you some feedback about yourself. Choose people who represent the different groups in which you mix, including family members, friends, work colleagues, and those who know you from your interests in the community, church, or a sports club. Ask each of them these questions:

- ✔ What am I good at?

- ✔ When have you seen me operate at my best?

- ✔ What should I do more of?

- ✔ What should I do less of?

- ✔ What can you rely on me for?

- ✔ Where do you think I can stretch myself?

After collecting feedback, look for the common trends and themes and think of ways to build them into your goals and development plans. If a number of people tell you similar things, it's likely there's some truth in the message and worth taking notice. (The odd negative comment from your nearest and dearest may be less helpful and more about their needs than yours – test it out.) Your attention then needs to be on working with the good stuff, stretching yourself and letting go of the rest. For example, if you have particular talent, look for ways to tell others about it and use it more. Consider delegating or changing the things people suggest you should do less of.

Feedback is just someone's opinion. The point of feedback is to take what you can from it in the way that's right for you. Listen to it, take what supports you in building your confidence, and let the rest go.

Picturing the Life You'd Like to Lead

Confidence is almost all about perception. Very few people are wholly confident in every area of their life. Those who appear to be so are probably good at acting – with themselves as the audience.

Imagine having a PhD in Confidence. Think about how your life would be different if you had studied the subject, taken the learning on board, and were supremely confident, firing on all cylinders.

Find yourself a quiet place to sit and contemplate for ten minutes. Picture yourself with your newfound super-confidence. Think of a real-life time coming up in your calendar where you'd like to be supremely confident in that 'I can conquer the world' quality. And start to notice. . .

- ✔ Where are you and who is with you?

- ✔ What are you doing?

- ✔ What skills and talents do you have now?

- ✔ What are your thoughts and feelings?

- ✔ What's really important to you about this newfound confidence?

- ✔ What would you do if you knew you couldn't fail?

Adjust the picture so that if feels right for you. Hold the picture for yourself and savour it so that you will be able to recall it whenever you want to.

Visualisation involves focusing your thoughts on the things you want to happen in your life and picturing them happening. Although it's a simple mental discipline, it can have dramatic effects. It's a powerful motivational tool that will help you take your confidence sky high.

Paying attention to what matters

As you become more confident, you start paying more attention to what's important to you in life rather than bowing to the pressures that those around you place on you. By the time you have read this book, we expect you to know very clearly what's important for you, and where you're going to choose to put your time and energy going forward.

Start now by answering one simple question: What really matters to you in your life right now? For example, do you want a loving partner or family around you, a successful career, or perhaps your health is your top priority. You may be working towards a very specific goal such as running a marathon or getting married.

Write your answer down and make this the priority for your confidence-building muscles.

Uncovering your confidence

You may still be curious as to what kind of confident person you can be at your best. This is a question that even the most experienced, capable chief executives and media personalities ask themselves regularly. Successful people stretch themselves.

You have enormous potential limited only by yourself. And it's up to you to realise it. Gandhi had to overcome acute shyness to take on injustice in the world and free his people. And the more you connect with what is important to you, the more you become true to your most confident self.

People often feel a fraud when they take a leadership role that's new and more senior to the one they are used to. If you feel this, then remember you've been selected for that senior job because your company believes you will do it well. It's not realistic to expect to have all the knowledge on day one. People invite you to join them because they know you can contribute, and they want you.

Not everyone wants or needs to be an international leader on the world stage, but you can see yourself as a leader in your own world. You can lead by your example. Look back over time to things that you may take for granted. You have learnt to ride a bike or drive a car, to operate a computer, or renovate your house. As your skills and competence grow, so you become more confident to take on bigger challenges. Something that seemed hard five years ago may be a piece of cake today.

Be your own sponsor as well as critic. You may be good at giving yourself a hard time by comparing yourself unfavourably with others: 'I'll never be as good as. . .' Comparisons with others are valuable in that they can help you to excel and raise your game as a budding Tiger Woods on the golf circuit, for example. But don't waste energy beating yourself up by not being as good as the expert who dedicates every day of their life to practice.

You are important in this world and have a real contribution to make. Support, mentoring, and personal sponsorship of various types can help you to be the very best you can be. Begin by assuming you are going to be successful, and surround yourself with people who honour you and support your growth.

So who are you really? The 'you' that you want to become is up to you, as you will find out when you follow your own direction.

In the words of Gandhi: 'You must be the change you wish to see in the world.'

Preparing for Action

When are you going to get started? You agree, we hope, that there's no time like the present. Confidence starts here and now. Yes, that means today. Not on Monday morning after the excesses of the weekend.

Getting your confident self fired up means adopting a new, positive mind-set, and getting rid of any doubts you have. You'll get help with this in the next few chapters by cleaning up on your doubts. So before you set off on the journey, first check inside yourself. Ask yourself:

- ✔ Is it okay to make this change and become a more confident me?
- ✔ What do I stand to lose or gain if I do?

Once you're happy that your answers are in the positive, even if it feels a bit scary, you're ready for the next step of the journey.

 If there's a part of you that is really unduly scared of change, it may be for a valid reason. Think about it, and if you're worried, check with your family or even a health professional about your physical and mental well-being.

Setting your intentions

As you set out on the journey, we want to state our intentions for you, the reader, and invite you to do the same. Our commitment is:

> We are committed to giving you our full support and sharing all our knowledge. We believe that you are a unique and special human being with your individual strengths. We also know that being kind and honest with yourself gives you the best results. We know that if you follow the tips and ideas in this book and put them into practice, you will build a more confident version of yourself to take out into the world.

Now, we ask that you make a declaration of your intent and speak it out loud to yourself three times with increasing commitment:

> I make a commitment to build my confidence in the way that's right for me, honouring myself as a unique and special human being. I will be honest with and kind to myself on the journey to be the very best I can be. I promise to have fun along the way.

Acknowledging the perils and perks of change

Any kind of change has its ups and downs. You can focus on the downside and say that you may be under threat from those around you who don't want a new confident you, you may find changing scary, and you may put yourself on the line and open yourself up to criticism and sarcasm. So what? The power of change far out-weighs the negatives. Just look around you and make your own judgement about who has the best life – the confident person or the shrinking violet. Confident people earn more money, have more fun, enjoy more freedom, and relish new experiences. They have a go, they discover, they have a zest for living. They love the power that comes from being confident to do the things that many of those around them shy away from.

A few tips then for riding the waves, the ups and downs as you change:

- **Flex your knees over the bumpy days.** Stay resolute and adapt your approach.

- **Look at the worst scenario.** Face up to it (it usually isn't all that bad), and then expect the best to happen. It usually does.

- **Ask yourself: What will this be like in a week's time, a month's time, or this time next year?** Taking a longer-term view usually strips away the anxiety.

Welcome on board the confidence train and happy travels!

Chapter 2

Identifying Your Sticking Points

In This Chapter

▶ Recognising when your natural confidence comes under attack

▶ Getting familiar with what pulls you down and holds you back

▶ Spotting new ways to break out of your inertia

*E*xuding confidence is a bit like being wealthy. Confidence, like money, only becomes a problem when it disappears. You've probably experienced times when you suddenly become aware of your confidence because you've lost it. You don't pay attention when confidence is coming at you in abundance and you have that pleasant, warm, 'can do' glow.

Now, we're not saying you should expect life to be 100 per cent perfect all the time. In fact, that's unrealistic. You can expect sticking points on any journey – times when your plans, hopes, and dreams don't run smoothly and you feel as if you're wading through treacle. The art of developing your confidence lies in minimising how long you let yourself stay mired in low-confidence land and how quickly you're able to let the causes go.

Getting on the road less boggy is what this chapter is all about. We show you how to face an underlying sticky mess, so that you can begin to let life flow for yourself. Rest assured that you may well encounter more tough times ahead – facing them is how you learn from life.

Soon you'll be ready to set your sights on your next destination, so for now, gather yourself together and prepare to jump down from the fence. It's time to get more decisive, make a commitment to change, and take responsibility for the results you get.

Digging Down to Root Issues

Cleaning up means digging deep to the heart of what really holds you back. You may not be fully aware of what gets in your way, but the clues are in what you say and how you describe your experience. Ever heard yourself utter things like 'It's *impossible* for me to leave my job', or 'I'm *always* going to have problems because I never went to the right school', or 'They'll *never* choose me for promotion because *everyone* knows they want someone who is younger/ slimmer/an accountant/a creative type/female/male/white/black' and so on.

Such statements are not based on reality, but on your perception of it. In fact, they are merely stories to frighten yourself with. These generalisations limit you and drain your confidence to have a go at whatever adventures lie ahead. They have the same negative effect on those around you.

The way you describe your world becomes your experience of it. As Einstein once famously pointed out: 'The most important question to ask, is: Is the universe a hostile or friendly place?' If you describe your world with hostile language, that is what you experience. Life becomes a nightmare if that's how you dream. Those who negatively distort reality suffer the most stress, anxiety, and depression, all of which get in the way of living confidently.

As you re-create your more confident reality, listen to your own words. Notice when your descriptions include words such as *always, never, everyone, nothing, totally, impossible.* Replace them or qualify them with more liberating words such as *I choose to, sometimes, possibly, almost.*

Getting past your past

As a lad of eight, John's secret dream was to be a ballet dancer, and he asked to audition for the school pantomime. When the school music teacher rejected him after a token interview, he overheard her say to a colleague: 'I could never have a fat boy like that in any production of mine.'

In spite of the teacher's unkind words, John went on to slim down and pursue his dream in Billy Elliott style. He had a highly successful international dance career before moving into the business world.

Forgetting the blame mindset

You know who the whiners and blamers are around you. If you have any sense of personal protection, you probably try to steer well clear of them or limit your time with them. When you're stuck in blaming mode, positive people begin to avoid your company and you end up building friendships with those who reinforce your blame approach so that you can double up on your whingeing and whining.

The blame mind-set is not a helpful place to be if you want to get on and succeed in this world. Blame limits your choices and your results. You find fault in others rather than taking responsibility for the results you get. You wait around for others to do things before you act.

Successful business leaders and entrepreneurs don't hang around blaming others or making excuses, they do everything in their power to bring about change. They take it upon themselves to make a difference without expecting others to bale them out.

This Parrot on Your Shoulder exercise can help you to shift your viewpoint and be more objective about your choices and your behaviour.

For one day, imagine that you are able to observe all your own behaviour – everything you do and say. You can be like a parrot on your own shoulder. Take notice when you think that a situation is due to what others around you are doing and when you make excuses for yourself. Then hear the parrot on your shoulder say: 'What are you *choosing* to do about it then?'

Your aim is to shift your blame mind-set into one in which you choose your outcome. Choosing your outcome can transform your world and open up new possibilities. You switch your focus of attention from what has gone wrong to what you want to have happen instead. You adopt an active and positive position rather than waiting and reacting defensively to others. Two key indicators of confidence are self-awareness and flexibility in behaviour. With the imaginary parrot's help, you can raise your scores on both counts.

Rewriting your role in your family

Family relationships are dynamic, meaning that they change over time. Part of being confident is recognising that it's natural for you to have a different relationship with your parents, siblings, and the rest of the family as you grow older. Just because your big brother

---

Being a child at 50

At the age of 50, Bruce appears to be a mature and confident man. He holds down a responsible lecturing job at a prestigious British university and has published works of academic excellence. For most of the year, he is bright, entertaining, and fun to be with. But that all changes when his parents come to stay for Christmas.

Over the years, he has loved and lost a string of live-in girlfriends who despair at his change in behaviour when his mother and father visit. At these times, Bruce reverts to being a 'good little boy', trying to please his parents by adopting false modesty. Each time, the current girlfriend is ousted from the double bedroom and placed in a guest room, and treated as a casual visitor in the shared home. Bruce feels that his parents will not approve of the live-in relationship he has chosen and pretends that he lives a bachelor existence. He behaves as if he still lives in the parental home, and he lacks the emotional maturity to be his own person, not acknowledging the true situation for fear of upsetting his parents.

Little wonder, then, that many New Year parties have been less than romantic for Bruce.

---

told you what to do when you were eight doesn't give him the right to behave in the same way 20 years on. Nor does it give you the excuse to slip into an unhelpful, child-like relationship with him.

Yet you may recognise that you cling to a pattern of behaviour with your family that's no longer appropriate to the confident you that you want to be today. Perhaps you bite your tongue rather than saying what you feel is true and right.

You can choose how you want to be with people, and the way you behave dictates the results you get.

The next exercise helps you to shift the dynamics in your family relationships by observing the current situation, then choosing how you would like it to be. It's very empowering, particularly if you feel stuck in old habits.

Think of a person in your family, including your in-laws or step children, who you'd like to relate to in a better way. Follow these steps:

1. **Write out the story of how you currently relate to this person.**

   Describe how you currently behave with this person. Note the situations that you find most difficult and challenging. Think about what you would like to change so that you can have a respectful, amicable, and mature relationship with this person.

2. **Write a second version detailing how you would like this relationship to be in three years' time.**

   Write in the present tense as if the change has already happened. Add as much detail as you like to visualise the new story with dialogue and your new feelings.

3. **Act as if you have already developed or changed this relationship.**

   Make a commitment to yourself that next time you have contact with this person, you will remind yourself of your new story. Visualising the future, behave as if the change you desire has already happened.

Benefiting from your life experiences

Sam has recently given up his computer sales business to teach yoga full time. He has that almost tangible inner strength of so many yogis and martial artists – a very centred kind of energy. One day at the end of a class, he commented that nothing fazes him after fleeing from atrocities in Uganda at the age of 15. He left his family and was sent off to Canada alone to meet up with one family contact who helped him to find a room to live in.

Although hopefully your tough times are not this tough, in a bizarre way, the awful times you come through provide the root source for your strongest confidence. They build your resilience and toughen you up to face the next hurdle.

Table 2-1 provides room for you to list some of the tough times you've faced in your life so far and how dealing with them benefited you. Your own tough times don't need to be as extreme as Sam's.

Table 2-1	Your Tough Times Index		
Tough Time	*Obstacles Overcome*	*Benefits*	*How to Put Benefits to Use*
Sam's example:			
Expulsion from home country	Separation from family		
Financial hardship			
	Self confidence		

(continued)

Table 2-1 *(continued)*

Tough Time	Obstacles Overcome	Benefits	How to Put Benefits to Use
Independence			
Resilience			
	Take risks with new ventures		
Follow personal dreams			
Your example 1:			
Your example 2:			
Your example 3:			

Cleaning Out the Negatives

It's spring-cleaning time – time to get started on some broad-brush clean-up action. Begin by facing up to some of that negative, confidence-draining stuff. Our belief is that you were born confident, and somehow along the way you let people and circumstances get in your way.

Working or living in a mess can wipe your energy. Just to get you in the clean-up/feel-good mood, take 15 minutes right now for a tidy-up. If you're at work, make it a desk sweep. Clear the decks, put your desk in order. If you're at home, take the space in the house where you spend the most time, and make it as attractive as you can for yourself right now. Already obsessively tidy? Then pat yourself on the back for being so organised, and lie back and relax for ten minutes.

Designing and creating your own life, as the next sections help you to do, is much more fun than spending all your energy constantly troubleshooting and problem solving.

Tackling unhelpful assumptions

You may be holding on to some unhelpful thoughts or assumptions about yourself – most people do – that prevent you from feeling fully confident. Perhaps you think that life or work has to be a huge effort and an uphill struggle all the way. Maybe you compare yourself unfavourably with others.

Some of the assumptions we hear in our jobs, which you may share, include:

- ✔ 'I'm not a confident person because I left school at 15.'

- ✔ 'It's easy for you to be confident at work because you have marketable skills.'

- ✔ 'I won't be confident until I can work part-time.'

- ✔ 'He comes from money, so he's bound to be confident.'

- ✔ 'I'll feel confident when I've lost my excess weight.'

- ✔ 'My boss has it in for me, so it's no surprise I lack confidence.'

- ✔ 'I don't have the right kind of friends to build up my confidence.'

Most of these comments are loaded with judgement and unfavourable comparisons with others rather than fact.

The trouble with taking on such unhelpful assumptions is that you act as if the assumption is true until it becomes a self-fulfilling prophecy.

Take a few moments to record some of your unhelpful assumptions about your own confidence that might be holding you back. Then write down an opposing, more positive assumption.

For example, an unhelpful statement may be something like: 'Since I've turned 40, I can't ever expect to feel confident going on a date.' Turning that around produces the more helpful: 'Now I'm 40, I can ask anyone out for a date with supreme confidence.'

Remind yourself of your new assumptions regularly. One way is to build them into an affirmation as in Chapter 20.

There may be an element of good fortune in any activity, but the more you practise, the luckier you get . . . as all top sports people will tell you.

Staying busy but not overwhelmed

If you love life, it's not surprising if you work to an action-packed schedule: So many people to see, so many things to do. But to function at your truly confident best, you need a balance between busy time and rest time. If you're constantly on the run, you start to feel off-balance, which eventually topples your internal sense of confidence.

Busyness does not equal effectiveness.

Recognising signals that you're at your limits

The following clues indicate that you're in danger of being over-whelmed:

✔ You run late for appointments or miss them altogether.

✔ You often forget what you were doing.

✔ You get easily distracted and start many projects without finishing any of them.

✔ You lose things like your keys, your mobile phone, and the shopping list.

✔ Your house or office paperwork is chaotic.

✔ You feel jittery inside.

✔ You snap at people you care about.

✔ You stop listening.

✔ Your eating habits are poor – you eat late at night or grab sandwiches from the local garage.

✔ You cancel dates with friends at a moment's notice.

✔ You catch sight of yourself in a mirror and look like a frightened rabbit.

If you ticked more than two or three, congratulations. You've recognised some of the signals of being overwhelmed and this is the first step necessary to making change.

Using the four Ps to take stock

If you feel that you've got too much to do and too little time to do it all, realise that you're not alone. Then realise that you can do something about it.

The best way to cut out whatever is getting in your ways is to stop and take stock – ideally at the start of each day. Follow these steps to assign a priority to each task on your to-do list:

1. **Draw up a list of everything you want to accomplish today.**

   (If you're well organised, you will have done that last night.)

2. **Colour code each item on the list.**

   - Red for **panics and problems:** The important, deadline-driven jobs you want to sort out quickly.

   - Green indicates **plans and opportunities:** The important, longer-term activities you'd like to spend time on. Include recreation as well as larger projects.

   - Blue for **pressing items:** The things other people are pushing you to do, but which are not top of your to-do list for today.

   - Yellow indicates **pootling issues:** The chats with friends and more trivial timewasters during which you drift around aimlessly.

   Your aim is to make the plans and opportunities list – the green one – largest of all and to reduce the size of the others. This area is most important because it enables you to put your energy on what's most important to you and save you getting stressed by deadlines, or just drift around listlessly.

3. Allocate your time today so that you can clear up some problems from your red list, build in space for the plans and opportunities in your green list, and see how much of the pressing (blue) and pootling (yellow) items you can cut out.

For now, it's important to become aware of what type of activities dominate your schedule most of the time. The colour coding is a quick visual guide to your effectiveness.

Redirecting those inner voices

For years I (Kate) had a little voice running in my head that said to me: 'Very correct . . . very dull.' At age 7 (back in the days of ancient history, as my girls so kindly say), I had written a short creative piece at Dulwich Hamlet Junior School. My teacher added this throwaway comment at the bottom in red ink – probably in a late-night book-marking session. Perhaps he was bored. Perhaps he never wanted to be a teacher. Perhaps he never even wrote those words at all, but that's what I remember. It's a filter, a negative inner voice, a naughty little gremlin I ran up against when under stress that questioned my confidence. 'Who are you to think you can write?' it whispered. This was despite the fact that I wrote professionally in my business career.

Over time this gremlin disappeared as I paid more attention to the voices that told me, 'You can do this. Your work makes a difference for people.' Part of this change happened by listening to encouraging feedback from various sources, and part was a personal decision to acknowledge that I was more than the words I put on paper. Today, with hindsight, I can recognise that my teacher had the very best of intentions to challenge me to develop my talents, and I thank him for that.

What about your inner voices? What do you say to yourself about yourself? Those inner voices, running in your head. As coaches, we often hear these busy, chattering gremlins in clients who say: 'The voice inside me says: Who do you think you are to take on this challenge? You'll get found out soon enough. You're a fraud. Are you good enough? Don't you think you should know your place? You're not a confident person, so what are you doing here?'

How can you tame these voices? In many creative ways, once you put your mind to it.

- ✔ Picture the friendly parrot on your shoulder (who flew in to the 'Getting past the blame mind-set' section earlier in this chapter) programmed with a positive message to repeat every time it hears a negative thought: 'I was chosen because I'm the best.' 'I can do this.' 'I am good enough.' 'I'm going to show you just how good I really am.'

- ✔ Imagine the negative voices playing on your CD player, then turning the volume control down to a hushed whisper, and finally gently flicking the off switch. Take the CD out, cut it up, and throw it away.

- ✔ Look for the positive intention of the negative voice. Figure out how it's trying to help you. Acknowledge it, thank it, and tell it to go away now that it's served a useful purpose.

You *can* clear out those unwanted messages.

Discovering What Drains Your Batteries

Confident people bounce with positive, focused energy – they're happy with themselves and life – and they're infectious to be with. They know where they are at and where they're going. Less confident people can drain the energy from everyone around them. Spend time with them and you're left feeling tired and exhausted. Ideally, you don't have many of what we call *toxic friends* because you wipe them out, park them elsewhere, or neutralise them before they wipe you out.

Then there are *toxic situations* – times and places that are just not right for you. In the following sections we invite you to line up all those damaging elements you're sticking with, and make the decision that you are no longer going to put up with them. You can get them out of your system once and for all. Freedom beckons!

Counting the cost of toleration

When we first met Julie, she was unhappy and exhausted at work, which resulted in a loss of confidence in her own technical skills. She had been off sick suffering from stress and depression, feeling unsupported in her job of delivering to tight deadlines for government projects. Her colleagues put more and more load onto Julie, who was conscientious about meeting deadlines, however unrealistic. Her energy was increasingly sapped in this toxic environment until she learnt how to push back the load and protect herself.

Now it's time to stop and consider what you might be tolerating that is gradually sapping your confidence. Table 2-2 gives you space to rate common confidence sappers according to how often you experience them. Go through the list in the table and mark the appropriate box for each item.

Table 2-2	Rating Confidence Sappers			
Sapper	*Rating*			
Work	**Never**	**Occasionally**	**Frequently**	**Always**
Overstretched/ long hours				
Talents unused				
Insufficient training				
Unfair pay or reward				
Bullying				

(continued)

Table 2-2 *(continued)*

Sapper	*Rating*			
Work	**Never**	**Occasionally**	**Frequently**	**Always**
Lack of support from boss				
Poor working conditions/tools				
Home and social				
Unfair allocation of chores				
Financial insecurity				
Unattractive/ untidy house				
Unpleasant behaviour/ negativity				
Excessive noise				
Lack of quality time				
Toxic friends who are very demanding				
Poor health				
Lack of exercise				

Now group your answers and rank them in order of their ability to sap your energy with the worst at the top.

- ✔ What is your number one confidence sapper, the thing that drains your energy the most?

- ✔ What is the effect on you of tolerating this?

  For example: Is it making you ill? Is it upsetting your relationships with other people? Is it costing you money?

- ✔ If you solved this one, what would be the bigger benefit in your life?

> For example: If you cleared the clutter in your house, could you invite a new boyfriend/girlfriend over for a romantic evening?
>
> ✔ What is your first step in dealing with this?
>
> Beyond your larger plan, think of something you can do to reach your goal *today*. Even if it's one tiny step forward, do something *now.*

You don't have to struggle on your own. Engage the help of friends, a mentor at work, or an independent coach or trainer who has only your interests at heart.

Trying to meet everyone's needs except your own

Busy people have a tendency to take on more and more because they see what needs doing and know how to get things done. Recognise the pattern?

It's very tempting to chase around the world helping everyone else except yourself. Doing so, however, can drain your energy in a drip-feed kind of way until you stop noticing it. You run around so much after other people, and dissipate your energy with your concerns about them, that you forget to look after yourself too.

As you begin to recognise more about where you are stuck in the confidence stakes and what holds you back, one very important question for you to consider is: How do you know when your needs are being met?

To answer this question, look at your life and see whether you sleep well each night; eat wholesome food; develop relationships; enjoy your work; and have time for hobbies, time out, and exercise. If not, then the balance may have tipped too much in favour of supporting others.

At the end of the day, do a final check to make sure you've done something good for yourself today, as well as supporting everyone else. If not, then put it top of your agenda for tomorrow.

The most confident people are generous to others and to themselves at the same time. They have high self-esteem – they know that they must value themselves and their time as well as that of others.

Chapter 3

Charting Your Course Ahead

· ·

In This Chapter

▶ Determining your path

▶ Choosing and using role models

· ·

*B*uilding anything is bound to be more difficult without specific information on what it is you are trying to build. And this is certainly true of building confidence. In this chapter, you look in more detail at the more confident you that you want to build and define the actions you need to take to realise that confident you.

Knowing Where You Want to Go

Many self-help books explain a variety of very powerful techniques to help you reach your goals. These methods range from the very practical tools used by professional project managers to the more gentle and esoteric methods of planting visions and feelings onto your future timeline and in your subconscious. These techniques all have one thing in common, though: You have to know what it is you want to accomplish or where it is you want to get to.

Does this ring any bells with you? You may be surprised to know how often people feel, that they need to strive to get somewhere really important with no clear notion of where it is they're going. You know you want to bring something into your life, but you haven't yet discovered exactly what it is. It's more of a feeling of dissatisfaction with the status quo, or a sense of knowing that you are capable of so much more. This is okay as far as it goes, but to take charge of the direction your life is going, you need to make some decisions.

Knowing precisely and in rich detail where you're trying to get to, and why that destination is important to you, is absolutely critical in achieving your dreams and becoming confident in the world.

Determining your areas of focus

A useful tool you can use to home in on areas you want to address, the *confidence wheel* is widely used by business and life coaches around the world. Figure 3-1 shows a sample wheel (decide upon your own categories and scores – we're just giving examples here).

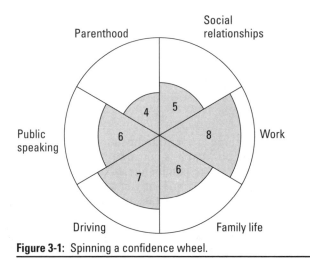

Figure 3-1: Spinning a confidence wheel.

To make your own confidence wheel, follow these steps:

1. **Make a list of the areas of your life in which your confidence plays an important part.**

   The list should include such things as social relationships, work, family life, and so on.

   You can have as many or as few as you like but six or eight is usually a good number to start with. These become the specific areas you work on to increase your all round self-confidence.

2. **Give yourself a score out of 10 in each area, in which 10 represents the level of confidence you would like to feel.**

   This score represents how confident you generally feel compared with how confident you would like to feel.

   For example, you may feel generally confident in your job and give yourself 8/10 for that, but perhaps you feel less confident in your social life and you score this at only 4/10.

3. **Draw a large circle on a sheet of plain paper and divide it into the same number of segments as you have items on**

your list. Label each segment to represent each area of
your life in which you want to develop more confidence.

4. **Draw a line in each segment to represent the score you
gave yourself in Step 2.**

If you score a segment 5/10, draw the line halfway between
the centre of the segment and its edge. You don't have to
be completely accurate, the idea is to create a visual representation of your confidence in the more important aspects
of your life.

The confidence wheel you generate gives you a comparative
assessment of the areas of your life in which you feel most and
least confident. You can use it to create more balance in your life
and to show you the areas that it would give you the most benefit
to work on. This information is useful in goal setting, and also in
understanding of how it feels when you are more or less confident
facing any new situation.

Taken in the round, your wheel also gives you an indication of
the degree of balance or imbalance in your confidence in various
aspects of your life. If this were a wagon wheel, how bumpy a ride
would you be getting? This is a useful insight into prioritising the
areas you may want to address first.

With this knowledge, you can draw a map to your destination;
without it, you are guaranteed to fail.

Mapping your own journey

The chapters throughout this book help you gain a deepening
understanding of your values and sense of purpose. For now, it
is enough that you have a few well-defined areas you would like
to change or improve while your deeper sense of purpose is
emerging.

The *SMART model* is a popular and easy-to-use system for making
change happen. You address the aspect that each letter stands for
in sequence. Think of something you want to bring into your life
right now and write down your answers as you work through the
following list:

✔ S stands for **specific.** Define what you want to achieve as
specifically as possible. If it's a car you're after, decide on the
make, the model, the colour, trim, year, and the price you are
prepared to pay. Find a picture or two of the *specific* car you
want and pin them up in strategic places where you will see

them every day. The more specific you are, the more effective your goal-achieving behaviour becomes.

✔ **M** stands for **measurable.** With an object such as a car measuring your achievement is easy – you either have it or you don't. But your progress towards some goals is more difficult to measure. Say your objective is to be more present with your family. First you must decide what this means *specifically* (the amount of time you spend at home, how long you focus on your partner's conversation, and so on) and then you can set up your equally specific *measures*. And don't forget to write them down.

✔ **A** stands for **attainable.** The trick here is to make your goal a challenge and a stretch without it being overwhelming. Athletes are good at this. They constantly set themselves new challenges, personal bests, and so on, pushing on their performance standards to new heights in challenging chunks. You can set intermediate goals if necessary to keep yourself moving in the right direction.

✔ **R** stands for **rewarding.** Asking yourself regularly why you want to achieve a particular goal and linking this to your growing confidence about who you're being in the world and what you're doing with your time are absolutely critical – and often forgotten. Having the *why* written down and available in your moments of weakness provides you with the motivation to carry on, to get through this tough patch, and to move on towards your goal. The bigger the reward, the stronger your motivation. With a big enough 'why' you will never give up.

✔ **T** stands for **time.** Having a deadline can be very motivating. It keeps you focused on achievement against plan and allows you to set up milestones for your bigger, more complicated goals. If your goal is to achieve your ideal weight by Christmas, then December 25 becomes your deadline, and you can work backwards from then to set yourself a series of intermediate goals.

Your increasing insights into how to set goals and achieve the things you want in life are an enormous support to your growing confidence. You can never know what is around the next corner, but you can rely on your growing skills and understanding to get you through it. Onwards and upwards!

When you're at your most powerful and confident, the things you take on in the world, the way you behave, your skills, experiences, and competencies, what is important to you, your beliefs, your sense of who you are and what you are here to do are all of a piece – making you, in self-help terms, congruent or aligned.

Setting milestones along the way

A good technique for broad-brush, big-picture goal setting is to think about how you want things to be in your healthy old age. Choose an age, say 85, and picture yourself at the centre of your network of family and friends doing whatever it is you want to be doing at that age. Focus on what you're doing, how fit and healthy you are, what your weight is, how you occupy your time, and what you enjoy doing.

Now figure out what you need to be like at 65 to make this possible, and at 50, and so on. By thinking backwards, you can add layer after layer of detail, as much as you want to give yourself a much clearer sense of what you need to make happen over the next five to ten years to give you the life you want.

Following the guaranteed success formula

There are many versions of the *guaranteed success formula,* and they all essentially tackle the problem of getting the result you want. You can use this simple six-step version straight away:

1. **Decide what you want.**

2. **Plan what you need to do to get what you want.**

3. **Take the necessary action.**

    (This is where confidence comes into it.)

4. **Notice what result you're getting.**

5. **Vary your action in light of your results.**

6. **Repeat Steps 2 to 5 until you get the result you want.**

Perhaps the most-cited example of the benefits of following this formula is Thomas Edison, the American inventor and entrepreneur, who is credited with having found 9,999 ways of *not* inventing the light bulb before getting it right.

A more up-to-date and less apocryphal example is how computers effortlessly achieve complex mathematical estimations. They sometimes perform millions of mathematical calculations in just a few seconds using the guaranteed success formula before presenting you with the optimal answer to the problem, using the guaranteed success formula to get the correct result.

Alcoholics Anonymous operates a highly successful personal improvement programme that literally saves lives. One of its teachings is that it is easier to act your way into a new way of thinking than it is to think your way into a new way of acting. Go on, change some of your behaviours and be sensitive to how people begin to behave differently to you.

Using the guaranteed success formula to improve your personal life

Say there is a person in your circle of friends you feel drawn to. You might even have entertained fantasies about taking long walks together in the country and having your feelings being reciprocated. Well, what are you going to do about it?

Using the guaranteed success formula, you decide what you want (to invite him on a weekend country walk) and you plan what you need to do to achieve that (get another couple to team up for a foursome). You then take action and ask him if he would like to come along, and pay attention to the result. Whether you get an enthusiastic 'yes' or a polite 'no', you need to be careful about how you interpret the answer. (After all, you aren't married yet, so you will need to keep on taking action and being sensitive to what comes back.) If his initial response was 'no', you may need to draw down on your reason for wanting this date. You may want to ask him if he would like to catch a movie sometime instead if it is important enough to you.

As long as you remain interested in the outcome, keep on varying your approach while remaining sensitive to the results you get. If you adopt this proactive, very conscious approach to goal achievement, you will remain clearer about what is happening and you will be far less likely to make a fool of yourself.

Choosing Role Models

One way of speeding up the trial and error element of the guaranteed success formula is to find an example of someone doing something the way you would like to and emulating, or *modelling*, not just what they are doing but also how they are doing it (including, as much as you can, what they are actually thinking and feeling while they are doing it).

Autobiographies can provide a very good source of insight into how prominent people have approached the achievements for which they are noted. The autobiography of someone in any area you choose, from sports, to business, politics, or philosophy, can be a very rich source of material for inspiration and emulation. A good autobiography gives a highly personal account of a whole person.

Finding reliable guides

Who do you most admire and why? If you want to be more like that person, then find out what you can about how they approach the things you would like to emulate and use this to inform your own application of the guaranteed success formula. The more precise and specific you can be about this the better.

Keep in mind that even true heroes have feet of clay – we all do. What you should care most about is how someone has achieved a standard of performance or developed a character trait that you want to emulate. Focus on the sporting excellence rather than the womanising, or the artistic brilliance rather than the drug abuse. Don't fall prey to the *halo effect* that occurs when you set your heroes on pedestals, then watch in horrid fascination when the tabloid newspapers and scandal sheets expose their faults and failings.

A useful metaphor is that of Steve Austin in the old television show *The Six Million Dollar Man*. After he was severely damaged in a near-fatal accident, scientists rebuilt Steve to be far faster, stronger, and all-round better than he was originally. You may want to run like Michael Johnson, be funny like Jerry Seinfeld, or score goals like Pelé. Whatever does it for you, be specific.

Enriching her life with theirs

Tanya is an avid reader of autobiographies and she finds them an enduring source of inspiration in her life of caring for her partner, children, and elderly parents while her career is on hold.

She loves the personal accounts of triumph over adversity such as that of Lance Armstrong, who beat cancer to set world records in cycle racing at the Tour de France and the Irish tenor and recording artist Ronan Tynan, who also set world athletic records after being born with defects that meant his legs and feet never fully developed.

Equally, she loves to read about those who set and achieve 'impossible' targets, like Sir Steve Redgrave, who won rowing gold medals at five separate Olympic games over a 20-year career at the very pinnacle of athletic performance.

Most of all, though, she loves to read about the awakening of the spirit, such as happened with the beautiful Queen Noor of Jordan who, as Lisa Halaby an American architect planner, met and married King Hussein and became an inspirational focus for the interests of women and children, education, arts, and culture in the Arab world.

In the first-hand accounts of all these true lives, Tanya finds the comfort, knowledge, and inspiration to keep her own standards high and her own performance on track for the life of her choosing. When she eventually restarts her career, she will bring a new depth and wisdom to her work based on the high standards and values evident in the great lives she has been steadily absorbing.

Becoming your own coach

You have the opportunity of becoming your own coach as you grow in understanding and knowledge of how to get the best out of yourself. This isn't as difficult as it might seem at first and you can make a start with just a few pointers.

Think about the attributes of a coach. Coaches take a dispassionate view of the client's performance. They look carefully to consider what is actually happening before making suggestions for change or improvement. Coaches see it and tell it like it is: no better, no worse.

Seeing it and telling it like it is, is a very useful skill that you can easily develop with just a little practice. Start right now. Stop for a moment and imagine yourself across the room observing the real you that is reading this book. Describe the scene in simple, clear, unambiguous phrases like: 'She is sitting and reading the text, she puts the book down periodically and appears to be thinking about something, occasionally she writes a note in the margin.'

Coaches tend to use simple, direct language in telling it like it is. There are no value judgements. There is none of the 'She seems to be daydreaming again, she seems unable to concentrate on anything for more than a few minutes; there she goes again, she'll never get this done' or any of the other things you may habitually say to yourself. When *you* are being the coach you first need to look and consider what is really happening, and only then think constructively about how best to move the performance or situation forward.

Becoming the hero in your own life

One of the most effective ways of raising your performance in anything is to 'raise your game'; that is raising your expectations and your personal standards. Who is the real hero of your life? You are, of course, and your standard of performance will be more influential than anything else in shaping the life you will experience.

Most people think of a hero as someone who is born with an exceptional character, courage, and bravery. Perhaps the hero has some externally imposed goal, such as the restoration of his birthright after a usurper stole his father's crown (think of Simba in *The Lion King*).

Real life isn't like this, of course, but that doesn't mean that no heroes exist in real life. Shakespeare reminds us that some are born great, some achieve greatness, and some have greatness thrust upon them. And this applies equally to women and men, even though the classical heroes are usually male.

So what does a real-life hero look like? Take a look in the mirror. Yes, a real-life hero looks a lot like you, right here, right now. Every life is a rerun of the classical hero's journey you read about as a child, and every one of us in our own way faces the hero's choices of good over evil, light over dark, right over wrong, and going forwards into growth or shrinking backwards into fear.

To become the star of the show in the drama of your life, follow these steps:

1. **Decide that you are going to take on personal change to enable you to achieve the things you want in life, and get into action.**

   Be kind and supportive to yourself. You aren't going to get things right first time, so expect setbacks and think about how you can manage and recover from them. Determine how to get yourself back on track efficiently.

2. **Decide where it is you are going, or what it is that you really want.**

   Set your goals using the techniques in this chapter. Some goals can be relatively short term and fun, others may be more serious and take you many years to accomplish. Reach for the stars: Your journey will last your lifetime and you don't want to complete it too soon.

3. **Plan your work and work your plan.**

   You always accomplish more – and more quickly and reliably – when you have a plan. But the plan itself is of limited use if you don't work it. Vary it, change it, but stick with it. Your plan is your friend – and a hero needs a reliable friend.

4. **Don't compete, create!**

   Don't view your life as a competition and the people you meet along the way as your competitors. On heroes' journeys, other people appear as messengers, allies, and resources. Sometimes they bring you warnings; other times they bring you keys and answers to the questions you are posing. Only rarely do you meet an enemy outside yourself – your enemy is most often found in the gremlins within you, holding you back, and you need to be creative to outsmart them.

5. Pay attention to your lessons before you apply them.

Hear the truths that strangers bring to you before you try to drown them out with your own truth and enthusiasm for your journey. Life tends to repeat the lessons you don't learn first time, so be alert and embrace what life teaches you.

6. Care for your companions on the journey.

As Shakespeare also said, the world is a stage and we all must play a part. You have changed your part to put yourself at the centre of your own heroic epic, but you need other characters to give your epic richness and colour. You don't want to end up a lonely old king living alone in your magnificent castle of dreams. Be kind to those whose journeys interact with yours.

7. Listen to your inner coach.

Your inner coach knows you and knows what you need. Don't neglect your daily needs in pursuit of your future.

As you gain new and powerful insights into what you do, why you do things this way and the choices you are making, you become more aware of your true potential. This awakening is an essential step on every hero's journey.

If you take on this way of being, you'll be amazed by the change you bring into your life. And if you ever take on a professional coach to help you, you will make faster progress through having learned to be coachable.

If the idea of your personal hero's journey intrigues you, you can find other tools on the Internet at www.yourmostconfidentself. com – the authors' Web site.

Part II
Gathering the Elements

The 5th Wave   By Rich Tennant

"I'm looking for someone who will love me for who I think I am."

In this part...

Y ou find out how to take action when your motivation is challenged. You're invited to connect with the ideals and goals that drive you and gain a better understanding of your deepest values. You delve into some emotional stuff as you learn to live with your mood swings – the highs and lows. Really importantly, you uncover more about your passions so that you can stop sitting on the sidelines and realise your dreams.

Chapter 4

Finding Your Motivation

· ·

In This Chapter

▶ Understanding what motivation means and what motivates you

▶ Applying motivation theories to your work and social life

▶ Using your understanding to engineer new opportunities for achievement

· ·

*Y*our personal motivation is the force that gets you out of bed in the morning and provides you with energy for the work of the day. Have you ever wondered why you seem to be bursting with it some days, and other times it seems to desert you entirely?

Understanding how motivation works so that you can access your natural motivation to help manage the life you want with more confidence and ease is what this chapter is about. It gives you the insight you need to keep moving forward despite the challenges you face.

The most important thing you can take from this chapter is that you don't have to put up with feeling weak and unmotivated. If you deal intelligently with blocks in your natural energy source, you can restore your energy, achieve more with less effort, and feel more at ease with life, more satisfied with yourself, and more confident and powerful in the world.

Driving Forward in Your Life

The more motivated you feel the more inclined you are to push yourself through the things that are holding you back. If you can increase your motivation, you automatically increase your confidence. In the next sections, we look at Abraham Maslow's influential hierarchy of needs to help you gain insight into what motivates you and everyone you come into contact with.

Rising through Maslow's hierarchy of needs

One of the founders of the human potential movement, Abraham Maslow is best known for his work on human motivation. He was fascinated by what makes some people face huge challenges in life, and what makes them refuse to give up despite incredible odds. He developed the model for which he is best known – his hierarchy of needs, shown in Figure 4-1 – to explain the forces that motivate people.

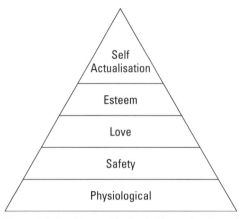

Figure 4-1: Looking at Maslow's hierarchy of needs.

Maslow saw men and women being constantly drawn on through life by the irresistible pull of unsatisfied needs. He grouped human needs into a hierarchy, which everyone shares and needs to satisfy from the bottom up. This model is widely taught in management development courses, but his work goes far beyond the workplace to the very heart of our humanity.

Maslow believed that you must first satisfy your basic physiological needs for air, water, food, sleep, and so on before any other desires can surface. As a member of modern society, these basic needs are largely taken care of for you, but if you have ever been short of breath under water you know and understand how this first-tier, physiological need dominates everything else until it is satisfied.

But once your physiological needs are met, you automatically shift up to the next level in the hierarchy to your need for safety, – and that now drives you. Again, modern society tends to provide safe environments, but whenever you do feel threatened, you experience an automatic physical response and cannot think of much else until the situation is resolved and you feel safe again.

At the next level, you have to make more personal interventions to ensure your needs are satisfied within the framework that society provides for you. Your needs for love and connection show up here; things you don't automatically get all the time. If your needs at this level are unsatisfied, and you feel isolated or lonely, you find it almost impossible to meet your higher-level needs in any meaningful way.

The next level is where your needs for self-esteem and recognition kick in. These may never have been an issue for you as you struggled to join your group, but now they can become dominant. It is no longer enough simply to belong; now you must have some power and status in the group too – drive a bigger car, become captain of the golf club perhaps, or chair of the school parent–teacher association. This is where most established adults reside most of the time today.

But thankfully, the endless striving does end, and with all your needs taken care of, you eventually arrive at the top of Maslow's hierarchy as a fully developed human being. At the exotically named *self-actualisation* stage, you decide what is truly most important to you in life and your major motivation becomes living and expressing this. Often, this is where you get to give something back to the world that has supported you so royally in your journey up the hierarchy.

Maslow's hierarchy of needs helps to explain so much of the variability in human behaviour. Different human beings can be operating at different levels, and be driven by different needs at any given time. Your motivation may be different on Monday from on Friday with the weekend looming. And of course, you may feel different at work from the way you feel at home. The more you understand what drives you, the better able you will be to use it to achieve the things you want in life.

Greeting the world with grace

Maslow is often associated with motivation at work, but his insights apply equally in social situations where you can use them to help put yourself at ease.

When you find yourself in a new social group – meeting new people at a party or function, for example – you can expect to feel anxious because *at this moment* you are at Maslow's second level, needing to be accepted into this new group. When you're in this situation, the first thing to do is to accept your mild anxiety about it. There's nothing wrong with feeling or admitting that you're nervous (in case the voice inside your head starts accusing you of being a wimp).

Beyond shyness into phobia

Neil had been an extremely shy and reserved person from early adolescence. And while everyone feels nervous in social situations from time to time, Neil's nervousness was not the normal kind but magnified on frequent occasions into disproportionate fear and anxiety.

His symptoms were intense with persistent fears of situations where he didn't know people and where he felt they would be judging him. This led him to avoid these situations to a degree that affected his social life and work. Even so, he still feared being embarrassed or humiliated and was particularly sensitive that others would notice him blushing, sweating, and sometimes even shaking. He was finally able to recognise that this was more than just shyness, and that his fears were excessive and unreasonable for the situations he faced.

Neil found out that when social anxieties become extreme like this and disrupt your life, they may have crossed the line into a medical condition known as social phobia, or *social anxiety disorder*. He checked into the symptoms on the Internet and was worried enough to seek medical help.

In Neil's case, the diagnosis was *global social phobia,* a condition that affects virtually all social situations and so can be easily confused with shyness. He was told that it can lead to substance abuse, alcoholism, depression, and even suicide, but that treatment was readily available.

His treatment was a combination of drugs to help balance his seratonin levels (seratonin is a hormone that helps keep moods under control by helping with sleep, calming anxiety, and relieving depression) and cognitive behaviour therapy based on the premise that it was Neil's own thoughts, rather than the situations he was facing, that were causing his extreme reaction.

Around 5 per cent of the readers of this book are likely to suffer from social phobia and soldier on in private, sometimes for years, avoiding and suffering in social situations. Only when they accept, like Neil, that they need medical assistance does it become possible to diagnose their condition and begin a course of treatment. The effects of medical intervention can often be liberating and profound, opening the door to a much more fulfilling and rewarding life.

Neil's seratonin is more stable now and he may soon be able to discontinue the drugs. The therapy has helped him to learn to think in a different way, just like the ideas in this book will help you to think in a more positive and helpful way, increasing your confidence in many situations.

Remember, everyone in the room fits into Maslow's hierarchy and is therefore feeling needy at some level. The people you're meeting who are not new to the group are operating at the second and third levels: some are anxious for acceptance, just as you are (and these people will be just as keen to be accepted by you as you are by them); some are motivated by their need for social esteem and need your respect.

Depending on the kind of party this is, you can expect to witness needy behaviours at all levels from hunger and thirst, through sex, connection, companionship, to a close approximation of self-actualisation on the dance floor. Don't judge your fellow partygoers too harshly. In fact, give everyone at the party a break, including yourself. Enjoy the spectacle!

Take on board these new factors in an otherwise ordinary and potentially dull social dynamic by paying attention to the curious and interesting display of need-motivated behaviours going on around you.

If you're curious about the people in the group and really take an interest in what's happening, you come across to others as attentive and a great conversationalist. This is more fun for you, and more fun for the people you meet. Pretty soon everyone will want you at their parties.

Bringing this more curious and attentive version of yourself into social situations lessens your anxiety, because you focus on the impression others are making on you rather than the one you're making on them. You always appear charming to those you meet if you give them the gift of your rapt attention. People are not used to this and they will love you for it.

Taking Charge at Work

Your personal motivation is critical to your performance and confidence in the world, but in work, your motivation is pretty important to your employer too. This has led to motivation becoming the focus of a lot of social science research over the last 50 years, and in this section, we show you how to use some of this for your personal benefit at work.

Looking at usable theory

Maslow's theory about human needs is universal, applying to everyone in all situations. Other important theorists, most notably Frederick Herzberg and William McGregor, have focused on your motivation at work, which is important to you and to your employer. In this section, you can find out how to take more control over your motivation at work and increase this if that is what you need. You will also find a self-test to help you to measure your progress.

Searching for satisfaction with Herzberg

Frederick Herzberg is another motivation guru frequently studied on management development courses (which means that your senior colleagues should have heard about him). His elegant theory reveals the factors that energise you at work and also those that take your natural energy away. He separates out those forces that motivate people, called *motivators*, from those that sap motivation, the *dissatisfiers*. He discovered that these forces operate in a surprising, seemingly illogical way.

Take pay as a universal example. You may think that the money you are paid provides you with motivation, and most employers act as though this is the case, but it simply isn't true in the long term according to Herzberg. Pay is a dissatisfier and not a motivator. If you aren't being paid the rate for the job, your poor pay rate can certainly make you feel dissatisfied, but surprisingly, of itself being paid over the odds doesn't motivate you any further than being paid a fair rate does (although it may bring other factors into play, such as recognition and team status).

Recognition, on the other hand, is a motivator. This is why a good job title, a word of thanks from the boss, or a mention in the in house journal for a job well done can be so motivating.

Table 4-1 contains a list of some of the main motivators and dissatisfiers that Herzberg identified. The dissatisfiers on the left have to be carefully managed or they can create serious dissatisfaction for you, but of themselves they cannot motivate you. The factors on the right are the motivators and give you the drive you need to do your best work, but they don't come into play until the dissatisfiers have first been neutralised.

Table 4-1	Factors Affecting Job Attitudes
Dissatisfiers	*Motivators*
Company policies	Achievement
Style of supervision	Recognition
Relationship with boss	Work itself
Working conditions	Responsibility
Salary	Advancement
Relationship with peers	Personal growth

Notice that the factors in the left column are external to the work itself and are largely imposed on you from outside. The motivators in the satisfaction column are much more personal, in that they tend to be more closely tied to the job you do. They are also more psychological, in that you have personal discretion over how much of them you feel.

If this insight starts to resonate powerfully for you, you may want to read up a bit more on Herzberg's motivation-hygiene theory before having a discussion about it with your boss. The dissatis-fiers present in your work may be easy for your boss to neutralise, leaving you unencumbered psychologically to bring your motiva-tion into play.

Unless you feel the presence of the motivators to a degree that has significance for you, you won't be motivated or satisfied at work no matter what else the company does for you.

Mapping McGregor's Theory X and Theory Y

Douglas McGregor's work is less well known to general managers and this is a shame as it focuses closely on management style (one of Herzberg's key dissatisfiers). McGregor brought out the effects of reactionary and over-zealous management practices and poli-cies in his two models: Theory X and Theory Y.

Theory X assumes that, as a worker, you have an inbuilt dislike of working and will shirk as much as you can get away with. Therefore, you need to be controlled to ensure that you put in the effort needed, and you need to be told exactly what to do and how to do it. This can be very damaging to your natural motivation, your job sat-isfaction, and eventually your self-belief and confidence. Studies sug-gest that if your boss treats you this way, you may begin to behave as if it were true. (If this is happening to you use the feedback model in Chapter 15 to make this point to your supervisor or departmental representative.)

Theory Y takes the opposite view. It assumes that working is impor-tant to you, and as natural to you as the other parts of your life. If your work is satisfying, it becomes a source of drive and fulfilment. You become committed to it and you require little in the way of supervision.

You perform better and are more productive if you are allowed to manage your own workload, output, and so on, because you know so much better than anyone else how to get the best out of yourself.

In these circumstances, your supervisor becomes a colleague you can consult when you need a second opinion and who can liaise with senior management to enable you to do the best job possible.

How do these two models compare with your own job situation? The chances are that your own supervision has elements of both Theory X and Theory Y. As ever, the onus is on you to take more control of an element of your life. Once you have knowledge you need to put it to use.

Taking action may require all the confidence you can muster, and in this case it will repay you directly by helping to build your confidence for the future.

The challenge you face is not so much individuals and their personal attitudes but organisation structures and the way jobs are organised. If you supervise a team, or even just work in a team, following Theory Y gives you a far better chance of getting the results you need. Educate your colleagues where you can and help to bring your teams into the 21st century.

Putting theory to the test

In this section, you see how to use the theoretical insights from the preceding sections to build your confidence as you engage with the world. And because most motivation theory is based on the workplace, you start there.

Whether you work for yourself or for someone else, you have to meet your motivational needs. Table 4-2 provides a self-test you can take in two minutes that measures your motivation response at work. If you work alone, modify the questions as necessary to suit your circumstances. Give yourself up to five points for each question – all five if you strongly agree, down to one if you strongly disagree.

Table 4-2　　Job Motivation Response Self-Test

Value Statement	Strongly Agree (5 points)	Agree (4 points)	Neutral (3 points)	Disagree (2 points)	Strongly Disagree (1 point)
I am entirely in control of my work environment. Provided I meet my objectives, I am free to decide how much I do and what work I do next.					

Value Statement	Strongly Agree (5 points)	Agree (4 points)	Neutral (3 points)	Disagree (2 points)	Strongly Disagree (1 point)
I have established a good working relationship with my boss. She gives me the room to do my job the way I want and I usually deliver what she needs.					
My benefits package and general working environment are okay. When something needs to be looked at, it's usually sorted out in a reasonable time.					
My work colleagues are generally supportive and don't get in my way. We are a good team and each of us serves the group objective pretty effectively. When issues arise, we are usually able to deal with them.					
I get a real buzz from the work I do. I feel closely identified with my output and put the best of myself into it. I wouldn't want it to be any other way.					
I feel that my employer values my work and is in touch with what is going on. They care about my career and look after things so that I don't have to worry about them.					
My work is very visible. People know that it is mine, and I take great pride in it. It is not unusual for people to acknowledge the good job I am doing.					

(continued)

Table 4-2 *(continued)*

Value Statement	Strongly Agree (5 points)	Agree (4 points)	Neutral (3 points)	Disagree (2 points)	Strongly Disagree (1 point)
I am allowed to take full responsibility for the quality of my work and for meeting my other objectives and deadlines. My boss knows that I know how to get the best out of myself and lets me get on with it.					
I feel that my work stretches me and allows me to grow. I have the level of challenge and variety that keeps me fully engaged without being overwhelmed.					
My work is an expression of who I truly am at some deeper level. Even if I were not being paid, I would still need to express myself through the kind of work I do. If I were unable to work it would be like losing a limb.					

Use these guidelines to evaluate your score:

- ✔ **40–50:** Congratulations, you may have found your life's work. You're working in a job that gives you most of what you need not only for motivation but for your growth and fulfilment too.

- ✔ **30–40:** This is still a very good score. You should be able to see the areas that are pulling you down and you can develop some goals for changing them. Use the SMART goal-setting technique in Chapter 3 to help create the changes you need.

- ✔ **10–30:** You already know this score is not so good. You may need to take more personal responsibility for your motivation at work, which can include changing your job or organization. Take a look at the techniques in Chapter 15 to help you take more control of your work.

Recognizing the importance of achievement

Achieving results in work is not just a matter of pleasing your boss and earning a bonus. It forms an important contribution to your personal sense of significance and wellbeing as you move up the hierarchy of needs (refer to Figure 4-1) and a sense of achievement is top of the list of Herzberg's motivators (refer to Table 4-1).

As you progress in work, you need to think more about what constitutes achievement for *you*. Consider what it is you really want out of your life and your work, and then, without working any harder, you should be able to secure more of it both for yourself and your employer. This increases your sense of fulfilment and satisfaction and provides you with more motivational energy for yet more achievement.

Your relationship to your work is a very influential part of your relationship to the world and all it contains. If you want to achieve your most confident and powerful version of yourself, you need to understand and manage your value and contribution through your work in the world.

Going for the next promotion

Like most people, when a promotion opportunity comes up, you may want to seize the chance to get it immediately (not least because if you don't get it someone else will). But think very carefully about what the promotion may mean for you before you go for it.

It is not uncommon for a successful and happy worker to win a promotion only to become a less successful and far less happy supervisor or manager. When this happens, the person can remain stuck in their new role where their poor performance rules out any further advancement and the organisational hierarchy prevents them from returning to where they were once good and happy.

If you know anyone who has been caught in this way, you understand that it's hardly a recipe for organisational achievement – much less for personal confidence and fulfilment. Armed with the knowledge of this chapter, absolutely no reason remains why it should happen to you.

Before you accept any new role, ask yourself:

✔ How did things play out for the previous person who held this job? Perhaps they went on to even higher things, or perhaps they were stuck in the role for a long time and didn't appear too happy in it.

✔ What is likely to happen to you if you remain a while longer in your current role? Is there an even better promotion coming up soon? Would your refusal to take on the promotion offered send a bad or a good signal to your management?

✔ How could you use the current situation to create the job you want? Would it be possible to change the new job into something that suits you better, retaining, say, some of your current responsibility? Or perhaps it would be possible to split up the new role and take only some aspects of it into your current role?

✔ How can you use the change on offer to let your colleagues and superiors know that you are thinking deeply about the work you do and are not just in it for the pay cheque? In the longer-term this may be the most valuable aspect of the entire situation.

Now, when the opportunity for promotion comes up, you have a far richer way of evaluating why you are interested in the new role, what it will bring to you other than money and what it will take away. And if you decide to go for it, you bring so much more to the table; making a good impression on your colleagues and leaving you with a big win whether or not you get the role.

Chapter 5

Sticking to Your Principles

In This Chapter

▶ Identifying your values

▶ Creating the life you have always wanted

▶ Leading an authentic life

*I*f you knew what was truly important in life and spent 70 or 80 years becoming really good at it, would the quality of your life be improved, do you think? Would this knowledge enable you to be a lot clearer about your priorities? Would it enable you to cut down on things that don't contribute to your fulfilment, and cut out altogether those things that actually take you away from what you want? You bet it would!

Defining what you truly want and how you want to live, and then sticking to your principles, is your most powerful means of achieving a life you love. In this chapter, you'll discover the things your life is really about and how to bring them to fruition.

Understanding Your Values

What do you value most in life – what is most important to you? These are probably the most important questions a human being can face and yet many people don't know the answers. If you want to bring your most confident version of yourself into the world and live a life truly worthy of you, it's important that you can answer them. You can then use your answers to guide you through life. This chapter is designed to help you discover your answers and live accordingly.

Discovering your values

It's an odd thing, but when you really get down to it, if you're like most people, you may have only a vague idea of how you want your life to be. You certainly want to be happy and may feel that in order to be happy you need certain other things: such as good health, a good job, a suitable partner, perhaps a loving family, maybe a nice home and a decent car (maybe even a *very* nice car). On top of this, you have certain values that you feel need to be fulfilled: values such as honesty, integrity, respect, and so on. Beyond this, many people are unsure.

If you're in this position, take heart. The work you do in this chapter helps clarify your values, leaving you crystal clear on what makes you happy, and making it far more likely that you will achieve what you need.

Think about this question: what do you value most in life? What comes immediately to mind? Is it very personal things – your health, your loved ones? Does it involve your work or sense of vocation – your art, your work at the hospital? Is your immediate thought of big, global issues – ecology, poverty, or world peace?

In discovering your most important values – those things that you believe will lead you to the feelings you most want in your life – go for those things that really engage you emotionally and leave out the things that you feel you *ought* to care most about; there should be no 'oughts' in this exercise (apart from that one!). With that proviso you are ready to begin:

1. **Write down your answer to the question: What is most important to you in your life?** Write down the single most important thing.

2. **Now answer the similar question: What else is most important to you in your life?** Write down the next most important thing.

3. **And finally, answer for the third time: What else is most important to you in your life?** Write down the third most important thing.

You can stop now, as you have three answers to work with, which is plenty for your first time; but you would only have to keep going to get more.

The answers you write down we call your *means values* because these are the means by which you are pursuing what you want in your life (don't worry if this doesn't make much sense to you yet).

There are no right or wrong answers. What you're finding out is what you want in life and ultimately how you can get more of it into your daily living. By doing the work in this chapter, you become able to include in your life the things that are most important to you. If you do this, you will care more about what you are doing and you will be more powerful and confident.

Uncovering your ends values

If your means values are your means to an end, then what is this end they're supposed to help you achieve? The answer to this is key, so are you ready for it? The answer is *feelings*! How you feel, at any point in your day, largely drives how you behave and how you *are* in the world. How you feel colours everything you do, and you learnt at a very early age to manage the way you feel by trying to have more of some things and less of others.

Your *means values* are your grown-up version of your need to satisfy your inner child's wanting to feel a certain way. They may not be the only ways you can get these feelings, and they may not be the best ways, but you have them linked together in your mind and are pursuing your desired feelings by these means.

Wow! So all those difficult things you've been pursuing in life are just to help you to feel a certain way? Yes, and it would be very helpful right now to work out exactly what ways you do want to feel. These are your *ends values*.

To elicit your ends values from your means values, follow these steps:

1. **Write down the first means value that you uncovered when you asked yourself: 'what is most important to me in my life?'**

   As an example, Dave is a married man whose first means value is his family.

2. **Now ask yourself the supplementary question: 'If I have this, what does it give me?'**

   Dave's answer to this question is 'a reason to get up in the morning to provide for them'.

3. **And now ask yourself the further supplementary question of the answer you just came up with: 'and what will *that* give me?'**

   Applying the question elicits from Dave: 'a reason for being active and powerful in the world'.

4. **Repeat Steps 2 and 3 until you arrive at a *basic emotion or feeling* (such as safety, love, connection, and so on).**

   In Dave's case, asking the question again gives: 'deliver my maximum value to the world', and once again gives: 'I'll be able to look at myself in the mirror', which finally comes down to 'self-respect'.

Dave can stop at this point, because self-respect is a basic feeling that he gets from looking after his wife and children. Providing for his family may also contribute to other feelings, but we'll stick with self-respect for now because this is what came up.

5. **Repeat the process with the other answers you gave to the question: 'What is most important to me in my life?'**

   By repeating the questioning process on all your means values, you eventually arrive at a few basic feelings, usually not more than half a dozen. These are your *ends values,* the basic feelings you want to experience regularly in your life.

6. **Write down all the basic feelings, or ends values, that you come up with.**

   Dave came up with the values of self-respect, connection, health and vitality, playfulness, and wisdom.

Congratulations! Pause a moment to reflect on what you have just achieved. In terms of your personal development, you're now ahead of 90 per cent of the people on the planet. *You know what you have been trying to achieve in your life so far and why.* These feelings on your list are your ultimate values and everything else is just your means of achieving them. You work with your list throughout this chapter.

Once you have your lists of feelings, or ends values, you're in a position to work with them in ways that can assist you to get them into your life more frequently and reliably. When you can do that, your values are satisfied and you're free to get on with your life in a whole new and liberated way. Your confidence is unbounded.

Resolving values conflicts

You may find that two or more of your means values are pulling you in different directions. For example, if you're like many people, both family and job are on your list of what's most important to you. Both enable you to experience the feelings of connection, achievement, success, and so on that you want in your life.

However, trying to honour both simultaneously may spread you very thin, and leave you feeling as though you're not doing well with your values in either area. At worst, you may feel when you are working that you should be spending more with your family, and when you are with the family you feel you should be working. From here you can become prey to feelings you definitely do *not* want in your life such as guilt, frustration, and dissatisfaction. If this sort of values conflict strikes a chord with you, take heart. Resolving such conflicts can add a lot to the quality of your life.

With a little work and application, it's possible to turn a 'no win' into a 'no lose'. Before you can do this though you need to know about values hierarchies and rules.

Rating your values

In Chapter 4, we talk about Maslow's Hierarchy of Needs and how to use it. This is a generalised model of values that illustrates the influences on everyone. But armed with the knowledge in this chapter, you can go a step further. Here you discover your own, very personal hierarchy of values. Although largely unconscious, your personal hierarchy has become tailored to the specifics of your life, and it is important to work with it to ensure that it serves you.

All your values are important, but you will always choose to secure one or two of them first in order to be able to enjoy the others.

Take a little time now to rank the ends values you discovered in the preceding 'Uncovering your ends values' section into a hierarchy, putting the most important one at the top and so on down to the last.

When you have completed this list, go on to the next section, which shows you how to make it really easy to have your values met, and much more difficult to feel that they have been violated.

Making your own rules

How is it that two people, on the same fairground ride, may have such a totally different experience of the ride? One may feel terrified and hate every second of it, while the other gets a "rush" and a sense of exhilaration. What's happening here? It comes down to a very particular set of beliefs they each carry around with them and use to determine whether or not their values are being met. These special beliefs – which you have, as well – are your rules about your values.

What's actually happening physically on the fairground ride is virtually the same for each person. But what each person makes that experience *mean* can be very different. Each of them is unconsciously applying a specific set of beliefs about their physical experience in the form of rules. The rule for one person may be something like 'I am putting myself in danger irresponsibly and pointlessly' and the rule for the other is 'I love the thrill of speed, it makes me feel so alive'.

All beliefs help you to make decisions quickly based on previous experience, but when they take the form of unconscious rules they may be working against you and causing you feelings that you don't want.

You don't have to worry about where your rules came from – whether you have an easy guess about the source or not. Because your rules are merely beliefs, that is, merely a sense of certainty, you can change them easily by applying a little common sense.

If you are in a similar situation, ask yourself: 'how likely is it that this fairground ride will crash in a serious accident, involving me as a victim, at this precise moment?' The real odds don't matter; the grounds for worry are so tiny. Is it a reasonable belief then, that you will be seriously injured on this ride? No, it isn't. Since there can be no certainty about being hurt, this belief doesn't stand up. Now, apply a similar logic to find any benefit that could ensue from your taking the ride and keep looking until you find some.

Beliefs like this, if they do not immediately respond to the logic treatment, may prove to be *phobias*. They can also be removed relatively easily but you may need the assistance of a therapist as described in Chapter 10.

The exciting part is this: What could you now consciously make a certainty about this situation instead of the false belief? Well, it would be frightening and exciting perhaps (call this *exhilaration*), and you would feel afterwards the glow of having achieved something that you haven't achieved before (call this *personal growth*). You could also share the experience of the ride with your friends now instead of waiting at the bottom with all the coats and bags (call this *connection*). You new rule could be that *you feel a sense of exhilaration, growth, and connection each time you stretch yourself to do something new with your friends*. How much better would this attitude work in bringing the values you want into your life?

To change any of your rules, you simply have to choose an alternative that works better for you – one that brings you pleasure rather than the pain of the old rule. You may reasonably question whether this is a bit artificial, and it is. But don't dignify your current rules as any more 'real'. They are no more real than the new set that you now choose, and if you choose your new rules well, they will be a lot more effective in allowing you to feel the way you want to feel.

For example, Raj's top value is to feel healthy and vital, but his rules for experiencing this are: I must have a good workout at the gym three times a week, and run five miles three times a week, and be within 3 pounds of my ideal weight, and be eating only nourishing, water-rich foods, and have no pain anywhere in my body.

Unfortunately, Raj wasn't able easily to satisfy these rules and so he didn't allow himself to feel healthy and vital very often. When he changed his rules, the problem was magically fixed. He expressed his new rules for feeling healthy and vital in the form of affirmations, which he can repeat as often as he needs to keep them firmly in his mind:

- ✔ I am aware of how healthy and vital I feel whenever I exercise to a warm glow.

- ✔ I am aware of how healthy and vital I feel whenever I go to bed without feeling exhausted.

- ✔ I am aware of how healthy and vital I feel whenever I avoid poor food or drink choices.

- ✔ I am aware of how healthy and vital I feel whenever I walk rather than ride.

- ✔ I am aware of how healthy and vital I feel whenever I meditate.

Ask yourself what has to happen in order for you to feel that sense of connection you want so badly. How about simply stopping for a moment in your busy day and picturing your partner, or children, or parents, whatever it is for you. That can be enough to flood you with feelings of connectedness. Don't limit yourself to one thing, though; add in some more.

Create half a dozen new rules that allow you to experience each of the values in your hierarchy. Make your own list of affirmations for each end's value.

Using your affirmations can ensure that you feel the way you want to feel most of the time, and it eliminates the values conflicts that come from the limitation of having just a few, hard-to-satisfy rules about fulfilling your values.

By giving yourself a variety of ways to feel good, you set yourself up for success and self-confidence because you can always fulfil at least one of your rules or affirmations.

Living Your Values Every Day

When you're conscious of your values, and you have a consistent set of achievable rules for experiencing their presence in your life, you have all you need to live your life as a series of near-perfect days. In the following sections you will learn how you can make this a reality.

Doing these few things, which take just a few minutes each day, can transform your daily experience of living more surely than anything else you can do. You would develop much more control over your achievements and experience of life. You could manage your values and feelings in a much more proactive way and create new and more powerful meaning every day. Try following the advice in the next three sections for a week, and you'll be amazed by the transformation.

Focusing on what's important

Every night before you turn out the light, write down the half-dozen most important things you want to do tomorrow. The tasks can be anything at all, so long as they're the important things. While you sleep, your unconscious mind works out for you how you can achieve your aims most easily.

In the morning, before you get out of bed, take your list and decide how you will fit the tasks and activities you have chosen into your day. If it looks like a tight fit, leave out the least important, and the next least until it looks sensible to you.

You now have a day's schedule that should ensure that both your time and your energy are focused on *the most important* activities of the day.

Sprinkling your values through your day

But this is not yet enough to create a day when you live and fully experience the feelings you most want in life. To help ensure you get these into your day, simply bring your ends values to mind one by one and use your value affirmations to see where in your schedule you have the greatest likelihood of feeling that value. The opportunity may be easily present in several places: just bring each occasion to mind and envision your day with all such opportunities taken.

Now you are much more likely to *live* your perfect day, focused on the important activities and rich in your most valued feelings. You have become present to the way the day *can* be and are much more likely to *experience it* that way.

Reviewing your day

At the end of your day, mentally review what happened and how you experienced it. Perhaps the day worked out pretty much as you planned it, but you didn't get everything done that you thought you would. You can learn from this; maybe you habitually give yourself too much to do. Instead of beating yourself up for not completing your to-do list, make a note to limit what you take on until you get the balance right.

Perhaps your day didn't work out the way you intended at all. Maybe there was an unexpected crisis at work or something else just came up. That's okay. Reflect on whether you managed to live your values anyway. Did you have that sense of connection, or feel the love when you thought of the family and took a moment to feel how lucky you are to have them?

Whatever happened is fine; Don't judge it, just look at what actually happened today and write down the most important things you want to get done tomorrow. Then go to sleep.

Living Authentically

By now you should be able to see that out in the world is where things are happening; inside you, an entirely personal set of experiences and meanings is being generated in response to what is occurring; and all these occurrences add to the totality of your life to date. In a very real way, you inhabit the inside world of experience and meaning much more than the external world of current events. This is a massive and transformational insight.

If meaning is largely a matter of your interpretation and choice, then your personal transformation is not only possible but can happen in this instant. For it to happen though you need to become *authentic*; you need to get free to interpret events and create meaning for yourself, without the need to consult or ask permission of anyone else (even in your own head). How you are experiencing life is inside you, and you have a lot more leeway and room for individuality than you may realise.

To aid your growth and to help you fine-tune your sense of who you are and what you can be and do in the world, it is important that you trust your developing self-awareness in the face of resistance from those who think they know you best, and even those who love you best. Be authentic, be true to yourself, and you really begin to make progress. This is the key to your power and confidence in the world.

There may be a time when you can lead those who most care about you through a similar journey of their own. For now, you need to be fully committed to your own development and you need to trust in your ability to see it through. All you need to do to become the fully authentic version of yourself is to stop pretending:

- ✔ Stop pretending to be what you're not; stop pretending not to be what you are.

- ✔ Stop pretending to care about things you don't; stop pretending not to care about things you do.

- ✔ Stop pretending to believe in things you don't; stop pretending not to believe in things you do.

Now ask yourself: What do I really stand for? What do I really care about? What do I truly believe in? If your answers to these questions begin to differ from those you worked with earlier in this chapter, you can start again and do the real work with your real answers. The difference will be transformational.

Developing your identity

Whilst it is critical that you begin to be true to yourself, it is also important that you let this developing version of yourself become known in the world. You need to let your friends and colleagues know that you have begun to think about things in new ways and that you are determined to take control of your life. This is an important step, but it can be a difficult one as your changing can easily unsettle or even threaten those around you.

The gay movement has a name for the psychological and social repositioning that accompanies a homosexual man or woman reclaiming their authentic identity: They call it *coming out.* Although your coming out as your authentic self is unlikely to entail the same social risks and consequences, the stages you have to pass through are similar.

The *Cass Model* describes six stages of developing identity; it has been adapted here to suit our present purpose.

Stage 1: Confusion

In this first stage, the identity you have always taken for granted is called into question. You may be confused as you begin to feel that your previous roles as reliable friend, helpful sister, caring mother, conscientious worker, and so on miss the essence of who you truly are. 'But who would I still be if I were none of these things?' becomes a legitimate enquiry in search of your more authentic self.

Stage 2: Comparison

By this stage, you may be accepting that you are in some respects more self-aware or otherwise different from your family, friends, and most other people in your social network. This can set off a fear of rejection and you may adopt strategies to minimise the risks (such as not telling anyone about your growing dissatisfaction with the status quo).

You may begin reading self-help books surreptitiously or see a coach or counsellor confidentially. You may conclude that it is only at work where you have issues, in all other respects you are just as you always were.

The best advice for you is to go easy on yourself. You cannot rush personal change and it is just as difficult to hold it back. You should let it take its course, reading any books and listening to any tapes that help you. You may not feel ready yet to take on the world and you don't have to.

Stage 3: Tolerance

By this stage you may no longer be satisfied with your previous experience of life (regardless of how successful you are in the eyes of the world). Although you may still be vague about your life's meaning and destiny, you are likely to be getting used to the idea of being on some kind of development journey.

You may have sought out a few like-minded souls, though the gulf between your growing sense of self and others all around you is growing even greater. This can be an especially trying stage if you have a strong need for peer approval and acceptance.

Stage 4: Acceptance

Publicly you may still be pretending to be as you always were, but inside you have accepted the difference and are feeling changed irrevocably. You are addressing the issues of 'Who am I really?' and 'How do I truly fit in?'

Stages 5 and 6: Pride and Synthesis

In these closely allied stages, you move from your growing 'them' and 'me' mentality into a realisation and acceptance that it is your experience of the world that has fundamentally shifted rather than the world itself. You remain a part of it all, just as you always have, with a heightened awareness of your authentic self-identity and increased ability to live your values and 'walk your talk'. Your authentic self is stronger and more confident and you feel less threatened by what the world may throw at you.

This last phase is your heroic identity, your fully authentic self delivered daily into the world through the medium of your chosen mission and values: your hero's journey. Your experience of living your values is powerful and complete.

Facing up to your demons

Your journey to your truly authentic self is a lifelong project. And just like the heroes of Greek and Roman mythology, and the super-heroes of comic books and Hollywood, you will choose to face your demons.

What is a demon in our modern world? It is anything that you fear, and fail to face. It is precisely the things that have been holding you back, and the confidence to take action is what you need to overcome them. This book is full of advice you can use to build your confidence so use it and get out there to live your life on a more heroic scale.

For the most part, you can face your tests with confidence and a keen sense of purposeful engagement. Some challenges, though, are frightening and lonely. During these trials, keep in mind that life was going to give you these tests anyway, and at least now you are getting them on your own terms and in a worthy cause.

In these dark moments, reflect on your progress so far and give yourself a pat on the back for achieving so much. If you are tired, take rest; if you are confused, take advice. You always have the choice of forward into growth or backward into fear. When you are ready, choose growth.

World champion track athlete Steve Cram said something that may help you get your head around all this. At the time he was the 1,500 metres world champion and world record holder. Injured, and temporarily laid up, he was doing a TV promotion at a charity event. The amateur runners had given their all and some of them were in terrible shape, collapsing on the line, being ill, and so on. On live TV a commentator asked Steve whether he could remember ever feeling so totally used up in this way. Steve's response: 'it is exactly the same for me every time I run. I feel the same pain as these guys, I just go a lot quicker.'

You have choices in life and you can expect highs and lows what-ever path you choose. Like Steve Cram, you can raise your stan-dards to those of the world's best and experience them from there. Why should you accept anything less than the world champion version of yourself? You don't have to, so don't.

Chapter 6

Making Friends with Your Emotions

In This Chapter

▶ Handling your emotions

▶ Paying attention to your moods

▶ Putting your hunches to the test

▶ Moving on from the grip of negative emotions

*T*hink back over the last week, and you're likely to recall running through a full gamut of emotions. Happiness, love, joy, fear, sadness, anger, and guilt are all natural human responses in everyday life.

Emotions are important in building your confidence because they drive your behaviour and how you feel about yourself. They also have an enormous impact on your body and your health; you can read more about the mind–body connection in Chapter 10.

This chapter helps you to get in tune with how you are experiencing the reality of life through how you feel – good and bad, up and down.

Getting a Grip on Your Emotions

When you make friends with your emotions, you listen to them and get to know them better. In this way, you gain vital information about what is happening to you and take responsibility for your response. By raising your self-awareness, you are in a stronger position to motivate yourself and take the action you want rather than reacting to other people and circumstances.

You may be asking yourself why you'd ever want to get angry or fearful – wouldn't it be good to drop these 'friends' out of your repertoire? No. Definitely not. Even your most negative emotions have their place in looking after you. They mean that you are alive and real. Your job is to notice your emotional reactions and focus the energy from them appropriately. In the following sections, we help you do just that.

Accessing your emotional intelligence

Popularised by author Daniel Goleman, the concept of *emotional intelligence (EQ)* relates to being able to rein in your emotional impulses, to read another's innermost feelings, and to handle relationships smoothly. The precepts of EQ are increasingly valued in business as organisations realise the tangible impact on profitability as well as in other walks of life such as education.

Emotional intelligence relates to a range of competencies around two aspects:

- ✓ **Personal competence:** How you handle yourself, your awareness of your feelings, and your understanding of your capabilities.

- ✓ **Social competence:** How you handle relationships with other people, in particular in how you manage your unhelpful reactions, how you exhibit empathy, and how much flexibility you demonstrate in dealing with difficult situations.

Whether you're a student or the chairman of a company, your ability to manage your emotions and bring out the best in others can make the difference between success and failure. Lose your temper and you lose an important customer or damage an important relationship – and the rest, as they say, is history.

The good news is that you can improve your emotional intelligence over time. Your EQ is not a given that you are born with and are stuck with. A number of formal assessment tools on the market help you understand the fine dimensions of emotional intelligence and how you score (see the Appendix for details).

To get the real benefit of a formal tool, it's useful to have feedback from other people as well as taking a self assessment test. Do this with the support of a coach because the information you receive may be challenging to handle on your own.

Pitting rational thought against emotion

Each time you think about an event in the past, you recall it slightly differently. Usually, over time, the intensity of the emotion gets less intense. However, some memories may continue to really annoy or upset you, especially if the memory is of something that was unjust or unfair or an event you feel embarrassed about. Part of you wants to be logical and rational about it, yet part of you still doesn't want to let go of it. Every time you think about it, the old tug of emotion gets to you. One way to move on is to separate your memory of an event from the emotion involved.

If a negative memory still conjures up strong emotion, you can try to distance yourself from the memory. Picture the event as something that happened a long time ago. See it as a faded black-and-white photograph with no colour, no life, no emotional pull at all.

Use the Event, Memory, Emotion, Knowledge, Action steps outlined here to overcome the negative effects of your memories:

1. **Recall the Event:** What was the event that happened to you?

    As an example, we use the case of Heather, who suffered from intense nerves and failed her driving test six times. The Event for her was her failed driving test.

2. **Recover the Memory:** What is your memory of that event?

    Heather's Memory is meeting the driving instructor and getting into the car.

3. **Evaluate your Emotion:** What emotion do you experience when you access that memory? On a scale of 1 (weak) to 10 (strong) how strong is your emotion?

    Heather's Emotion is a feeling of fear and worry in her stomach, which rates an 8 out 10.

4. **Uncover the underlying Knowledge:** What knowledge can you take from the memory that can help you in the future?

    Heather's Knowledge is managing her nerves when driving with a stranger in the passenger seat.

5. **Decide on an Action:** What action can you take as a result?

    Heather's Action is to book her next three driving lessons with three different instructors.

By going through these steps, you can extract the value of the memory and take the lesson forward while letting go of the downside of all the negative emotion.

Sharing the love at work

Beppe is the managing director of a building company. Through attending a personal development course, he realised just how hard he had found it to express his emotions, and he discovered how to tell his family how much he loved them. At work, he was also used to operating in a macho style, always looking at the financial figures and productivity measures. One day when business was tough, he decided to be courageous and express his feelings to his fellow directors. He began the monthly board meeting by going to each member of the team around the table and saying what he really valued in them. The team was surprised and also delighted to see this more human side of the MD.

As a result, the meeting got straight to the heart of difficult issues and made important decisions that people had been holding back on.

Connecting creativity and confidence

The last 30 years have seen a tremendous amount of research into how the brain functions; the field of neuroscience continues to broaden understanding of the human experience. However, taking a straightforward, practical concept of division of labour in the brain suggests that the two hemispheres of the brain process information in different ways. The left hemisphere is responsible for verbal, analytical, and logical processing, while the right side processes information in a more global, intuitive, and creative way – and it needs unpressured time and space to do that.

Creativity is about using imagination to make something new that didn't exist before –whether it's a idea, or something more tangible like a piece of art or literature. It usually involves seeing the connection between seemingly unrelated things. Most successful individuals deliberately allow time and space for their creative imagination to get to work – which is right-brained activity. Unfortunately, with business pressures growing, many companies overlook the need to allow people time to brainstorm and think outside the box.

Building your own confidence involves finding new ideas, approaches, and solutions. To do so, it's essential that you use all aspects of your brain and allow the creativity to flood in rather than shutting part of it down.

Take regular time out on your own to think and re-charge your batteries.

Finding courage to voice your emotions

Trusting yourself to express emotion takes courage. It may be particularly hard if you are used to operating in a cool, factual, and rational way. Yet it is through your emotions that you can connect with yourself and with others in a deeper, more powerful way.

Clearly it isn't appropriate to tell everyone at work your innermost emotions or pent-up feelings, but you probably have room to express yourself more fully than you're currently making use of. Consider whether there is one area of your life in which you are holding back your emotional reactions and feelings. Do you ever feel there's something important to say but you never quite manage to say it? Try to determine the long-term benefit if you voice what you really think and feel. Any relationship based on an open and honest expression of feelings has a strong chance of staying fresh and engaging – it will continue to grow rather than stagnate.

Tracking Your Moods

During the course of a day, you experience a number of *moods* – temporary states of mind or temper. Think of your moods as a temperature gauge, registering hot and cold at different times according to the weather.

When you're in a particular mood, it affects your behaviour and in turn the results you get. So there's a real benefit to paying attention to how you feel. Your mood shows through your expressions and gestures as much as by what you say or don't say, and thus has a knock-on effect on others around you.

If you are aware that you are not in your best frame of mind, then you know instinctively that today is not the best day to make important decisions. And if your mood isn't helpful, then you may decide to change it.

Staying in touch with your mood patterns

As you refine your awareness of your mood and that of others, you heighten your observation of what triggers a change in mood for you – whether for good or bad.

As you become more aware of your moods, think about the colours and hues of your underlying emotions and feelings, the fine difference in temperature that you detect in yourself and those around you.

Take a typical day in your schedule, once a week and make a note of your mood at key points in the day – early in the morning, at midday, mid-afternoon, early evening, and finally as you go to bed. Start to pay attention to how you are feeling and the nuances of how you describe those feelings. On the down side, you may say you are sad, grump, sullen, nervy, melancholy, or cross. And when things are on the up you may be happy, content, peaceful, excited, or joyful. Start to build your own repertoire of language to describe the subtle changes in your mood, and pay attention to what happens to trigger the change. You may then decide you want to make some changes in your day to prevent dropping into a negative mood.

Becoming more aware of your natural state

When Kate is walking along, she often finds herself involuntarily humming a familiar piece of classical music – *Vltava,* by the Bohemian composer Smetana. Her humming transports her to a happy, sociable time when she heard it played in a concert. She takes her humming to mean that all is well with the world, she's in a good state and that her life is flowing steadily.

Your *state* is more than just a mood – it's a way of being, as opposed to a way of doing. To find your natural state, your baseline state on a day-to-day basis, you need to determine your normal way of being. For example, are you naturally laid back about life most of the time, or do you go through life with a purposeful energy racing inside you? Do you have a strong sense of nervous excitement, anxiety, or guilt, or do you live in limbo waiting and anticipating what will happen next?

Make a note of the words you use to describe your baseline state. Write down the pictures and feelings that come to you.

Your baseline state is how you are used to being as you go about your life. It's become a habit. You may be happy with it or want to change it. By noticing what it's like, you're in a good position to adapt it if you want to.

At the start of each day, set your intent for the state you want to be in for the day. Check in with yourself at intervals in the day to see how you're doing.

Facing up to overwhelm

Jhoti is a businessman who has built up a profitable food manufacturing empire. As a hard working entrepreneur he lived his life in a constant state of stress and being overwhelmed. He rushed from meeting to meeting, never taking time out to think or plan but responding to an increasing number of crises. He became aware of the effect of his mental anxiety on his body and the stress on his heart and blood pressure. He realised that it affected his ability to make decisions clearly, and chose to employ a coach to work with him on re-assessing his personal and business goals.

Life has a natural rhythm of ups and downs. However, if you are regularly experiencing negative feelings of being overwhelmed or anxiety – more than, say, 20 per cent of the time – then make an appointment to see your doctor or medical practitioner.

Trusting Your Intuition

You have it, but how well do you use it? Intuition is your gut feeling, the magical sense inside that can guide you if you listen to it. Intuition often comes in a flash of insight, an 'aha!' moment. *Intuition* can be defined as 'the direct knowing of something without the conscious use of reasoning'. It's what you have when you pay real attention to your kind and helpful unconscious mind. When you get in touch with your intuition, you connect with what you really want in your life – and follow that true sense of direction that confident people have.

Tuning in to the gifts of intuition

Listening to your intuition gives you valuable information about what is really going on for you at a deeper level. When you listen to your inner self, you become connected to the energy within your body – physically, emotionally, and spiritually. Your intuition may or may not give you the 'right' answer, but it can be incredibly valuable to work with it rather than against it. Your intuition can help you to:

- Find new ways around problems
- Make sense of a situation
- Improve your decision-making abilities
- Notice things that need your attention
- Achieve your goals

How can you know when your intuition is kicking in? When you find yourself thinking: *This is strange*, or *how bizarre*, or *what a coincidence*. You may get an insight that you are letting go of the rational and logical thoughts and just going with what feels right. To find out more about how to access your intuition. In the UK, The Art of Intuition offers workshops and information on their Web site at www.artofintuition.co.uk. You can also check out Laura Day's www.practicalintuition.com US site.

Listening to your inner self

Einstein said that problems can't be solved at the same level at which they are created. Great scientists as well as great artists, musicians, and leaders in every field act on their hunches to achieve breakthroughs in their thinking.

You can release your own intuition by using your imagination to think about problems in a completely different way. Use this exercise when you are grappling with a challenge:

1. **State your issue to yourself.**

2. **Let go of the facts and quiet your rational mind.**

3. **Sit in silence without interruption for 15 minutes.**

4. **Open yourself to the intuitive insights that come to you.**

   You may become aware of visual images, sensations in your body, or a connection with a particular person or place.

5. **Allow your analytical mind to wake up and get to work on the intuitive thoughts.**

The saying goes: 'People buy on emotion and justify on facts.' Whether you are selling yourself at an interview, promoting an idea, or selling a product to a client, take notice of the emotional undercurrents at play as well as the factual evidence. You can be sure that these play a part.

Faking it

Traditionally it's women who've had the edge on the 'sixth sense'. Maybe now the tables are turning. It would seem that men are getting in touch with their intuitive side, according to a study carried out at Edinburgh Science Festival by the University of Hertfordshire. Researchers asked 15,000 people to look at images of smiling faces and pick out the 'real' grins. Men spotted 76 per cent of the women's fake smiles, while women only identified 67 per cent of men's fake smiles.

Harnessing Your Darker Emotions

Dark emotions are part of life and part of who you are, just as night follows day. Remember that all your emotions are valuable – they provide feedback about what is happening to you.

Some emotions stimulate your energy while others depress it. Fear and anger, for example, stimulate you to action. Meanwhile, sadness and guilt act as depressants, causing you to hold back and lie low.

Unless they are diffused, emotions can build over time to a point where they erupt uncontrollably. Picture the emotional events in your life like a bracelet of beads on a string. Imagine experiencing anger over the years and not being able to express your feelings: At age 5, your favourite toy is given away without your permission; at age 11, you get bullied in the school playground; at age 15, the first person you have a crush on dumps you for someone else; at age 18, you lose out on a competition prize because someone else cheated; at age 25, you get gazumped on a house purchase. Finally, at age 30, you fail to make your putt on the final hole, lose the golf tournament, and your anger blows up uncontrollably.

Such seemingly unprovoked or over-the-top reactions often result when you subconsciously join up a number of 'angry' moments over your life into one big grievance. The explosion is way larger than the small, last-straw event that triggered it. Unless you discover how to break this pattern, you're in danger of falling out with people unnecessarily – not an emotionally intelligent place to be.

In the following sections, we look at some examples of finding the daylight in the darker moments.

Turning your anger into energy

To handle situations in which you're angry with someone else, you need to express your anger effectively. Knowing the difference between making a complaint and conducting a personal character assassination helps:

> A *complaint* is about the action; a *personal criticism* is about the person. It's important to separate the 'deed' from the 'doer'.

A personal criticism leaves the other person feeling emotionally charged and defensive, which then puts them back on the attack, and you both end up in a vicious downward spiral. Saying to someone 'You're thoughtless, self-centred, and lazy' is a personal attack that encourages the anger to build.

Better instead to go for the complaint approach, being very specific about what someone has done and how you feel as a result. A more productive complaint is: 'You left all the washing up for me to do, and I feel fed up in the kitchen doing it on my day off.' Follow that with a request for action: 'Please will you do your washing up after you've finished dinner?' You express your anger and make a reasonable request for change. A complaint allows for the energy to shift towards a resolution rather than wasting it in a red-faced exchange of temper.

When making a complaint, follow these steps:

1. **State the facts.**

2. **State your feelings.**

3. **Request a simple action.**

Letting go of unhelpful emotions

Emotions such as jealousy and bitterness wreck your sense of confidence. They eat away at you, taking up inordinate amounts of time and energy, and they prevent you from moving forward. Often these feelings dissipate over time, but you can help them on their departure using the Event, Memory, Emotion, Knowledge exercise in the 'Pitting rational thought against emotion' section earlier in this chapter.

Forgiveness in the animal kingdom

Offering forgiveness to those who do you wrong is a sign of compassion. Studies among animals demonstrate amazing capability to sort out arguments and move on. Animals can't afford to hold a grudge in situations where they depend on each other for food or for competing against other groups. Yet humans seem to find conflict resolution much harder.

A *New Scientist* report ('Kiss and make up', 7 May 2005) looks at disputes between various animals from hyenas to dolphins. It's the chimps who get top marks for instigating reconciliation. In one field study, researchers observe a male chimp leader slapping a female as he passes her. Within 15 minutes, she has licked her wounds and is the first to make amends by going to her attacker and offering the back of her hand for a kiss. Very quickly, the group is happily reunited, cuddling and sharing food once more.

Reprogramming phobias

Some emotional responses are particularly sticky to change. A *phobia,* which is a severe response of fear related to something that happened or somebody you met in your past, can be tenacious and difficult to dislodge. Phobias don't appear to be logical, and you may have no conscious idea of how the fear developed. Whether the phobia is of flying, escalators, motorway bridges, spiders, frogs or anything else, the impact on your life can be hugely restrictive.

As coaches trained in Neuro-Linguistic Programming, we work with clients using the *NLP fast phobia cure,* a technique that enables you to detach the emotional content from the memory of your experience.

The cure is explained fully in *Neuro-linguistic Programming for Dummies* (Wiley), of which Kate is co-author with Romilla Ready. Essentially the treatment is about separating yourself from the memory of a phobic response. The technique enables many people who have suffered phobias for years to have a cure within 20 minutes. The relief and pleasure of freedom from a phobia are extraordinarily powerful. Most importantly, people who overcome phobias regain control of their emotional responses.

If you still find yourself going over and over old wounds or grievances, seek professional therapeutic help to get closure on them. A Time Line Therapist can work with you to clean up on the negative emotions holding you back from enjoying life to the full.

Allowing yourself to forgive and move on

The art of developing mature relationships lies in the skills of managing yourself and empathising with others. Daniel Goleman, in his work *Emotional Intelligence,* suggests that the roots of morality are to be found in empathy.

To have a mature relationship with someone takes *empathy* – the ability to enter into and share another person's emotions. When you face a difficult situation with someone, try to step into their shoes and understand what life looks like from their perspective, how they might be thinking or feeling about the situation.

Empathy is an attribute notably lacking in criminals. Bear this in mind if you are attacked or victimised, and always make your safety your prime concern.

Holding onto grievances from the past can deplete your energy. The memory of it can get in the way of you moving on with your life.

Give a message of forgiveness to someone you feel has upset or wronged you in the past by writing a letter to that person. Write down the facts around the incident that happened and how you felt about it at the time. Tell them that you forgive them for their part in the experience. You don't need to post the letter. You can now tear it up and see it disappear into the rubbish knowing that you have let go of whatever it was that upset you.

Chapter 7

Unleashing Your Passion

. . . .

In This Chapter

▶ Understanding how to use your passion

▶ Raising your game

▶ Committing to your hero's journey

▶ Leading others with your passion

. . . .

An important part of living your values (a topic we cover in Chapter 5) has to do with the intensity with which you live. If values are colours on your artist's palette, you'll want all your favourite colours, of course. But to paint a full and rich picture of your life, you surely want those colours in both bright and pale shades. You may not always want to paint with the most vibrant hues, but you certainly want those intense colours available for when your life warrants them.

It's the same with your ends values, your feelings. You don't always choose to live in a state of high passion or excitement, but you want to be able to access your passion at will, especially during those times when you need to be passionate to get the result you want. Passion is your key to intensity. Finding it and gaining access to it are what this chapter is about.

Discovering Your Passionate Self

Take a moment and recall the last time your heart ached for something. Did you find the energy it brought you empowering? Did you achieve the outcome you felt so passionate about? Could you have achieved this outcome without the passion?

People of Anglo-Saxon origin tend to be uncomfortable with powerful emotions, and passion is about as powerful as they get. Apart from passionate sexuality (which can often give rise to all manner of problems), passion is most likely to be associated for them with negative outcomes and emotions such as revenge, jealousy, and hatred. This is a great pity because adopting this narrow view of passion cuts you off from one of your most powerful emotional drivers.

If you are committed to confident living and to getting as much as you can out of each day, passion is an essential emotion in your toolbox. With passion in your armoury, you can take on bigger challenges and achieve greater results in the world.

But while a part of you longs for access to the more vital and more passionate parts of your nature, another part of you is wary of living without holding back. You are probably afraid of making mistakes, of not looking good, of being shown up or otherwise embarrassed by trying too hard and falling flat, and you hold back to avoid such embarrassment.

Holding back becomes a habit and avoiding embarrassment becomes self-defeating as you lose access to the power of your passion. Even worse, the bottled-up emotion you're either avoiding or denying has a nasty way of biting you back in the form of physical illness or mental breakdown.

It is better by far to take on this rich opportunity to extend your emotional range and embrace passion as one of your most powerful expressions of your being in the world.

Passion is an emotional intensity; it's a charged-up version of excitement; it's a supercharged motivation. It is a tremendous force that can meet almost any challenge head on. It is nature's way of giving you the power you need to achieve an outcome that you care deeply about. You can't do without, so it is worth your while to understand your passionate side and find out how to use it.

Becoming more passionate

You have the same capacity for passion as any artist, orator, or athlete (or any other group noted for their passion). What you also have, probably, is a series of blockages that stifle your natural passion for living and make it difficult for you to unleash your most passionate self into the world.

To unblock yourself and let your passion flow (some of them you will already be doing as you study other chapters of this book), you need to open up your heart a little to counter the voices in your head that tell you what you *should* be doing. What this really means is that you need to get present to your *ends values,* the feelings you most want in life, and start to give them the priority they deserve (Chapter 5 explains how you can do this).

Nothing is more important to you right now than the way you *feel*. How you feel dictates the meaning you make of the things happening to you and determines what you do about them.

The feelings you most want in your life can be a reliable guide to what is most appropriate for you. And, provided you then *act* in accordance with these feelings, you begin to unlock your blocked passion. Robert Dilts, the American psychologist who developed the model of neurological levels we explain in the next section calls acting in accordance with your feelings *congruence*, which is a very powerful idea.

Exploring your neurological levels with Dilts

Being guided by your feelings alone can be a bit like being a castaway on a desert island – it can be beautiful, idyllic even, but unless it is also purposeful, meaningful, and engaging, the experience pales and fades with time and may even end in disaster. You need a consistent purpose; and for a powerful, passionate life you need a big purpose – one bigger perhaps than you could realistically expect to be able to fulfil in only one lifetime.

To help you to understand congruence of feelings, thoughts, and actions, and to develop it, you can use Dilts's *neurological levels* – a difficult name for a simple and powerful way of looking at how human beings operate in the world (Kate's book, *Neuro-linguistic Programming For Dummies,* published by Wiley, covers neurological levels in more depth).

Looking at the levels

Dilts believes that you experience yourself in the world at six distinct levels. These combine to make up your complete human experience. The levels are self-contained in a way that leaves room for them to become misaligned. When this happens, you become *incongruent*, meaning you lose your natural power and the confidence to be passionate and take decisive action.

Following is a description of the levels, and how you usually experience them:

- ✔ **Environment:** This is your experience of where you live and work, with whom, the prevailing culture, and how things get done. You co-create these environments with others by the way you allow them to be and the way you interact within them.

- ✔ **Behaviour:** One of the most powerful ways you affect your environment is the way you act in it. Often you feel totally in control of what you do. Sometimes, though, things can get unpredictable, including the way you act and react to events.

- ✔ **Capability:** Living demands a high degree of capability. You have to communicate, and you need to develop social and economic skills. You have to predict how others will behave and accommodate this in your interactions with them.

- ✔ **Values and beliefs:** In their purest form, your *values* are the emotional states you want to feel. *Beliefs* are your rules of thumb about what feelings to have. They let you make fast decisions but, unquestioned, they may trap you in the past.

- ✔ **Identity:** This is your holistic sense of who you are really. It rolls up your perception of your environment, behaviour, capabilities, values, and beliefs into a whole, allowing you to relate to the larger systems of work, family, and nation.

- ✔ **Ontology or spirit:** This is your sense of why you are here and what you are here to do. It may be clear to you, or unclear. Many religious practices, meditation, and personal development techniques attempt to expand your sense of self at this level.

You can consider these six levels as your total sense of *being* in the world. To be truly confident and powerful, you need to achieve a high degree of congruence throughout the levels (they need to support and reinforce each other and not conflict). When you achieve this, all these elements of your being combine harmoniously to take you in the same direction.

This fully congruent version of yourself is the awesome version you feel in flashes on the inside but often struggle to present consistently on the outside. Becoming more congruent is your key to personal power and your ticket to total self-confidence.

Exposing your levels

In this section, you use the Dilts model to work out what you know and feel to be true about yourself. Write a simple paragraph about your experience of life from each of the six levels starting with your environment and working up to your spirit. When you have done this, write out a separate description of your experience of the six levels *as you would like each to be*, only this time start with spirit and work down to environment.

By completing your own personal analyses, you get a new sense of how closely your life today compares with how you would like it to be. You can then use the gaps to set up change goals for yourself. Use Nigel's analysis, shown in Figures 7-1 and 7-2, as an example.

Don't be surprised by the degree of congruence you are already achieving in life. You have immense capabilities and power that you take entirely for granted. What you do instead is focus on and sometimes get hung up about the areas that need your attention. Take a look now at anything in your model you know is a problem and take steps to resolve it as Nigel does. Nigel's initial self analysis is shown in Figure 7-1.

Nigel's experience of himself at the six neurological levels is distorted by how he feels right now and by pent up emotions such as regret, guilt, and frustration. On the outside he looks to be a very successful businessman, but he clearly feels he has given up a lot to achieve this.

He now has the opportunity to re-experience himself as he would like to be at the six levels. This time, the instruction is to do it top-down starting with Ontology. Nigel's view of himself in Figure 7-2 is aspirational – it doesn't exactly reflect what he feels today, but it is still recognisably Nigel and it is within his sense of what is possible for himself.

In contrast to Figure 7-1, Nigel's new description of how he wants his levels to be is much more congruent. Much of what he is saying he wants he has already, he just isn't experiencing it that way. Other things that he could easily do, or emphasise, come to mind as he thinks about how he wants things to be. He now has an aspirational target for change.

To unlock your true passionate self, you need to address those uncomfortable inconsistencies you've been ignoring. If you do this, your experience of life will be transformed.

Analysis of My Levels

<u>Environment</u> – I live with my wife and our four children. We live on the edge of the green belt outside a large city giving me easy access to work and providing a nice country life for my family. I'm in professional services and I serve some of the world's biggest corporations. I don't always support their trading policies, nor the products they create, but the people are usually really great to work with, fair, and decent. I am well paid and this provides private education for the kids and a provision for our life-style and old age.

<u>Behaviour</u> – I think of myself as an easygoing guy, preferring professional behaviour where everyone gets on with things and doesn't require close supervision. I am embarrassed sometimes by the need to correct people at work, and I'm not very good at it. At home I prefer to avoid difficult situations with neighbours, which makes me a little reserved. I guess some people find me standoffish, though I'm not really.

<u>Capability</u> – I am educated to degree level and have worked in my industry over 10 years. I am well known for an original line of analysis and have an established and faithful client base. I have an enquiring mind and a good track record in innovation, often beating my younger colleagues in coming up with powerful new ideas and implementing them. At home I'm not much of a handyman, but I consider myself to be a patient husband and a skilled and loving father to my four children.

<u>Values and Beliefs</u> – I was brought up in the 1950s and 1960s when we thought we could change the world through free thinking and challenging the status quo. I value my free thinking more than almost anything and am disturbed when I see its lack in others. I worry about the world today and see little evidence of the 'better tomorrow' we thought we were building. My liberal politics seem to be falling out of favour again after a brief resurgence in the 1990s. We are destroying the planet and there seems little political will to do anything about it.

<u>Identity</u> – although I no longer worry about being 'found out', I do still feel a bit of an impostor sometimes. I have enjoyed a successful business career without feeling I fully belonged in it. I have worked successfully with people whose values are very different from mine. I feel I have been out of touch with the real me for long periods and have tended to define myself by what I am not and what I don't want rather than what I am and what I stand for.

<u>Ontology or Spirit</u> – I feel like a caged spirit. Who knows what my life would have been like if I had accepted my calling in my 20s instead of selling out to a business career? I have encouraged my children to follow their passions and I've given them permission to think for themselves. Perhaps now, relatively late in life, I can finally fulfill my destiny and contribute to the wellbeing of the planet through responding to my sense of calling.

Figure 7-1: Nigel's analysis of his six levels today.

Aspirational Re-Alignment of Neurological Levels

Ontology – I have always felt a deep and profound sense of connection to the universe, to nature and to the planet. I feel the need to live in harmony with the planet, including its ecology and its entire people. I feel I was put here to represent the holistic viewpoint and was meant to express it in the world, to my fellow man, to business and to our youth. I would not describe myself as religious, though I have tried various religious paths. My path is pure, free spirit, respect for all and personal responsibility for our individual decisions and contribution.

Identity – who I am, is the embodiment of freedom, tolerance and respect for all. I choose to be an example of an educated, enlightened businessman. When I am at my best I feel supported by an invisible force of nature, a force that orders the world and keeps me honest. I am clear on my roles and contribution and choose them with care. I am reliable: I will always deliver what I have promised. Others see me as a role model, as an inspiration and as a force for good in the world.

Values & Beliefs - I accept and respect the need for commercial integrity, financial propriety, and profit – but profit is not the only important thing in business and I would never put it before people, or before honesty and integrity. I believe there is an order in nature and through the universe, caused by forces we do not fully comprehend. I believe that the good we do in the world comes back to support us in so many ways we are not always aware of. The most important thing in life is the freedom to become who we were meant to become.

Capability – I am a skilled student of life with a commitment to lifetime learning. I am a skilled businessman with a rich and varied experience. I am a skilled speaker and teacher with a keen interest in others' learning. I have vision, passion and energy. I can become excited by new possibilities and I have the passion to enthuse and enroll others into their causes. I am a loving and committed father, and partner to my wife. I can do anything I need to do to fulfill a cause I have taken up.

Behaviour – I am calm and reasoned. I am focused and dedicated to my tasks. I am convivial and respectful of others (but not at the expense of doing a good job or achieving some other committed undertaking). I prefer to live and let-live but I can also be assertive and have no issues with taking stands, of even being one against a crowd when I believe it is warranted. I consistently go with my beliefs and values, people know this about me and don't expect me to do otherwise.

Environment – I prefer to live in situations of calmness and order, where objectives are clear and outcomes are agreed. I choose to be with people who tend to be the same as myself, and in any case accept me the way I am. When disagreements arise, they are resolved before they develop into conflicts and enmities. I operate in successful businesses where people know what I stand for and what I can deliver and they value my contribution.

Figure 7-2: Nigel's analysis of his preferred six levels.

Tapping into your natural passion

Perhaps the fastest way to unlock your natural passion is to become clear on what you want, why you want it, and what you can do to get it. The philosopher Friedrich Nietzsche said, 'If a person has a why to live, he can handle almost any what!'

So *why* do you want whatever you have decided you want? Does it support your values? Is it consistent with your sense of who you are? Is it worthy of someone put here to do what you have decided you have been put here to do? Are the actions you need to take appropriate to a person with your beliefs and values? Do they support or undermine your sense of who you are? Would you be proud to read about them in the newspaper? Would you want your mother to know about them?

If you answer "no" to any of the preceding questions, you're sapping your capacity for passion, you're draining it away just as surely as trying to fill up the bath with the plug out. Here are some more drainers to avoid:

- ✔ **Fear:** Fear is the opposite of confidence. This book is full of recipes you can use to help banish it for good.

- ✔ **Doubt:** Why do you want to pursue a certain course of action? You need to be clear and you need a big enough reason to get it done.

- ✔ **Risk-aversion:** Risk-aversion is another manifestation of fear. Don't view risk as something to be avoided, rather see it as something to be managed.

- ✔ **Procrastination:** You put off doing tough things to make life more pleasant, but it always does the opposite. Get into the habit of doing the tough thing on your list first. This releases your passion for doing the rest (if procrastination is a particular problem for you, there is a more detailed analysis of it in Chapter 9).

Being passionate and powerful come naturally to you when you are engaging with the world over something you care deeply about. The magic key to more passion is more caring. Think through what you want in life, and why you want it. Then use the tools in this book to act more decisively, powerfully, and consistently to achieve your goals.

Realising your dreams

Dreams can be a good way to connect to your passion – both sleep dreams and daydreams. Do you have dreams? Sigmund Freud famously ascribed the cause of dreams to unfulfilled desires, and the dreams themselves to wish fulfilment. It seems that deep longings must find a way into our consciousness if we are to be healthy.

But all dreams are not equal. You can have big dreams and small ones; dreams that are worthy of a life being well lived and others that are less worthy compared with your goals and values. You must always choose whether your dreams merit the resources, energy, and time you must put into getting them.

In today's consumer society, you're bombarded by sophisticated propaganda designed by experts to implant dreams and desires you didn't have before. These manufactured dreams are so powerful that it can be difficult to distinguish what you truly want from what you want in the moment only.

The response of many people to all this is either to succumb to the consumer pressure (and very often get themselves into debt), or to resist it, switch off, and, so far as they are able, refuse to play the game. It makes no difference which camp you are in; the result is the same: You all too easily lose touch with what you truly desire and with what will bring you fulfilment.

If, like wealthy celebrities, you can have pretty much anything you want, instantly, what does this do to your life? Does it bring you fulfilment? Patently not if the newspapers can be believed.

So what kind of dream supports the growth of your confidence and power in the world and where can you get it? You get it from doing the work in this and other chapters designed to help you understand how you want your life to *be* and by worrying less about all the stuff you want your life to *have*.

When you pursue your dreams of *being,* you start on a journey to become all you want to be and more. When you dream of *having,* you lose touch with the person you're becoming in the process of getting the things you are pursuing. You become as Faust in the legend, who traded his soul for the prize he sought.

Putting Your Passion into Action

Is it realistic to expect an ordinary person to have big dreams and to live them? Evidence suggests that it is: Books, films, and newspapers are filled with stories of people who have done exactly that, often producing the most incredible results. But in a way, this is missing the point.

Any life, when carefully enough examined, contains all the ingredients of the epics we all read since childhood. One of the 20th century's greatest novels, *Ulysses* by James Joyce, dissects one 24-hour day of its very ordinary hero, Leopold Bloom. In doing so, Joyce shows how this one life contains all the drama and heroism of Homer's original epic about the journey of the Greek hero Ulysses.

Your life, too, is an heroic enterprise, and you are living through it every day. You don't have to make it anything that it isn't already. What you may choose to do is to become more aware of what is really going on for you and give yourself more experience of what you most want. You may even choose to become the hero of your heroic enterprise, the hero of your own life. What a thought!

Starting your journey

Your own life is already your hero's journey, but in all probability you are sleepwalking through it with most of your emotions well buttoned down – most people are. Here and now you have the opportunity to wake up! Why not? If your life is destined to be a journey, why not make it more of an epic?

If you want to live more intensely every day, begin to become more absorbed by your life by viewing it as an epic adventure. You are obviously the central character, but other heroes surround you playing large and small parts in your story. Their heroism is revealed by their character, and by your attention to the detail of what is really going on in the story.

Joseph Campbell described the fundamental steps of the hero's journey, which you can use here to think through the key stages of your own life adventure. Assume that whatever you choose to do you will ultimately succeed. Like our heroine, Jan, in the exercise below, if you don't give up, you simply cannot fail.

1. **Accept your calling.**

   What is your sense of what you are here to achieve? This may have emerged when you were thinking about your neurological levels in the earlier sections in this chapter. Your calling can be a major sense of vocation or simply something you dream about.

   If you have no clear ideas, imagine yourself in your healthy old age telling the gathering of your clan the story of your wonderful life, and just make it up. Your journey will contain many twists and turns anyway, so make a start and trust that your calling will become clearer. By accepting a calling you are confronting your limitations and breaking through them.

Jan is a nurse who serves as an example for this exercise. She had always wanted to be a nurse, but her experience of nursing in the NHS didn't match up to her expectations. Very long hours of heavy and often menial work left her exhausted with little of the satisfaction she expected from helping sick people recover their health. She decided from this point to see herself on a hero's journey and to respond to her calling in a more positive way.

2. Cross the threshold.

Do whatever you have to do to summon up the confidence to take that first step. In stepping out, you are immediately in new territory that your old maps don't cover and where your past experience may not help you. Have confidence that you are able to rise to new challenges as they come up with new solutions you develop to fit the situation.

Jan confronted the idea of quitting nursing to retrain for some other profession. But she couldn't imagine giving up on her dream of helping others. Instead, she decided to take on further training to become a more specialised and more valuable nurse – to go forward into growth and not backward into fear.

3. Find a guardian and face your demons.

The saying goes: 'When the student is ready, the teacher will appear.' Having stepped out, you're in a position to find the guidance and sponsorship you need. Trust in this and be sensitive to the guidance that comes your way.

Realise that demons aren't necessarily bad or evil, they are just energy (inner fears, competitors, crises). To move beyond their influence, you have to face them and remove their hold over you.

Jan now began to seek advice. A friend asked her what she most loved about nursing, and what she would miss most if she gave it up. She began to realise that it was the impact she could have on families that was most important to her, especially dealing with mothers. She decided to specialise in women's health and in family management.

But this meant going back to school for more formal training, and she had struggled to pass all of her nursing exams in the first place. Was there a way around this? No, in the end she had to weigh up the consequences of not going back to college and, with her husband's pledge of support, she decided to give it a go.

4. Transform the demons and complete your mission.

Your defeated demons can become resources you can use on your journey. This may be in the form of new skills, resources, or tools that enable you to fulfil your calling.

In fulfilling your calling and completing your mission, you create a new and bigger world to live in, and a new map by which to navigate. These incorporate the growth and discoveries your journey has provided for you.

As a mature student, Jan found college a different experience from her first time. She was much more focused on what she had to learn and get done. She tackled her assignments early and usually managed to get things in on time.

Still, the exams were always going to be the big trial. When they came around though, she was well prepared and wasn't fazed as much as she had feared. She was even able to help several of the younger students, who weren't so well prepared, through their ordeal. She passed with distinction, an experience that transformed her beliefs about her capabilities and her fear of exams.

5. Find your way home.

You are now living your life at a higher level. In finding your way home, you're able to share your discoveries and experiences with your loved ones and pave the way for others to follow their dreams and embark on their own hero's journeys.

Even with the new qualifications, it was difficult for Jan to find exactly the role she wanted, but she found it eventually in a local community health centre. After she settled in, her new boss shared with her why she had been the preferred candidate. It was because there was something special about the way she carried herself. Even though other candidates were even better qualified, Jan had impressed with her presence, her maturity, and her bearing. It was as though 'she knew what she wanted' and the health centre was proud to have been chosen by her!

You can build these classical elements of the journey into your day, your week, your month, and your lifetime. You are in command of all of this, so take control. Make the journey of your life equal to the power, passion, and brilliance you have at your disposal.

Sit with these ideas for a while and reconnect with some of the aspirations of the younger you. What would this level of desire bring to your life today? Do you have a sense of calling? Do you feel deep down that you are not living the life you are meant to lead?

What will happen if you change things? You can. Allow yourself to believe and use this to access your passionate self. What may happen if you do? How will the world be changed?

Using your passion to lead

The British Prime Minister and statesman, Harold MacMillan, said that the world needs a theme. Back in his day, with Europe recovering from World War II and the standoff of the Cold War well entrenched, this may have been true, but not today. In today's world, great global themes unite all of humankind, but true leadership is hard to find.

What the world needs now is leadership at all levels; and this includes you. Why else do you want to become more confident if not to be more influential in the world and better able to lead others with your vision of the way life should be? Why else would we write this book to enable you to bring the most confident version of yourself into the world?

At whatever level you choose to engage, you need passion to lead.

In business, character-based leadership is a hot topic. Many have finally woken up to the fact that leadership is about leading people – people with ordinary lives but sometimes exceptional hopes, dreams, and aspirations. Leaders who are able to help us to connect to and realise our dreams can achieve extraordinary new levels of performance. But no gimmicks can achieve this, only authentic (no pretence), honest-to-goodness character.

Warren Bennis, the world's leading authority on character-based leadership, says that the process of becoming a leader is not very different from that of becoming an integrated human being. A great leader then, is an integrated human being on a great mission, on a great journey to a better future.

If you have done the work in this chapter you are this person and your destiny is leadership. Don't fear it, take it on. This is the ultimate destiny of your passionate, powerful, and confident self – the self you are creating.

Part III
Building Your Confident Self

"We're looking for someone with a high level of self confidence, Mr. Anthony. Unfortunately, I think you're over qualified."

In this part...

A key insight in this part is that you need to forget being perfect if you want to be most effective. You discover that you operate at your peak by paying attention to how your mind and body connect and find out how to make that connection.

Chapter 8

Using What You Already Know

● ●

In This Chapter

▶ Turning your life's experiences into your confidence fuel

▶ Facing your fears

● ●

*A*t certain times in your life, even if you can't recall them instantly, you've felt on top of the world, you've tasted moments of extreme joy, happiness, courage, excitement, empowerment, high energy, a sense of being truly invincible. As you flex your confidence muscles, your task is to build on the wealth of experience in your life and turn it to your advantage.

You actually have loads of confidence locked inside you pushing to get out. It may just be that you need help to release it. So this chapter is about unlocking that inner, intuitive, confident way of being. We explain how to flip over your fears and transform them so they give you energy rather than reducing it. Specifically we help you look at how you can take more useful action by getting into a strong way of 'being' – what is known as a sense of 'flow'. It's what sports people describe as being 'in the zone'.

Accentuating Your Positives

Peak experiences are those on-top-of-the-world times, and the memory of these can give you a valuable inner source of confidence when you face a difficult or fearful moment.

Kate likes to play mind games when she feels challenged. She remembers when she is at her most enthusiastic in the great outdoors – skiing off mountain tops, nurturing baby plants in her greenhouse, running along a sandy beach. She aims to bring those peak moments to mind in everyday life. So, for example, when she's sitting in the dentist's chair or about to do an important presentation, she pretends she's off skiing. You can tap into your own feel-good moments; the following sections tell you how.

Expecting the best

There's a saying that goes 'Be careful of what you dream about, as it might just happen.' The same is true of what you think about. If you begin with negative thoughts, you almost always get a bad experience. If you want positive outcomes, start with positive thoughts. Expect that good things will come to you.

Some years ago, when we first began to run personal development workshops, we met a lady who was an awesomely confident trainer. She positively oozed a powerful sense of presence and was a very positive role model for how to work confidently with large groups of people. We were intrigued as to how she did it. The most useful tip was her thoughts on standing up in front of a group for the first time. She said: 'I never know how an event is going to turn out. It's always different to the way I expect it because I'm working with people. I just know it's going to be fun. And it always is.'

Duplicating positive results from the past

Ivana is a young design engineering graduate, recently out of college and looking for the first step on the career ladder in a graduate trainee role. When we met for a coaching session, she was preparing for a series of highly competitive assessment centre-style interviews and feeling extremely nervous about them. One interview was with a serious management consultancy firm in London for a client-facing role, and another with a very successful entrepreneurial manufacturer as a product designer.

Once we had rehearsed her answers to the obvious questions the recruiters were likely to ask her, I invited her to think of a great time in her life, the time when she felt she could conquer the world and be at her best. She brought to mind the experience of rebuilding her old Jeep and taking it out on the open road. My next request to her was: 'Hold that feeling in your body, and notice all the sensations, smells, taste, sound, and any pictures.' When the experience was most vivid, I 'anchored' the sensation by pressing firmly on her knuckle. My request to Ivana was that as she walked into the interview, she would press her knuckle in the same place to trigger her 'I can conquer the world' memory.

A couple of weeks later, Ivana called with the results of the interviews. She had performed well at both and enjoyed the experience without feeling nervous. However, she was thrilled to have been offered the place in product design and felt quite lucky she had not been offered the consultancy role, which in her own words 'was just not me, but I felt I *ought* to go for it.' The anchoring had enabled her to overcome her nerves easily, and the assessors had recognized her natural talents and interests.

When you trust that things will turn out okay in the end, they usually match your expectations!

Distilling the essence of positive outcomes

You can help yourself to attract more of what you want in your life by accessing your memories and drawing help from them.

The following confidence-comparison exercise helps you extract some useful advice for yourself from your moments of low confidence. We offer an example in our friend Jimmy's experiences.

1. **Think of three times when you felt at your least confident.**

   Jimmy's three moments are when he got dumped by his first girlfriend, when his mobile phone was stolen and the thieves ran up a £600 bill he had to pay, and when he got rejected by the promotion panel.

2. **Think of three times when you felt at your most confident.**

   Jimmy felt confident when he danced in the Salsa competition, when he got married, when he received an unexpected bonus last week.

3. **Notice the patterns or trends present in your responses to Steps 1 and 2.**

   Jimmy noticed that his confidence is about being loved and accepted, competing and winning, and feeling financially secure.

4. **Determine what you can do differently as a result of your realisations.**

   Jimmy came to recognise that not everyone is going to love him but that he can work at his marriage and at being lovable. Also, he accepts that he's not always going to win, but knows he benefits simply by competing. He's prepared to see his finances go up and down unexpectedly, but determines that saving his bonus as a buffer in case of problems is the smart choice.

Going with the flow

When we talk about the *flow state,* we mean experiencing a sense that your skills and your challenges are balanced and that you are

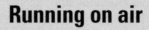

Running on air

Marathon runner Michael knows that after around 15 miles into a race, he typically hits a tiredness hurdle that gets progressively worse. As he senses the pain increasing, he plays mental games to raise his energy and ability to break through the barrier.

'At this point, I change the way I think. I bring to mind the image of a colourful helium balloon that I allow to raise me in the air so that I feel as if I am not running at all. I imagine this balloon tied to my running shoes and then, it's as if I am running on air. This image enables me to get into what I call a flow state, a kind of zone which is like a trance that takes me across the finish line. I also use the energy generated from the crowd who are constantly shouting words of encouragement. Instead of allowing this to be just a nice feeling I absorb the flow of energy and direct it to where I need it most, i.e. my legs – in this way the energy generated becomes integrated into my overall state of flow.'

At the same time, Michael uses the power of music. 'I play two pieces repetitively before the race. "It's a Kind of Magic" by Queen, and "We Share the Same Dream" by Belinda Carlisle. When the going gets tough, I raise the volume on these songs in my head.'

completely focused on what you're doing – nothing distracts you, your self-consciousness disappears. You are living life and swept up with it. It all seems effortless and natural. The flow state is what happens when your sense of thinking and doing become integrated. It is a joyful state of creative absorption. Often music can help get you to your flow state, as can encouraging yourself with positive self-talk.

When you go with the flow, life becomes easier, you reduce anxiety and fear, you are relaxed, focused, and functioning at your best. You achieve stronger results, and faster, in anything you do – whether it's writing a proposal at work, doing the chores at home, or playing your favourite sport.

You can start to experience more flow in your life by putting your energy into doing the things you're good at and by living according to what's important to you. (For more on living your values, turn to Chapter 5.)

Managing Your Fears

In Victorian times, people's biggest fear was being mistakenly certified as dead and buried alive. Coffins were equipped with a bell so that a 'deceased' person who came to in a coffin could ring for help. Today, your fears are more likely to be quite different – fears of public speaking, spiders or snakes, or flying. No matter what your fears, liberation from them is a positive way forward.

A simple way to manage your fear reaction is through practising the 7/11 breathing technique:

1. **Inhale to a count of seven.**

2. **Exhale to a count of eleven.**

Follow these two steps until you feel relaxed.

Avoiding the trap of fear

Fear is a trap you can stumble into unexpectedly. For example, when Verity tripped over on a pavement slab while out running, for some weeks she became fearful of going out of the house alone in case she repeated the accident. This sudden loss of confidence can show up in your tentative movements and facial expressions. It's so visible when someone close to you has that look of a frightened rabbit startled by a car's headlights.

A sense of being out of control, of being trapped, can be debilitating. The way to move on is first to notice and acknowledge what is happening, and then to find some strategies and resources that help you to move on.

From fear to function

Jeremy recounted his wife's reaction to a foreign posting to a country whose culture appeared quite alien to a Westerner. Soon after he and his wife moved, he realised the toll the relocation had had on his normally buoyant partner. She grew to hate buying food, as the supermarket staff took on a surly demeanour if she did not have the correct small change available in her purse.

For several weeks she tolerated the sour treatment until one day she blew a fuse, and shouted in English when they refused to serve her. By standing her ground in a completely different style to her polite normal way of responding, the staff took notice and began to serve her in a good-humoured and direct way.

Even though she couldn't speak the language, she earned their respect by standing up for her right to be treated as an equally important customer. She began to take control once more of her experience.

Use this exercise to confront and diminish your fear:

1. **Think of something you don't want to look at, something you feel fearful of that is coming up in the future.**

   Notice how it feels.

2. **Get a strong picture in your mind of what that looks like.**

   Look at it straight out in front of you.

3. **Now put a frame around the picture – a strong black frame that contains the image.**

4. **Look at the picture, and shrink it to a smaller and smaller frame.**

5. **Move the picture and frame to the bottom left-hand corner of the room until it's a tiny little black dot in the furthest corner.**

6. **Notice how it feels now.**

Making the fear smaller in your mind's eye reduces its power over you.

Transforming your fears into confidence

Fears are largely about experiences that may happen in the future: after all, human beings are hugely creative at imagining catastrophes.

Your worst fears can trigger you to action, so your experience may lead to a real benefit. If you can take energy from the fear and let go of the emotion, notice how empowered you feel.

To let go of your fear and strengthen your confidence, it is important to face up to what really unnerves you. We list some common worries:

- ✔ **Fears of loss and rejection:** Will I be left alone?

- ✔ **Knowledge:** Do I know enough about the subject?

- ✔ **Fluency:** Can I find the right words under pressure?

- ✔ **Judgement:** I don't want to face criticism or have others assess me.

- ✔ **Privacy:** What will happen if I tell people about me?

> ✔ **Bad experiences:** I have some unhappy memories from the past.
>
> ✔ **Being seen:** I prefer hiding in a corner.

You may well have some of your own particular fears to add.

Table 8-1 contains an exercise that helps you to break down your sense of fear into manageable parts and get to the root cause. It's particularly useful during times of change – say when you are leaving home to go to college, changing your job, or taking on a large financial commitment.

The first row offers one example so you can see how it works. Fill in the blank rows with your own fears. Note that the final column is really important – taking the first step is often the hardest, but without any action you won't make the switch from feeling fearful to acting with confidence.

Table 8-1	**Focusing on Your Fears**		
What Do You Fear?	*How Did This Fear Begin?*	*What Ideas Have You Got to Change It?*	*What Action Will You Take and When?*
Taking on a large mortgage to buy a flat.	My grandparents told me I shouldn't ever owe anyone money.	Talk to friends who have mortgages. Work out a plan for the repayments with different interest rates.	Speak to John after rugby on Saturday. Call to meet the financial adviser to get some detailed breakdowns.

Once you know what you're scared of and put it in black and white, you can find ways to make facing it more manageable.

Chapter 9

Moving beyond Perfection

- -

In This Chapter

▶ Freeing yourself from the perfection pressure

▶ Finding your own way of living happily

▶ Taking things one step at a time

- -

*I*t's impossible to attain and hold perfection, and striving to do so positively damages your confidence. In any case, is there any fun in being perfect? You know it's horribly boring to be with 'perfect' people. So in this chapter, we look at how you can be the best you can without driving yourself insane or collapsing under the stress of trying too hard.

Keep in mind that you're a human being; you're not some sort of superhero. As a human being, you're already perfectly fine and doing your best. So as you travel through the next few pages, chuck out your 'perfect expert who must be in control of life' view of yourself and adopt a simpler, more philosophical way to move on. Already you and those around you are doing the best you can, and your best will get better as you gain more knowledge.

Letting Go of Unreal Expectations

The poet Robert Browning said: 'A man's reach should be beyond his grasp, or what's a heaven for.' It's wonderful to have goals and dreams, the things you're going towards in your life. And we fully encourage you to aim for the stars. Yet there may be times when the goals you set, and the speed at which you want to attain them, put you under really crazy pressure. It's like expecting to be Prime Minister or the next President of the US when actually becoming a local councillor or standing as Member of Parliament is a more than acceptable step on the success ladder. You may find you have more practical impact in your community and a better quality of life at a less senior level.

In moving forward, you may want to keep your sights closer to home too.

Admitting that you can't be perfect (and that you don't want to be)

Liz grew up as the only child of parents who adored her. They told her she was perfect – beautiful, talented, and able to do anything she set her mind to. Yet the continual pressure on her to be top of the class, the most popular student, as well as good looking and slender became a burden as she hit her thirties. She suffered from stress-related illnesses that affected her job as a project manager for an international firm.

Expecting perfection from yourself brings problems: one is that you make unfavourable comparisons with other people all the time; another is that you set yourself on a pedestal that's all too fragile. Being on top the pedestal at all times isn't a healthy place to be. You never have a chance to re-charge your batteries and soon wear yourself down. It's like being a pop star on tour all year, or a perpetually flowering plant. You never get a chance to just chill out if you are constantly looking for the next achievement.

Similarly, being regarded as the expert in your field is good for your ego and confidence in one way, but it can also be a very lonely position that alienates you from the rest of the team or organisation and puts you under huge pressure to solve problems single-handedly.

Turning perfection into an excuse

John had a dream to move house in his retirement and live by the sea. He shared it with his new partner Juanita. She bought into it and was inspired by the idea – she too had always wanted to live by the sea.

John spent two years taking Juanita on 'away days' around estate agents in English seaside resorts looking for the perfect house to move to. Unfortunately, every house that she thought was great, he found something wrong with. His requirements for the perfect house and location became increasingly stringent and uncompromising. He gave up the dream as an impossible move.

Meanwhile, Juanita set off on her own, sold her flat in the North, and moved to one in a pleasant small town on the South Coast. Now she is very happy to walk along the beach every day or cycle along the promenade and take in the sea air and her new-found feeling of freedom. The flat is excellent without being perfect. She's living the life she dreamed of. John is still searching for it.

How can you overcome the perfection pressure? Our strategy (when as business consultants, we're sold into a project as the experts) is to step off the perfection pedestal. We prefer to share our knowledge as peers and invite others to do the same. In this way we capitalise on the team's strength and protect the individuals in the team from too much stress and the illness that ensues when each member tries to do it all.

Think about an area – at work or home – in which you're trying to be perfect. Now acknowledge that you can't be perfect and let the pressure roll off your back. Feel it go and gently land at your feet. That's better.

Focusing on perfection distracts you from excellence

Instead of perfection, try adopting excellence as a more useful objective. When you aim for excellence, you simply go for the best, aiming high and accepting that there will be times when you don't quite reach the summit. Substituting excellence for perfection doesn't mean you don't have high standards and expectations – you do. But it does mean you can be easier on yourself and in so doing you are more likely to succeed in what you really want to achieve.

How can you develop excellence? Think of an area of your life that's important to you. Maybe you'd like to create a happy relationship with someone significant. How will you know when you've got it? Picture what it will be like when you succeed, what will you see yourself doing, what will you be saying and feeling? Make a note of it now and write it in the present tense to make it more real for yourself. For example: 'I have a wonderful relationship with this person and I prefer to spend my time with her to being with anyone else. We have fun when we go out together and enjoy quiet evenings at home in each other's company. I am telling her that I care about her and I have a sense of contentment just being close to her.'

Getting clear about what it is that you want puts you on the way to achieving it.

Being Generous to Yourself First

In order to support other people, you need to be generous to yourself too. Many people run ragged putting themselves after everybody else, including their mother-in-law's dog. The result? Resentment builds, alongside ill health and unhappy relationships.

Practise being generous to yourself – give yourself the unconditional love of a parent for a child. Make time each day to be alone,
even if it's only ten minutes.

When considering the requests on your time, ask yourself: What
does this do for me? Does it fit with my agenda and values? Politely
let go of others' demands, pressures, needs, and perceptions. You
have needs too, which are just as important.

Acknowledging your successes

Jonnie is a learning junkie. He's taken several degree and postgrad-
uate courses and a vast array of private courses – everything from
garden design and photography to software programming and
business negotiation. His cupboards are stashed full of manuals,
CD learning sets, and certificates. Yet he's so caught up in courses
that he never has time to apply what he's learnt and in every new
project compares himself to the specialists in that field.

Do you ever catch yourself running so fast through everyday life
that you forget to stop and realise what you've discovered and
achieved? A 'done it, toss it over the shoulder' mentality is at work
here. When you're always looking to the future rather than the
here and now, it's easy to notice what hasn't happened and what
you haven't done rather than what you've already completed. You
may be piling the pressure on yourself to do more, to earn more
money, to tick more off the list, and your to-do lists become longer
and longer. Even holidays become busy tick lists of where you've
been and what you've seen and done.

Such competitive pressure can zap your confidence.

It's important for your sanity that you pay attention to what you've
achieved rather than just pushing yourself harder. So, look back
over the last year and acknowledge your accomplishments and
successes.

1. **Put on your success sunglasses and take out a large piece
   of blank paper.**

2. **Write down every success you can think of.**

   What new things have you found out? What relationships have you nurtured? How has your life moved on
   in some way?

Acknowledge the everyday successes as well the big ones. Perhaps you've nursed someone through an illness, supported a friend, or completed a course of study. Perhaps you discovered the importance of time to chill out. Maybe you joined a new team at work or prepared food 365 days of the year. Don't forget to count the money you raised for a charity or your kids' school.

3. **Keep writing until your blank page is full.**

4. **Now sit back and give yourself a pat on the back.**

Well done. You're already a success.

At any point when your confidence dives, just take a look at your success list – remind yourself of how much you've achieved to keep positive.

Accepting help and delegating

It takes confidence to recognise that you can't do everything yourself all the time and to let some things go. So how about relinquishing control and asking for help? This doesn't mean stepping on people's toes, but sharing the load fairly.

The evidence suggests that women find it harder to delegate than men, given that they take the majority burden of domestic chores in addition to working the same hours as their partners outside the home.

I am enough

One of our favourite stories on letting go of perfection is told in Naomi Remen's *The Search for Healing*, about her experience of attending a seminar given by the therapist Carl Rogers.

In the seminar, Rogers tried to analyse what he did as a therapist by giving a demonstration of unconditional positive regard in a client therapeutic session. He said: 'I realise there's something I do before I start a session. I let myself know that I am enough. Not perfect. Perfect wouldn't be enough. But that I am human, and that is enough. There is nothing this man can say or do or feel that I can't feel in myself. I can be with him. I am enough.'

Remen was stunned by this and says: 'I felt as if some old wound in me, some fear of not being good enough, had come to an end. I knew inside myself that what he had said was absolutely true: I am not perfect, but I am enough.'

In either a work or home context, list the tasks you find most time consuming or burdensome (for example, updating the customer database at work or doing the laundry at home). Ask yourself:

- ✔ What would I most like to have help with or delegate to others?

- ✔ Who could help me and what's the benefit or reward for them?

- ✔ Putting time and money to one side for now, what's really stopping me accepting help and delegating?

- ✔ What will I do to get help? And when?

Whenever you're feeling overloaded, go back to your list and find something to delegate. You'll find the lighter load so much easier.

Overcoming Procrastination

Question: What's your procrastination all about?

Answer: I don't know. Can I tell you later?

If confidence is about focusing your energy and acting decisively, then procrastination is the direct opposite. Procrastination scatters your energy and puts off acting at all – sometimes you avoid even deciding. You postpone and postpone. You dither about. Perhaps you have a proposal or essay to write and you keep putting it off and putting it off. Maybe it's the tax form to fill out, the cupboard to tidy, the difficult phone call to make, the button to sew on, the cobwebs to dust off the ceiling, or the medical check-up. It – whatever the current it happens to be – never happens.

Unless you're hyper-organised, you probably have something sitting on a 'to do' list that hasn't become urgent enough yet to do something about it. If so, you're qualified to join the procrastination club – if only club members could get a date and venue organised to meet up. Maybe next week.

Procrastination is the ultimate waiting game: waiting for someone else to take the lead; waiting for something else to happen first; and above all waiting for everything to be perfect before you do anything. Procrastination comes when you lack focus and energy. When you're high on focus and energy, the positive result you get is purposeful action – a livelier place to be.

The quick secret to bust through procrastination is to do something, anything, but just get moving. As writers we face the blank page each day. So we start writing anything, even if it's pure rubbish.

In the next sections, we look at practical ideas to allow you to move on with confidence.

Breaking the gridlock

Clients often come to coaching because they are stuck in what we call the *X then Y gridlock* scenario. They have a goal, a dream, something they want to realise, and yet it's not happening. Instead the conversation is around: 'I can't do X until Y.' These are the kind of messages we hear that signify people are putting their lives on hold. Some may be familiar to you:

> 'I can't do the training course until the children are older.'
>
> 'I can't turn professional until I have sponsorship.'
>
> 'I can't travel to Australia until my health is better.'
>
> 'I can't leave/change my job until my partner's business has taken off.'
>
> 'I can't buy my cottage house by the sea until I'm rich.'
>
> 'I can't get to the gym until I change jobs, and I can't change jobs until my wife is working too . . .'
>
> 'I can't lose weight until my wife stops cooking delicious dinners every night.'

. . . and on it goes. The treacle gets stickier by the day. This stuck situation becomes debilitating and reduces energy and focus to an all-time low.

In order to achieve a big dream, most people quite rightly argue that they are limited by not having enough time, money, or energy. However, these are not the sole reasons people get stuck. Essentially, they are struggling because they haven't broken the job into steps.

Try this step-by-step approach to breaking this pattern of gridlock for yourself and for others.

1. **Put aside the idea that you do not have enough time, money, or energy – assume the lack of any or all these elements is not the real problem.**

   Imagine that you are rich enough in time, money, or energy.

2. **State your goal or dream in a positive way and write it down.**

   For example: 'I want to move to a cottage by the sea.'

3. **Ask yourself Question 1: 'Can I do it today?'**

    If your answer is yes, everything is in place, hey presto your dream is complete. However, if it's not – and this is the most likely scenario – then proceed to Step 4.

4. **Ask yourself Question 2: 'What needs to happen first?'**

    Break out all the separate tasks you need to do to accomplish your goal.

    In the example of the house by the sea, the tasks divide into three main activities: Researching the location, Finding a more flexible job, and Getting the family's agreement.

5. **Loop around the questions in Steps 3 and 4 for each task.**

    Ask yourself Question 1, 'Can I do it today?' and if not, then Question 2, 'What needs to happen first?', until you arrive at a list of activities that you can either do today or you have negotiated with yourself to do on a set date that you write in your diary.

Get the idea? In this way you have broken through the gridlock, and are moving towards your dream.

Biting off smaller chunks

Patience and persistence are valuable qualities to help build your confidence. And when you calmly stick at things, breaking large tasks into smaller ones, you're more likely to get closer to perfection than if you rush at a job looking for a quick fix.

Bob calmly tackles stressful challenges in his job in a global IT team as well as in his hobbies by keeping his cool and seeing large projects as simply a collection of smaller chunks. At work, his job is to help transform the efficiency of an international airline – a seemingly impossible task. Yet he breaks this down into a series of smaller and smaller chunks. First he identifies the critical business processes, then maps business processes onto the existing IT infrastructure. From there he looks at process performance measures, identifies issues, and sets up smaller projects to tackle improvements that will make a difference.

At home, Bob takes a similar approach to large challenges, whether it's building a garden, renovating the house, or flying a glider. When he first decided he wanted to learn to fly, he did his research, found a gliding club, booked on a beginners' course, and set himself a series of challenges that he has quietly ticked off one by one: Flying solo, flying a single-seater glider, an endurance flight, a long cross-country flight. None of these has required any great fuss, as his practical approach is just to 'get on and have a go', knowing that he will gain confidence as he finds out more.

In order to break your own projects into smaller chunks, follow these steps:

1. **Set your big goal.**

    For example, perhaps you want to write a novel.

2. **Set a reasonable and realistic timeframe.**

    Writing a novel could take a year.

3. **Break your goal down into a series of small activities to accomplish within the timeframe.**

    For writing a novel, these activities may include finding a publisher, firming up the story line, and developing your creative writing skills.

4. **Set specific timeframes for each activity.**

    Each novel-writing activity could take several months of work to complete.

5. **Break each activity into a series of daily habits or short projects.**

    So developing your creative writing skills may translate to attending a creative writing evening class and writing for an hour each day.

Organising a project into manageable tasks lets you tackle the largest task with confidence.

Taking Time Off – for You

All work and no play makes for a dull life. It's also highly unproductive. If you stay at work for crazy hours, you know how your productivity dips very quickly after the main shift.

What would it be like to slow down a bit and keep things simple? The information in the next sections gives you a glimpse.

Slowing down

You may be used to acceleration, working in top gear, speeding from place to place by the fastest route possible and rarely stopping to think. Society today is geared to fast – fast food, fast cars, fast computers, fast results, and instant gratification. 'I want it, and I want it today.'

Yet when do your moments of inspiration come? Most often in the quiet moments when you give your brain a chance to unwind a bit: On the day you take off of work; in the shower; on the gym bike; ambling around the park; working in the garden; walking along a country lane. Rarely does your best thinking occur when you're buzzing around like a busy bumble bee in a flower patch.

Your brain may work wonders in fast mode, in logical, rational mode. But it works so much better if you give it a chance to relax at regular intervals. Perversely, going slow speeds up the results you get. Take a break, a complete break, and you come back refreshed.

Meditation offers a calm sea to support you in negotiating the choppy moments. That's why millions of people around the world now practise meditation each day. Here's a two-minute meditation you can do yourself before an important meeting or before the baby awakes – whenever you'd like to slow down gently and savour time for yourself. You may like to read it out aloud to yourself or record your voice saying it and listen to the recording. For more on mediation ideas, see the Appendix.

Let your mind be free . . . free of any thoughts or worries. Let them go. Allow them to float away gently on the breeze. Take your awareness to your breathing. Simply notice as it rises and falls gracefully in your chest and abdomen, with no comment from the mind. Allow your thoughts to come . . . and then to go. Observe the colours and pictures around you, take in the light, and bathe your body and mind in its generous warmth. Hear the sounds in the room and beyond. Let them soften to the furthest corners of your mind, then let them go. Feel the movement of the air on your face and on your body, and bask in that cool stillness. Smell . . . taste the delicacy of the silence. Rest in that calm awareness for a few moments. And when you're ready, come back to now – refreshed, energised, and ready to move on.

Adopting the 80/20 principle

When Kate worked in corporate advertising, she knew the rule that roughly 20 per cent of her advertising spending produced 80 per cent of the results in any campaign. The problem was always to know which 20 per cent was really working. Fortunately, there are some less fickle areas of life where the data is clearer to gather and interpret, and we examine those areas in the next sections.

Explaining the split

Pareto's law, or the *80/20 principle,* is named after the 19th-century economist Vilfredo Pareto, who discovered that 80 per cent of the land in Italy was owned by 20 per cent of the population. He also, allegedly, noticed in his garden that 80 per cent of the peas he harvested came from 20 per cent of the pea pods.

Over the years, the same generalised principle has been applied to interesting effect in many other areas beyond land ownership and gardening. Most importantly for you, it suggests that 80 per cent of your results come from 20 per cent of your effort, and, in turn, it takes the 80 per cent of your remaining resources to shift that extra 20 per cent from 80 per cent to 100 per cent. All of that is good evidence of the real cost of perfection. To squeeze out that extra 20 per cent is going to cost you four times the effort. Some things are worth that effort and some are not.

The 80/20 rule is a rough approximation to what happens in reality, but here are some examples of where you might spot Pareto's law in action:

- Twenty per cent of your cleaning effort gets 80 per cent of your home sparkling.

- Twenty per cent of your customers bring in 80 per cent of the sales.

- Twenty per cent of the people in your office create 80 per cent of the results.

- Eighty per cent of your progress comes from 20 per cent of the activities on your to-do list.

- Twenty per cent of your clothes are worn 80 per cent of the time.

- Twenty per cent of the meeting time results in 80 per cent of the decisions.

Adjusting the split as needed

Recently, a friend was studying for a qualification that involved writing clinical essays. Writing is not her favourite pastime and she became increasing anxious about this piece of work until she decided she could take pressure off herself. 'I'm working on an 80 per cent essay – one that will be good enough to get me the marks I need and still have time for the family and me.'

It was an eminently sensible application of the 80/20 principle – to do her best in the time she had, and then to stop rather than trying to extract the extra marks and suffer unduly in the process.

We believe that busyness is one of the biggest challenges that ordinary folks face. By aiming to do 100 per cent all the time, you dramatically lose energy and focus. If you were to apply the 80/20 rule, you could cut out 80 per cent of your activities and increase your leisure time dramatically.

Identify an area where you are struggling to achieve 100 per cent perfection. Decide on an 80 per cent result that is acceptable to you. Now allocate 20 per cent of your time to focusing on purposefully achieving this result.

Generating Realistic Standards of Behaviour

We hope that you have the point that perfectionism and procrastination are both ultimately time wasters in most circumstances. They take vast amounts of your energy. Naturally, you want to be your best, and circumstances exist where you are competing to excel and want to give it your 100 per cent. The point is to get real as well as having a vision.

Most successful people recognise the benefit of keeping things simple, as in the famous acronym *KISS – Keep it Simple, Stupid.* The harder and more complex you make things for yourself, the more you are likely to make a mess when it's too tough, and lose your confidence in your ability to succeed.

Adjusting your goals to the circumstances

You know from the previous section that 80 per cent of your results come from 20 per cent of your work. In moving towards your own vision and goals, it's essential to adopt habits that stop your dillydallying procrastination and keep your energy focused. There are some questions to ask yourself as you constantly re-evaluate your route forward.

✔ What's the vision now? (And reconnect with why it's important for you.)

✔ What am I doing that I can delegate to others?

✔ What am I doing that doesn't need to be done at all?

✔ What can I do that no one else can do to achieve this vision?

Capture your answers and refer to them whenever you need to stay on track. Refer to them at least once every month, and ideally more frequently.

Staying positive while keeping it real

There will be times and situations when your confidence plummets due to external factors over which you have little or no control. Here are some tips for staying positive and holding it together.

- ✔ Think about a time in the future when none of this will matter.

- ✔ Plan a series of small treats for yourself, even if it will be a while before you enjoy them.

- ✔ Imagine that you are in a movie, and this is the bad bit, but you know the movie has a happy ending. Write your own happy ending.

- ✔ Go to bed early with a hot water bottle.

- ✔ Eat the best-quality, healthiest food available and drink lots of water.

- ✔ Take a walk and marvel at the sky, the air, the greenery.

- ✔ Remember everything that has gone smoothly, however small the event.

- ✔ List out the things that are perfect about this most difficult situation right now.

Increasing your flexibility

For years, long-distance running was Joanne's favourite exercise and form of stress release. She was part of a close-knit running club, ran several miles before work through all weathers, and enlisted for competitive runs at weekends. Running at speed was a theme for all of her life in the fast lane – a high-powered job as a board director for a large firm with a demanding travel schedule. Her children rarely saw her, and her husband felt as if he was a single dad much of the time, bringing up the children on his own.

A hamstring injury enforced a break in Joanne's running schedule. On the advice of her physiotherapist, she exchanged her running routine for swimming and yoga practice at home, and clawed back more time to create an attractive environment in the cottage and relax with her husband and children at weekends. The enforced change of routine encouraged Joanne to take stock of her working life and day. She realised that she'd been stuck in a rut of the same exercise and mixing with the same group of people.

Once she became more flexible in her exercise routine, she allowed more flexibility and space in her life for her family, and redefined her company role. Her relationships and energy soared once more.

Think about your daily and weekly routines with an eye towards looking at areas where you may be stuck with certain habits that do you no favours. Where would some change, however small, have the most impact? Consider the routines you've developed that have become less than inspiring. Do you, for example, always mix with the same people, spend your weekends in the same way each week, or visit the same places time after time?

Examine the things you *always* do, feel you *ought* to do, or *never* do and try something different. Perhaps you've got into a boring rut. If you always eat Sunday lunch with your mother or tackle the house-work every Friday morning, experiment by doing something differ-ent. What would happen if you took your mother to the beach on Sunday for a picnic or spent Friday morning playing a round of golf?

Flexibility is a route to freedom. The more adaptable you become, the less you are harnessed to the pressure of perfection.

Chapter 10

Stretching Yourself Mentally

● ●

In This Chapter

▶ Exploring your comfort zone

▶ Looking towards the future

▶ Receiving what you need

▶ Developing your power

● ●

*T*he truth behind the advice 'Enjoy life; this is not a dress rehearsal' underlines the fact that you cannot always prepare for what life throws your way, and if you attempt to insulate yourself from the unexpected, you end up missing out on so much of the richness that life has to offer.

Do you remember the test in the fairytale, *The Princess and the Pea*? To find out whether the visitor is royal, the courtiers trick her into sleeping on a pile of ten mattresses with a simple, garden pea hidden underneath the bottom one. Being an authentic princess, she is unable to sleep due to the discomfort this causes her, and next morning she is full of complaints about the lumpy mattresses.

This is as much as we learn about this princess, but we know from other fairytales that princesses are often unable to eat normal food, they are allergic to dust and grime, cannot bear to be questioned or contradicted, are paralysed by the least setback, and their lives seem much less easy than they should be. Despite all their privileges (or because of them) fairytale royalty seems less able to cope with life than simple, ordinary folk.

Like a lot of folk literature, there is a truth at the heart of these princess tales. They are about human beings who have shrunk in stature and capabilities because they have never had to stretch to meet a challenge. Facing up to difficulties is one of the most important drivers of all human growth. In this chapter, we show you how to embrace the challenges life places your way and use them as stepping stones to your full confidence and power in the world.

Expanding Your Comfort Zone

What we mean by your comfort zone is a lot more than your physical environment. *Comfort zone,* a term in widespread use in psychology and personal development, mostly refers to aspects of your mental environment, the one you have created for yourself. Think of it as your den, the place where you feel truly relaxed just being yourself. It's familiar, it's easy, and it's comfortable.

You can readily see how even the most comfortable of dens becomes boring and over-restrictive if you never get out of it. But your psychological comfort zone is different from your den at home in one important respect – it's slowly shrinking! Unless you take steps to expand it again, it will squeeze you to death.

To be a healthy human being, you have to be able to stretch your mental environment from time to time. You grow much more quickly in confidence if you accept your need to expand.

Here's another useful analogy. Imagine yourself lying in bed on a cold and stormy night. Outside the wind is howling and you can hear the rain lashing against the windowpanes. Inside, though, you are cosy and protected under your duvet. As long as you stay put you *feel* that you can see the storm through in comfort.

But how good a guide are your immediate feelings of comfort? If the storm goes on for a while, you are liable to get hungry, and if the wind takes off your roof, you are going to be extremely uncomfortable and perhaps fall into danger. In these circumstances, your bed isn't going to offer you any real protection, and you need to get out and find a safer place. You won't find your storm cellar so comfortable but it's a better place to be in a storm. You might want to prepare one.

Comfort is a poor guide in life; it's an illusion that is entirely subjective and relative to the moment. You may usually baulk at a cold shower, but if you're on a camping safari and the temperature outside is 105 degrees, a cold shower out of a bucket might seem a luxury. Comfort always depends upon context.

Understanding the limits of your zone

Think of your comfort zone as your routine living, working, and social environments; those places, activities, and relationships where you feel most at home. There is nothing wrong with living in this zone most of the time. Doing so makes it possible for you to get through your days without continually having to re-evaluate every nuance of every situation. But, just as your beliefs are decisions about what things mean that can keep you trapped in outmoded thought, so never venturing beyond living within your comfort zone can render you unfit to face the adventure of life.

ANECDOTE

Coming alive

In his youth, Mike was a fine athlete. Small in stature, he was nonetheless strong and quick, with a winner's spirit born out of competition with his four brothers. When he was married with children of his own and the responsibilities of a demanding job, his time for sports was squeezed out. When he became responsible for an entire region, he spent more and more time traveling, both entertaining and being entertained, and living mostly on hotel and restaurant food. He put on weight and began to worry about his physique for the first time in his life.

Another promotion saw him transferred back to head office. When his new team members asked him to make up their numbers in the indoor football tournament he accepted. But when he went out for a training run with them he had to work very hard to keep up and he didn't enjoy it at all. He missed the other two training sessions due to 'pressure of work', but the truth is that his body was hurting. He decided that playing would be less arduous than training and he decided to 'wing it'.

But on the evening of the tournament Mike's life changed. He ended up with torn ligaments and a leg broken in seven places. Lying in his hospital bed, after several operations, he yearned for the simple pleasure of a walk in the park with his wife, and the time to enjoy it. He knew that his 'accident' could have been so much worse. He reappraised his life and work and decided to make changes.

He had always gone where the company needed him without question and done what his employer asked. In return, he received regular salary increases, pension rights, a steadily improving company car, and an expense account. What he had lost was his natural affinity for decision making, competition, risk taking, growth, and self-determination. Mike realised that although he enjoyed the trappings of success he had lost touch with a large part of his physical being. He had lived in a shrinking physical comfort zone for the previous 15 years.

After his recovery, he quit his job to set up a small enterprise with his younger brother. They now arrange and lead adventure holidays and corporate leadership safaris. Now Mike's whole life is a stretch and he is fitter in all dimensions. 'I feel like I'm alive again,' he reports. 'I'm enjoying being active, thinking up new ideas, responding to new situations. I never know what next week will bring. My life is an adventure and my work, helping people to break out of their own comfort zones, is a joy.'

Just as you need to stretch your body's muscles and ligaments regularly to maintain your physical strength and wellbeing, so you need also to give your mind a stretch to maintain its power and flexibility. Just as you must use your muscles or lose them, so it is with the growth possibilities that life presents to you. You must seize them when you can or settle for living in an ever-shrinking comfort zone that constricts and stifles you, that steals your possibilities for love and joy.

Everyone has a tendency to avoid painful or potentially difficult situations. However, each time you do this, you withdraw a little bit farther into your comfort zone. Unless you deliberately stretch yourself from time to time you are eventually hiding under the mental equivalent of your duvet with storm demons raging all around you.

The next time you feel awkward or embarrassed and want to withdraw from a situation for no good reason, remember that choosing not to exercise your mental powers – hiding in your comfort zone – is the very opposite of confidence; you need to be on your guard against it. The knowledge you gain from this book can help you break through your glass ceilings and limiting beliefs.

Decide now to become more proactive in your family life, work, and other relationships and you can begin to use any small opportunity for growth. These regular small stretches make you familiar with feeling challenged, and the more familiar you are with a feeling, the less you fear it. When bigger challenges show up in your life, you're in a far better position mentally to take them on.

Stretching your boundaries: Expanding your zone

Just as you may advocate regular visits to the gym and the lifting of light weights that can be gradually increased, so it is with your mental stretching.

If you are terrified of public speaking, for example, it may overstretch you to lead a funeral oration or to deliver a witty and gracious personal tribute to a beloved boss on her retirement, though you can aspire to these things and easily achieve them over time. Remember, the journey of a thousand miles begins with a single step. The best way to start in public speaking is to take any small opportunity to speak up in a group, in a routine weekly meeting say, or informal social gathering.

One of the most revealing aspects of the Comfort Zone Theory is that *any* stretch expands your capacity in all areas simultaneously. To examine this point, say that you are facing these challenges in the next few months:

Look at the diagram Figure 10-1.

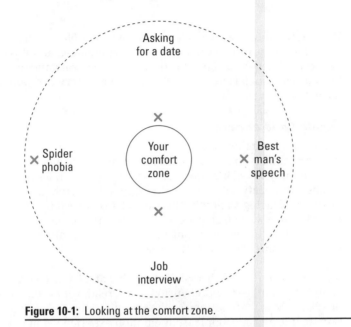

Figure 10-1: Looking at the comfort zone.

> ✔ You put yourself forward for a promotion you feel you have earned and now have the important interview to get through.
>
> ✔ Your oldest friend is getting married and you have been asked to be the Best Man. You felt honoured to accept but now you have to make the dreaded speech.
>
> ✔ You're attracted to a young lady in Accounts, and she seems to be interested in you too. Your workmates have begun teasing you and putting pressure on you to ask her out.
>
> ✔ You have a life-long fear of snakes and yet you have agreed to accompany your young nephew, who idolises you, on a visit to a snake farm. This will entail handling the snakes, something that fills you with dread.

Right now *all* of these things are outside your comfort zone. You can see yourself doing the first two, at a stretch, but asking your colleague for a date has you feeling queasy, and you have no idea how to deal with your snake phobia.

The best thing you can do in this situation is to start where you feel the most stuck. By getting help with your snake phobia, you increase your capacity to deal with the other, seemingly unrelated, situations as well. It's amazing and true! It's as though when you expand your comfort zone in any direction, you expand its radius, bringing many other things within your new, expanded circumference.

Phobias are most easily dealt with through simple therapies such as hypnotherapy or Neuro-linguistic Programming, and if you seek this kind of help you can also address any general anxiety you may have around social situations like speeches, interviews, and asking for dates.

Facing up to anxiety

Faced with something that scares you, or that seems well beyond your present capabilities, you may experience dry mouth, butterflies in the tummy, knocking knees, and so on. You may refer to these feelings as anxiety, but a better description is apprehension at the prospect of facing something unfamiliar. It is normal to feel a little apprehensive when facing a specific, new stretch, and it is a good indicator that you are engaging in growth activity. Apprehension is your friend; anxiety is something else.

Anxiety is not related to anything specific at all. It is a complex combination of fear, apprehension, and dread, very often accompanied by physical sensations such as palpitations and shortness of breath. It is a vague, unpleasant emotion experienced in anticipation of some usually ill-defined misfortune. Because of its vagueness it can interfere with lots of areas of life.

The normal antidote to occasional anxiety is common sense: thinking about your situation in specifics, spelling out your requirements in detail, thinking through your actions carefully. If this approach doesn't bring relief and anxiety and symptoms persist, you may need more specialised help.

Recognizing anxiety disorders

Don't confuse a mildly anxious response to a situation you find challenging with a range of more serious anxiety disorders. These conditions can fill people's lives with overwhelming discomfort and fear. Unlike relatively brief anxious feelings, anxiety disorders are chronic, often relentless, and can worsen unless treated.

Around 10 per cent of the population has some form of anxiety disorder and around 1 per cent experience panic attacks (although twice as many women as men report them).

Common among such anxiety disorders, *panic attacks* are experienced as feelings of terror that can strike suddenly with no warning. They are so frightening that sufferers live in fear of the next one, which makes their lives a misery.

So how do you know if you're suffering such a disorder? During a panic attack, you're very likely to sweat, to experience a pounding heart, and feel faint or dizzy. This is often accompanied by feelings of nausea, shortness of breath, or chest pains. You may have a sense of impending doom or believe you're having a heart attack. In the midst of a panic attack, it is common to feel you are going to die.

Panic attacks are readily treatable and left untreated can become very disabling. Sufferers tend to avoid situations where they fear an attack could strike such as swimming, driving, using a lift, being in a confined space, and so on. About a third of sufferers' lives are so restricted that they can become housebound.

Although the chances of it are only 1 in 10, it is important to seek medical advice if you feel you may suffer from any form of anxiety disorder.

Driving Safely in the Fast Lane

So you've made up your mind to become proactive and more open to new challenges. You've done the mental equivalent of 'consulting your doctor before commencing any vigorous programme of exercise'. You may be feeling a little apprehensive or even scared, but underneath that you are also feeling more alive. A wellspring of joy is evident that can become your motivation to stretch yourself. Congratulations: You're growing again.

Creating a haven for yourself

You are surrounded by a whole personal development industry that offers you tools for development, and there are many in this book. One of the most useful at this early stage of your journey is to create a haven for yourself where you can be calmed and nourished by things that trigger the appropriate neurological and physiological responses in you.

If you see life as a great expedition, as peaks to be conquered, then this haven can become your growth base camp. Just as climbers establish a base camp that contains everything they need to sustain them as they make their ascents on the peaks, so you need a place for rest and recuperation (R&R) – a place you can rely on to restore you quickly and efficiently to your normal, well-balanced condition.

The key attributes your haven needs to provide are:

- ✔ A means of restoring your physical state from agitated to restful and alert.

- ✔ A means of restoring your spirits from careworn to inspired.

- ✔ A means of restoring your energy from depleted to abundant.

It is possible to restore your body, mind, and spirit very efficiently through a combination of physical rest and relaxation, focus, and routine. Your objective is to create a system that delivers to you the three attributes in the preceding list in 30 minutes or so.

Creating your haven may be easier to do than to describe, so follow these simple steps. Later, when you get the hang of it, you can vary it to suit yourself, but keep it consistent each time you do it, as the habitual element of doing it the same way every time is an important part of the process.

1. **Go to a quiet corner in your room, your house, park, or garden where you can sit comfortably and be undisturbed for 20 to 30 minutes.**

   Just sitting quietly in this place allows your body and mind to quieten, which can do a lot to restore you when you are feeling a bit frazzled by events. The more you use your haven the more powerful this immediate calming becomes as your mind and body anticipate the rest that is to come.

2. **Breathe into relaxation for 4 to 5 minutes.**

   Breathing is a lot more complex than you might think. It's been the subject of intense study by mystics, philosophers, and physicians for thousands of years. All you need to know right now is that breathing is an important aspect of your mind/body coordination, and you can use it to create any effect you want. Right now you want to be relaxed and centred.

   When you are stressed or anxious, you breathe shallowly. This happens very naturally but can take quite a long time to get back to normal; meanwhile you continue to feel the effects of the physical conditions that shallow breathing creates in your body.

   To change your breathing instantly, you merely have to take it under conscious control, and the traditional way of doing this is to count monkeys!

A. Exhale all your breath.

B. Breathe in again to the count of four monkeys (one monkey, two monkeys, three monkeys, four monkeys).

C. Hold your breath for four monkeys.

D. Exhale for four monkeys.

E. Finally, hold your breath with your lungs empty for four monkeys.

   If this final step makes you feel dizzy, reduce the count to two monkeys until you become more used to the exercise and can comfortably hold for the four-monkey count.

You may find this conscious way of breathing very odd at first and it may seem uncomfortable and artificial, but stick to it. Breathing in this way settles you down as your body eliminates the neurochemical residues that keep you excited.

You need only do monkey breathing for five minutes, but come back to the monkeys if, at any stage in the process, you begin to revisit the scenes that cause you anxiety and you feel yourself getting tight again.

3. **Do 20 minutes of visualisation.**

   In *visualisation,* you engage your visual creative imagination by imagining yourself on a seashore, in a mountain meadow, or in any other idyllic place of your choosing with a gentle breeze, warming sun, and a sweet place to rest your head.

   Be creative and engage all your senses in planning how you will do this:

   • You can use gentle, instrumental music or natural sound recordings such as waves on a shore or rainfall. (This is *not* the time for heavy metal music, emotionally loaded words, or anything else that's likely to create excitation in your nervous system.)

   • You can simultaneously use aromatherapy oils or incense to engage your sense of smell. Using the same scent during visits to your haven helps create a powerful connection to your restful, contemplative state and strengthens the habituation effect, which helps to make your haven totally reliable in giving you the R&R you need.

- If you have a relaxation tape, this is the perfect place to play it. You can write your own script and tape-record it so that it perfectly suits your imaginative haven.

During this visualisation phase, focus on relaxing your mind, body, and spirit. The calm, untroubled environment you cultivate here is what makes your haven so valuable.

4. **Start taking your leave.**

When it is time to end your session, take a few minutes to return to the real world gradually. When your body is in this restful state, your brain waves tend to change into an alpha rhythm. This provides a lot of the R&R effect and is the perfect antidote to the stress of the day. Coming out, you need to allow your brain a few minutes to return to the beta rhythm of your normal waking state.

Switch off your music, take a few deep breaths and stretch; then sit quietly and contemplate for a few moments your experience in your haven. If you had a particularly pleasant visualization, you may want to jot down any new elements so that you can use them again. If you think you fell asleep, think about how hard you have been pushing yourself. Whatever, give yourself a moment or two and then say goodbye to your haven until your next visit and come to rejoin the mainstream.

The rule is that whatever works for you is okay. Experiment with the suggestions we provide to find a way that really delivers for you. When you find your combination, stick with it and all of these sensory stimuli will become triggers for your relaxation. Once you become habituated to this routine, your haven can restore your calmness and peace on even the most trying days.

If you take the trouble to create it and tailor it to your needs, always respecting it as a revered space, you will come to love your haven and it will give you the protection and nourishment you need to maintain your busy life of accomplishment.

Your haven is also a good place to visualise your day, your perfect sales presentation, or whatever stretch you may be facing that you want to get just right. This is not only your place of safety and restoration; it can also become a place where the more powerful versions of yourself can be born into the world in quiet perfection. The more you use it, the stronger and more dependable it becomes.

Your haven is a wonderful place for creating a vision of your future and the more detailed planning that flows from it. As you become familiar with the process and turn it into a daily routine, you can begin to develop more powerful thinking habits that will serve you for the rest of your life.

Preparing for the future

The great trick of preparing for anything is to think about what you need to achieve the perfect result rather than focusing and worrying about what might go wrong. The latter has a place in planning, but it is a lot less significant than you might believe.

In *Neuro-linguistic Programming for Dummies,* the authors (one of whom is Kate) describe a powerful planning tool called Well-Formed Outcome, which is a very effective way of thinking about any result you want to achieve.

The tool describes seven conditions that any decision or goal must satisfy in order for you maximise your chances of achieving it. You can understand these conditions most easily if you consider them as the following list of seven questions.

1. Is your goal something you want or something you don't want?

In other words, are you heading *towards* an outcome that you positively want rather than running *away from* something you don't want? Knowing what you want is the most powerful first step to achieving anything.

The thinking of the 1960s generation that 'we've got to get out this place if it's the last thing we ever do' led to rejection of the austere values of the immediate post-war period. Unfortunately, it also led to many unpredicted problems, because the desire and energy for change weren't directed towards anything specific.

There are very few situations in life where you can truly say 'absolutely anything would be better than this', although you may feel that way at the time. Even your escape from a burning building will go better if you know which door leads to the fire escape. So accept and embrace your dissatisfaction with the status quo, but think through what you want instead, and state it in the positive.

2. Is this your goal and is its achievement within your control?

The next thing you need to determine is whether the goal is really yours or whether someone else is imposing it on you. Your mother may have impressed on you the need for a good education, but her regard for learning is unlikely to get you through college unless at some point it becomes something you want for yourself.

You also need to ensure that the achievement of the goal is within your control. You may have a real desire to be loved by everyone who knows you, but such a goal isn't within your control and never can be. It is easy to see how your life's energy can be squandered by pursuing such a goal. On the other hand, a goal of being loving to everyone you meet is within your control. If this is your chosen outcome, a likely by-product is that many of the people you meet will be loving back to you. The key difference is that you are focused on what *you* can control.

3. How will you know when you are succeeding?

In a crazy dream you may get into a game with no way of knowing whether you are winning, which is exactly what people do in real life. If your goal is to be better at your job or to become a more sympathetic spouse, how will you know you are achieving it?

You need to set up your way of measuring success, and the clearer and more objective you can make your measure the better. In business these are often called *key performance indicators* or KPIs. The great thing about KPIs is that they are objective, clearly identified, and readily monitored. Try to do the same with your evaluation measures.

4. Do you know where this desire is coming from?

It is very unusual to want something out of the blue. All your wants and desires come from somewhere inside you, and you benefit from knowing where because this may modify how you feel about them.

For example, if you want a two-seater sports car, ask yourself why. Well, it's a great car you might say, with fabulous engineering, wonderful performance, and a grand marque. It's a status symbol that will let everyone (and you) know that you've arrived. And you have wanted one ever since your first job when you were 20.

Figuring out why you want what you want is all part of the context of your goal-setting decision. Having brought all your reasons to mind, you may decide that now you're 25, you should go for that two-seater before it's too late to enjoy it. If you are 35 though, with a wife and three children, and this is to be your main family vehicle, you may want to modify your choice to a larger four-wheel-drive, with wonderful performance of course, providing just as great a status symbol, and more seats!

ANECDOTE

Desert island dream

Gerald Kingsland had a very unusual long-term goal: he wanted to experience life on a real desert island. He meant to live this dream for a lengthy period, so it involved lots of preparation and the acquisition of real survival skills (hunting, fishing, building shelter, and so on).

Because very few people had ever done this and survived, he knew he would be properly prepared only to the extent that he had thought through everything he would have to do and taken steps to ensure he could provide all he would need (he even advertised in the newspapers for a Girl Friday and acquired Lucy Irvine as a partner for his desert island adventure).

All of this took several years, and the resulting events nearly cost the pair their lives, but they did survive and you can read their individual accounts of the story in *The Islander* by Kingsland and *Castaway: A Story of Survival* by Irvine; or see Lucy's account of it in the 1986 film, *Castaway*, with Oliver Reed and Amanda Donohoe in the roles of the castaways.

5. What resources do you need to achieve your goal?

When you have your goal clearly stated, in the positive, with your KPIs clearly identified, it becomes far easier to identify the resources you need to achieve it. For some of your goals, you already have all the resources you need and can make a start straight off the bat. For others, though, you may not have all you need and your first steps should be to secure them.

As you continue to think about your future, your thinking naturally expands to include other people and resources that you don't have currently. That's okay. It is important first to identify what you need and then to come up with plans to get what you need by the time you need it.

6. Will accomplishing this goal take away anything else that you value?

When you ask yourself what the future will look like when you achieve your dreams, also consider what will be left behind, or what will disappear. When you are rich, in your mansion at the top of the hill, you will certainly leave today's poverty behind, but what about the positive parts of your life now: The friends, the sharing, the helping each other through difficulties. If these are also giving you things that are important to you, you need to find a way to keep them in the picture. You're far less likely to achieve your goals if they don't incorporate your core values.

7. Does the goal identify the first step you need to take?

Well begun is half done, goes the saying, and dreams most often become reality through action. Knowing what needs to be done is imperative, and getting started is the critical first step. When you take an action, the world reacts and gives you something to work with. When you marry this action with commitment, you have an unstoppable combination.

As WH Murray, a great Scottish mountaineer, wrote (in a quote often attributed to the German poet Goethe):

> Whatever you can do, or dream you can do, begin it.
>
> Boldness has genius, power, and magic in it.

You should be identifying your next actions constantly – and taking them.

Attracting More of What You Want

Many self-help books tell you that you can get anything you want in life, and to an extent that is true. But you have to think carefully about what it is you really want.

Let's say that you and your friend free a genie from a bottle and are each granted one wish. Your wish is that everyone you meet loves you for the rest of your life. This is easy for the genie: in a puff of blue smoke, you're transformed into a little puppy, critically injured in a road accident with only minutes to live. Now everyone you meet will love you for the rest of your very short life.

Your friend wants everyone he meets to give him money. Puff of blue smoke, now he's become a slave, chained to a bridge collecting toll money for the stinking troll who guards it. He's doomed forever to receive money from everyone he meets, and nothing else.

That's the way it is with genies: Be careful what you wish for. The point of this is that life, just like the genie, has a habit of delivering to you exactly what you focus on.

You tend to get what you spend most time thinking about, so just as with the genie, you have to be very careful about how you frame your requests and desires.

Getting back what you give out

Suppose money was tight when you were growing up, and you saw your parents having to do without the things they wanted in order to put you through school. You're likely to feel a combination of gratitude and guilt as a result, maybe tinged with a little anger that life was so unfair for your parents, and perhaps frustration that they had been unable to handle their affairs better and so landed you with all this guilt. These are all common human responses.

But underneath this, you may also have formed a steely resolve that you will make sure that you and your children never have to make such difficult choices. This is also a common result. Now, how this resolve shows up in the world is very influential in determining how wealthy you will become; and it may not give you the result you want.

It's a simple, though strange truth: You tend to get what you think about. It's all too easy to fall into the trap of thinking most about what you don't want!

If you think most about being rich, you tend to become rich; if you think most about being poor, you tend to become poor. If you think most about being as healthy as possible, you tend to become healthy; if you think most about becoming seriously ill, you tend to become seriously ill.

You see the obvious link to a well-formed outcome described in the 'Preparing for the future' section earlier in the chapter. If you state your goals in the positive, your self-talk and the focus of your thinking is positive too, and you're much more likely to get your heart's desire. If you don't form your intention well – and this surely is the strangest secret – you may deliver just as surely the very opposite of what you want, the things you most don't want. Earl Nightingale, the early personal development guru, sold a million records across the USA in the 1950s describing this strangest secret.

The mystics have a name for the power in the universe that reacts to human actions. They call it karma. *Karma* has had a poor press in the Western world and is often associated with New Ageism and freakery. In truth, the theory of karma is much subtler and richer than it's usually credited with being. At its simplest, it seeks to explain how the action you take in the world creates the environment within which you live.

The Bible too gives 'karmic' advice: 'As ye sow, so shall ye reap' is a belief that many in the West choose to live by whether or not they are otherwise religious. Other traditions also have their versions of this universal law.

Your experience of life appears to be very closely tied to the way you are in the world, whichever theory you prefer. What you get back does, in a very real sense, reflect what you put out, so use it to help you create the world you want.

Finding what you're looking for

This book contains many tools and techniques to help you create the life you want and attract to you the people and material things you need to make it happen. But there is no mechanism that will deliver to you what you want and need unless you are clear and consistent at some level about what that is.

Our definition of *ultimate confidence* is your ability to take any action you need to take in order to achieve any outcome you want to create. But it's all worth nothing if you don't know what you want. That's why so much of this book is about helping you to work out what you truly want from life, at your most confident best.

Feeling Your Power

When you really start to get the results promised by the thinking in this book, it greatly enhances a wonderful power in your life. You have a wider sense of choice and a greater appreciation of your own free will.

The way you achieve this is by using your will to break the endless patterns of action and reaction, and superseding them with your own free choices that create new patterns of action and reaction.

In earlier times mercy and grace were the ultimate expressions of princely power. A powerful prince could defeat his enemies, 'enemies unto death', and then, through the exercise of clemency, let them off scot-free. And this was considered something that no ordinary human being was able to do. Well, you can do it too, in many areas of your life, and doing so liberates you. Once you are on your own chosen path, refusing to let other people or events divert you, you're free.

Appreciating a new way of being

Once you master your ability to take action consistent with your core values and in pursuit of your chosen life's purpose, you are, to all intents and purposes, unstoppable. You can then adopt the *guaranteed success formula*.

This is: you know what you want, you decide on your strategy, you take the action and then the next appropriate action steered by the reaction you got to the previous action. You have total behavioural flexibility, well-formed outcomes, and the drive and desire to achieve your goals that can only come from the core of your being. You won't stop until you succeed.

This is the most powerful version of yourself, free in the world to do your work. You will have total freedom of choice and action. You cause effects because you *will* them to occur. You need no other reason. The formulation of your goals and their acquisition become two ends of a seamless continuum.

This is a new way of being, and it is based on your willingness to understand who and how you are being today, and then assiduously working through everything that is holding you back. The key to this new way of being is your ability to take action and your belief in yourself as an integrated human being, more than equal to anything life throws at you.

Trusting it will be okay

Because you are confident in your ability to do anything you need to create the life you want for yourself and your family, your life takes on a simpler structure. You become like a good golfer on a beginners' course. You drive beyond the bunkers and render them irrelevant. You hit over the corners and the water hazards, arriving on the putting greens with shots in hand. Because you're always ahead of the game, you're comfortable and relaxed in your putting, feeling less pressure and making fewer mistakes. You build momentum as you progress through your round and play an even better game at the end than you did at the beginning.

Even if you don't play golf, this is a great metaphor for your life. In golf, you have a ball and a maximum of 14 clubs of differing sizes to hit it with. Once you start, no help or external intervention is available until you finish. You play your best golf when you are confident that wherever your ball ends up, no matter what bad luck strikes you, you will always be able to play the next shot. Even when you make a mistake, you can learn from it and become a better golfer in time to play the next hole. And you continue in this way until you finish the course.

In life, too, you can learn to trust yourself and make your plays. They will come off more often than not and what you take on will exhilarate and challenge you in equal measure. Live this way and trust it will be okay. This is how you are meant to live.

Listening to the voice of reason

Everyone has the little voices in their ear playing good cop, bad cop. Bad cop is your harshest critic, chastising you and telling you how you've always messed things up and you always will. As you develop your confidence, you hear less of the inner critic.

The critical voice is replaced by a voice of reason with an accumulating body of evidence that demonstrates conclusively that 'you don't always mess things up' on the contrary, more often than not, you get things right and there is no reason why you won't get your next action right also.

This natural growth through the incessant babble of the inner critic allows your innate ability for right action in the world to emerge more powerfully still and your confidence grows with this momentum.

And once in a while the voice of reason will say to you: 'You know what, I've never done this before and I don't know what to do next – wow, something new. Now who can help me to get this right?' And you ask someone who can give it for the help you undoubtedly need.

Chapter 11

Developing Your Physical Confidence

● ●

In This Chapter

▶ Noticing how your body affects your thoughts and deeds

▶ Getting more comfortable in your own skin

▶ Holding out a healthy vision of yourself

● ●

*D*o you jump out of bed in the morning raring to go, knowing that your physical body is in good shape, fit, healthy, and free of pain, ready to enjoy the day ahead? Or do you sluggishly grab for the first coffee, croissant, or cigarette to get you on your feet and force you into action?

When you get yourself in the best physical shape you can, you've a strong foundation for being your most confident best. Confidence takes energy, and this chapter is about getting the energy flowing for you.

Lark or owl?

Health guru Gillian Burn of Health Circles advises that your body clock relates to times of day that you feel more like doing certain things. She says: 'Our bodies have natural body rhythms and biorhythms which affect us. It's certainly true that some of us are "larks" – at our best in the morning, waking early, and preferring to start early in the day. Other people struggle in the mornings, are happier in the afternoon and evening, and work well late into the night. These are the "owls".

'In terms of confidence, a useful starting point is to understand your personal body clock and whether you are more like a lark or an owl. Then you can choose the best time of day to perform certain tasks or projects. Don't fight your body, listen and go with it.'

Brain boosting the biceps

Just as physical exercise can boost the brain, it's been found that how you think can boost the body. The *New Scientist* reported on a study in 2001 at the Cleveland Clinic Foundation in Ohio. Researchers got volunteers to spend just 15 minutes a day simply thinking about exercising their biceps. After 12 weeks, their arms were 13 per cent stronger. And all this happened without any physical training.

Connecting Your Mind and Body

Think of your body as a car, and then realise that your body is the most complex vehicle on the planet. Some 50,000 million cells make up your body, forming your bones, muscles, nerves, skin, blood, and other organs and body tissues. None of these systems works in isolation – they all communicate through highly sophisticated pathways of information signalling.

As you consider your mind and body as one system rather than as two separate and unrelated parts, you notice how the two are inseparable. When your state of mind is calm, clear, and focused, your physical performance is likely to be at its best. Conversely, if your mind is confused and frazzled, then it's likely that you will be off balance physically, experiencing symptoms from clumsiness to butterflies in your stomach.

Breakthroughs by neuroscientists over the last 30 years indicate that when an emotion is triggered, your physiology shifts even though you are not consciously aware of this. This shift sends a message back to the brain affecting virtually everything the brain does. So your performance, your ability to act with confidence, is inextricably linked with your physiology.

Many mantras, prayers, yoga, and spiritual practices can have a beneficial effect on wellbeing. By practising disciplines such as yoga, meditation, Tai Chi, and martial arts, you can develop the discipline to calm your mind and centre your body for effective action.

 One of the quickest ways to get your physiology regulated is through changing your breathing patterns. Practise simple deep breathing exercises every day and focus your energy on your heart as you do so. When you find yourself in a situation of tension, breathe through the situation rather than reacting with anger or negative emotion. Breathing helps you conserve your reserves of energy.

Considering What Makes You Healthy

What does healthy mean to you? Perhaps your measure relates to the food you eat, the exercise you take, whether you floss your teeth each day, or the medical treatment you receive. Take a moment to write down what makes you feel healthy.

In Europe today a rising tide of people is becoming chronically obese, which in the longer term, produces severe health problems, including heart disease and Type 2 diabetes. Regular exercise combined with a healthy diet is essential if you want to live to a healthy old age. And feeling healthy makes a huge difference to your overall confidence.

If you're struggling to increase your exercise, cultivate an exercise buddy to walk or run with you or join you in a sport regularly. Kate has been playing tennis with friends each week for many years, turning the game into a social occasion that is friendly and fun as well as healthy.

Health and fitness are not the same. You can be superfit, yet damage your wellbeing from over-exercising or poor eating habits.

Releasing stress, staying healthy

Stress is a key factor in modern living and working as your time, money, and energy feels the squeeze. Financial pressures plus family issues such as divorce or caring for young children and elders take their toll at home. Increasingly, business research highlights that modern workers experience substantial job insecurity, longer working hours, increased travel, and lowered morale. Workplace stress also damages health, happiness, and home relationships.

Stress is not all bad – it can create excitement, innovation, and motivation. Yet when it crosses the dividing line from a positive stretch to a negative pressure, you feel out of control. An excess of stress leads to hypertension and greatly increases your risk of heart disease.

You may think of stress and depression as strictly psychological problems, but they have an effect on the whole body, not just the quality of your mental processes. You suffer physically as you become more gloomy and pessimistic. Your confidence and physiology are so closely linked. That's why it's so important to manage your stress levels.

Normal everyday stress affects your body and can:

✔ Raise your blood pressure

✔ Make your heart beat faster

✔ Restrict the flow of blood to the skin

✔ Deplete your immune system and resistance to infection

✔ Disrupt the digestive processes

✔ Create a feeling of edginess inside

Stress can become extreme as a number of work and domestic issues get compounded. This happens, for example, if you are working long hours for a period of time and can't see the end to it, then you suffer the death or ill health of a loved one, face financial difficulties, or your marriage breaks down.

Your body is pre-programmed with a basic 'fight or flight' response to keep you safe. This may show itself as flight, as when you physically can't get out of bed to go to work or you experience panic attacks – or fight, when you lose your temper or lash out at someone unexpectedly.

Getting stress out of your system

To get negative stress out of your system involves building good everyday habits. By this we mean regular practices that keep your system functioning smoothly.

Don't wait until you feel bad, make sure that you develop stress-reliving habits while all is well so that you're better prepared when your immune system is most vulnerable.

Delegates on Kate's 'Balancing Act' workshop create their own set of everyday exercises to stay centred and quieten the mind. These range from physical postures such as the Yoga sun salutation – a range of movements to stretch and energise the body – through to problem solving strategies and mentally creating a quiet place which they can visit in their heads to feel calm.

Talking things over with a friend or mentor can help give you a better perspective on the issues underlying your stress. You need to objectively identify the causes and remove them in order to move on happily. Joining a support group of people in a similar situation is also helpful – whether this is a group of mums of toddlers or a job-search group.

Raising the feel-good factors

What gives you the feel-good factor? In Figure 11-1 there's space for you to evaluate the positives in your life from various angles. Then when you're feeling down, you can spend a minute circling round each spoke of the wheel inhaling the good vibes. This unlocks the endorphins in your body that boost your immune system.

For each section of the wheel, capture two or three positive suggestions. This may trigger a memory of an event or place that made your feel good or a reminder of something to do like playing a piece of music, looking at a favourite picture or object. The categories are

- ✔ **Places** you have visited or would like to – cities, beaches, mountains, gardens, galleries, or buildings.

- ✔ **People and animals** can be those you know and others you don't but who inspire or interest you.

- ✔ **Exercises** include your favourite sports as well as mental exercises.

- ✔ **Objects** are things of beauty; items that trigger a happy memory.

- ✔ **Events** such as holidays, anniversaries, and celebrations – important times in your life.

- ✔ **Pictures and symbols** may be items of art, postcards, icons, and photographs.

- ✔ **Smells and tastes** are your favourite food and aromas.

- ✔ **Words and sounds** include music, poems, mantras, and affirmations.

Make a note of these in each sector of the wheel shown in Figure 11-1 as a reminder to give you a boost when you need it.

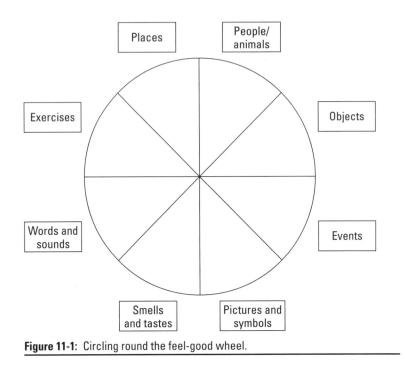

Figure 11-1: Circling round the feel-good wheel.

Following the golden rules for a healthy diet

You wouldn't consider putting the wrong kind of fuel in your car, so why do it to your body? What you eat and how much water you drink has a major impact on your energy and thus your confidence. So eat well and with awareness.

Put the brakes on your eating at moments when feeling stressed, anxious, or over-excited, because it's easy to lose awareness of what is going in your body, how hungry you feel, and what the best food is for you right now. Instead of grabbing fast food on the run, step back, choose the more healthy option, and get ready to savour every mouthful.

✔ **Drink water:** Unless you want to end up as a dried-out prune, drink 1½ to 2 litres of pure, clean water every day. Your body naturally loses several litres of fluid each day. Water is critical to help you cleanse your body eliminating waste and toxins. Often when you think you're hungry, you are actually thirsty.

✔ **Examine your oils:** Avoid chemicals and additives in the fats and oils you choose. Hemp seed oil is one of the richest sources of essential fatty acids omega-3 and omega-6.

✔ **Choose brown, not white:** Brown rice is more cleansing for your immune system, and go for wholemeal breads and pastas every time.

✔ **Snack on seeds:** The zinc in pumpkin and sunflower seeds boosts your energy. Seeds are instant and tasty.

✔ **Don't add salt:** Save the salt for when you swim in the sea. Cut back on salt and look after your blood pressure.

✔ **Go with greens:** Eat leafy greens every day. Watercress, spinach, cabbage, lettuce, swiss chard, mint, and parsley are rich in minerals and vitamins.

✔ **Avoid tobacco:** Get away from all forms of smoking. Whether it's your smoke or someone else's, smoking depletes the nutrients in your body.

✔ **Re-educate your sweet tooth:** Eating regularly and well will keep your blood sugar stable and save the need for sugar fix. As well as cutting down on sweets, biscuits, and cakes, beware the hidden sugar in processed food such as flavoured yoghurt, fruit and carbonated drinks, and sauces.

If you're good at keeping to the healthy rules 80 per cent of the time, you're well on your way to making a healthy diet a natural way of eating.

Believing in your health

Beliefs are the working principles on which you act. They are not proven facts but working assumptions. To develop your physical confidence, it's helpful to believe that it's possible and desirable to look after your wellbeing to the best of your ability.

What is your real age?

At www.realage.com you can measure how fast your body is aging. The idea is that whereas your calendar age simply reflects the number of birthdays you've had, RealAge gauges the physiological age of your body and measures your rate of aging.

Certain health choices can slow and even reverse the rate of aging. In highly stressful times, your RealAge can be as much as 32 years older than your calendar age. Laughter, learning, and vitamins are just three of 44 factors that promote age reduction. And the good news is that even choices made late in life make a difference. People who start exercising in their fifties and sixties, or even later, show considerable health benefits.

The following belief statements can support you. Try them on for size by taking one principle a day and acting from that position.

- ✔ When I'm healthy my confidence levels rise.
- ✔ I can create a healthy life for myself.
- ✔ It's never too late to start being healthy.
- ✔ I have a strong appetite for physical exercise.
- ✔ There are many different ways in which I can look after my health.
- ✔ My health is my responsibility.
- ✔ I can accept an injury or illness and still be a healthy person.
- ✔ I can learn from a number of role models.
- ✔ Fun and laughter play a great part in my wellbeing.
- ✔ It's important to keep moving.
- ✔ My vitality and wellbeing are infectious.

Looking Forward to Your Healthy Future Self

What you do today has a direct impact on your health in the future. Your health is one area of your life that you cannot afford to ignore.

Sports coaches often film you playing your sport and then compare your movements, shots, strokes, or swings with a sporting hero. If you had a video camera, what picture would you record of your own physical wellbeing right now? Now fast forward that image and see what you look like one year, five years, and ten years from now, and at the end of your life. Imagine the image you're going to see if you carry on as you are doing just now and feel how that affects your confidence. What, if any, changes do you want to make?

To be healthy and energetic, you need fuel from good-quality food and water, adequate rest, a healthy environment, sufficient exercise, variety and challenge in your work and play, and supportive people around you.

Part IV

Communicating Your Confidence

The 5th Wave   By Rich Tennant

"No, it hasn't anything to do with my presentation. But wait until you see how much confidence I convey with it sitting next to me at the podium."

In this part...

This part shows you how you can demonstrate your newly built confidence to the outside world through how you look and sound. You also see how to hold on to confidence when reality hits.

Chapter 12

Raising Your Voice

In This Chapter

▶ Telling your truth with confidence

▶ Speaking out with integrity

▶ Using more than your voice

*P*ublic speaking to a group or large audience, and even regular speaking in a business meeting, can feel very artificial. If you have ever sat through a dull committee meeting you may have mused that too many people like the sound of their own voice. But actually, for every one of those people there are a dozen who hate to hear themselves speak or else don't believe they have anything worthwhile to say. To become more powerful in the world, you need to feel able to speak up authentically in all situations.

It's a truism to say that your voice is one of your most important links to the rest of humanity, but have you ever really stopped to think about how fundamental it is, and how debilitating it can be to your life if your 'voice' in the world is less powerful than it should be?

A powerful voice in this context doesn't mean the power to fill an auditorium with sound, like a Shakespearian actor. It means giving authentic voice to the real you as you live and breathe, and go about your work in the world. This is the voice that links you to the rest of the world. In this chapter, you discover how you can use your voice to project the more powerful and confident you into the world.

Speaking Out with Confidence

Why is public speaking so nerve wracking? Why, when confronted unexpectedly by their dream date or their boss, do sitcom characters become incoherent, mumbling idiots (and you laugh because you recognise yourself in the situation)? How can it be that something so natural as speaking, which you've been practising more or less continuously since you first learned to do it, can at times become so difficult?

Children joke about the centipede who loses his ability to walk when someone asks him how he does it; it's the same with speaking. When it becomes self-conscious, for any reason, you get caught up in its mechanics and lose your easy, natural groove.

To find your public voice and gain the confidence to speak out, you need something to say and someone to say it to. And you need something connecting you in that moment to the person or group you're speaking to, which is commonly called *rapport* – a shared view of the world within which there is room for disagreement. To achieve all this, you need to deal with anything standing in the way.

Listening to yourself

Have you ever heard yourself speak on tape? Did you find it a shocking experience to hear your own voice 'from the outside'? It sounds so different from your voice as you experience it from inside your head that you may assume the recording quality is at fault until others confirm that you sound exactly that way in real

---

What your accent says about you

Spoken English is a language with a rich and varied heritage. In the North of England, certain dialect words have remained unchanged since mediaeval times. Off the coast of North Carolina in the USA, the speech of isolated communities still closely resembles that of the west countrymen who left England to settle there in the seventeenth century.

Received pronunciation (RP) is one particular accent of British English based on the speech of the middle classes of southeast England. It's characteristic of the accent used at the public schools and Oxford and Cambridge Universities. It is the accent adopted by the BBC at the advent of public broadcasting, and after World War II, became the national standard of the educated English.

Today, this domination of broadcasting by the RP accent has been rightly consigned to history. Now it is becoming as common for the upper and educated classes to try to cover up their posh accents as vice versa. A new egalitarian accent, Estuary English, has been born (popularised by the Prime Minister, Tony Blair). Today's Britain is at last becoming more interested in what is being said rather than the accent in which it is being said.

life. You may have been surprised or dismayed by the poor quality of your diction, or the strength of your accent, and have made an unconscious decision to do something about it or else never speak in public again. However, deciding not to speak in public for any reason is ridiculous and undoable.

Speaking with the local accent and in the regional dialect can be a great help in building rapport. Be proud of your accent, it is part of who you are, but do be prepared to work on your public speaking skills a little in line with the advice in this chapter.

The most common problems with speaking in public are clarity and diction. As your first schoolteacher probably told you, if you sit up and speak clearly you will be heard – heard all over the world.

Breathing to improve your speaking

Shallow breathing is a common problem when you're faced with any kind of public speaking.

Rapid, shallow breathing can reduce the level of carbon dioxide in your blood, which reduces the flow of blood through your body. Then, even though your lungs are taking in all the oxygen your body should need, your brain and body experience a shortage. This can leave you feeling tense, nervous, and unable to think clearly.

The solution, which is well known to singers and those who play wind instruments, is to breathe deeply from the diaphragm or abdomen. If, like most people, you have little idea how to do this, read on.

Feeling how you breathe

First, locate your diaphragm: Place your right hand flat on your stomach just above your navel and below the bottom of your rib cage. Now take a series of short sniffs as though you are trying to detect the smell of something on fire. You should feel the area under your hand moving in and out. This is your diaphragm.

Now, place your left hand on your upper chest just below your collarbone, keeping your right hand over your diaphragm. Take a few normal breaths.

If you're breathing correctly, you feel the rhythmic rising and falling movement of your breathing in your right hand. If you feel

Practising to avert disaster

When Oliver faced the daunting prospect of making the best man's speech at a large wedding, he turned to his father for help. His dad was an experienced public speaker and consulting him seemed very natural as it was his wedding and Oliver was only 13 years old.

Dad gave him permission to tell a few jokes in the tradition of the best man's speech and over a couple of weeks they worked out a nice but funny speech that would take 8–10 minutes to deliver. Oliver typed it into the computer. There were three weeks to go to the wedding, so he was ready nice and early.

He was still nervous but felt much better now that he knew what he was going to say. Then Dad delivered his bombshell: he wasn't going to allow Oliver to read his speech from the prepared paper. Instead, Dad recommended that he read it out loud in his bedroom 12 times before the day, then prepare five or six bullet points to act as his only memory aides.

Oliver probably read his speech more like 20 times over the next two weeks. Then the week before the big day, his Dad helped him to pull out five bullet points that would help him to remember the key structure so he could speak in a natural way when he came to give the speech. He practised this in his bedroom and although it was a bit shorter now, at six minutes, he found he was able to do it.

Then on the day, disaster! As the company sat down to the meal, with the speeches the next item on the wedding agenda, Oliver's wedding nightmare came true: He had misplaced his bullet points, and had no time now to think about them, or ask his dad who wasn't even sitting next to him. He was scared witless.

When it was his turn he stood up to speak, took a deep breath, and started – but nothing came out. He started again, his mouth moved, but no sound came out. It was now or never. He took a small drink of water and, with the audience literally on the edge of their seats, he began, a little hesitantly at first but soon gaining momentum.

He found he could remember the bullets, and even whole sentences. As he went along the words came, and when he realised he had missed out a piece of information he needed for a joke he went back to it, quite naturally, as he would have in a conversation. His audience of family, friends, and relatives laughed at the jokes and were spellbound. Oliver felt a binding rapport with them as he told his stories.

At the end, the applause and shouting were amazing. He seemed to have been on his feet for only a couple of minutes but the wedding video, which captured every nuance and detail, confirms that it was 10 minutes exactly. He stole the show, and there was nobody more pleased than his dad, who even had a tear in his eye. Would he do it again? Yes, definitely – but not for a while.

movement under your left hand, you're breathing from your chest, and this is not what you want.

Discovering how to breathe through your diaphragm

Breathing through your diaphragm gives you the powerful voice you want. To make use of this technique, follow these steps:

1. **Place your right hand over your diaphragm and your left hand on your chest.**

2. **Purse your lips as though you're about to whistle, and breathe out slowly to a count of five monkeys (count one monkey, two monkeys, and so on to yourself) while tightening your stomach muscles.**

   (Chapter 10 has a complete explanation of monkey breathing.)

3. **Breathe in slowly through your nose to a count of three monkeys.**

   Feel your right hand rising with the diaphragm.

4. **Pause slightly for two monkeys and then breathe out again to a count of five as in Step 2.**

If you practise this for just a few minutes before every meal and again at odd times throughout the day, you soon become habituated to this more effective way of breathing. Once you get your muscles trained, your diaphragm can do 80 per cent of the incessant work of your breathing for the rest of your life. Proper breathing gives you the platform you need for a powerful voice.

When you're comfortable with diaphragmatic breathing, you can add in another two steps to improve your voice quality further:

- ✔ In Step 2, instead of pursing your lips, add in a gentle 'Ah' sound for the full exhalation stage. Keep this 'Ah' going until you run out of air.

- ✔ When you have the rhythm going, drop both your hands to your sides and bounce your shoulders gently but rapidly up and down as you breathe out to 'Ah'. This releases tension from your vocal cords and helps to prepare your voice for speaking.

Now your voice is ready, what are you going to say?

Saying What You Mean and Meaning What You Say

A good rule for effective communication is always to say what you mean and mean what you say. This isn't an excuse to be rude to people, or haughty, but it is a very solid basis from which you can come to know your truth and speak it out. Following this rule is good for your integrity and very quickly cements your reputation as a communicator of real power and persuasion.

Holding onto your integrity

What does it mean to you to have integrity? Perhaps you immediately think of things like keeping your word and not telling lies or otherwise being dishonest. Integrity does mean these things, and more besides, and it is an essential element of the most powerful, confident you.

Think of your integrity as your inner sense of wholeness, coming from a consistent sense of who you are being in all parts of your world. When you do anything with integrity, you're being authentic; you're acting or speaking without pretence, *not even to yourself.* Having integrity is critical to your power and congruence in the world, and is at the heart of your confidence to take action.

Sadly, your personal integrity and authenticity can be too easily sacrificed on the altar of rubbing along with your friends and neighbours or looking good to the boss. This can be a massive own goal in your game of life that can cost you far more than you bargained for. A white lie over here, a little 'talking up' over there, and pretty soon you won't know who you are or what you really stand for.

The single most powerful step you can take to improve your confidence and power in the world is to restore your integrity.

Table 12-1 contains an integrity checklist. Each time you violate any item on the list, you leak personal power and confidence. Each time you honour an item on this list, you become more powerful in the world and build your reserves of confidence.

Before you start your personal evaluation, draw a mental line under everything you have ever done in your life, good or bad, until this moment. Wipe your slate clean. Your new integrity account is now open for business.

Table 12-1	Integrity Checklist
Actions that Increase Your Personal Power and Confidence	*Actions that Reduce Your Personal Power and Confidence*
Honouring your word and keeping your promises	Failing to back up your words with actions
Being honest with yourself and with others	Acting or speaking in a way that causes real harm to others
Accepting people as they are and judging only their actions	Acting superior to others or browbeating someone weaker than yourself
Treating others with respect and candour	Failing to act in the right way because no one is watching
Letting people know where you stand on important issues	Not giving of your best
Being genuine and transparent with people. Not deceiving through silence or inaction	Not following your conscience
Being true to your values and purpose	Not practising what you preach
Living up to your standards and always doing the right thing	Manipulating or misleading others (or yourself)
Admitting and accepting your own mistakes	Telling white lies to look good or to avoid looking bad
Saying what you mean and meaning what you say	Using bluff or bluster to get your own way
Walking your talk	Pretending to be anything other than your authentic self

Having difficult conversations

So, you've opened your new integrity account and are determined to take only those actions that increase your power and confidence. Then your wife comes into the room wearing a new outfit that makes her look dumpy and sad. 'How do I look?' she asks (at this point you mentally run down a few relevant items on your list: being honest, saying what you mean, treating others with respect, not speaking in a way that causes harm to others). What do you do?

Only you know the honest answer to this. The scenario is a set-up, of course, and deliberately difficult. It would have been a lot better all round to share your new insights and intentions with your partner before she asked you the fateful question. But the harsh truth you may discover here is that the communication in many of your relationships lacks integrity, and that damages the relationship more than you may realise.

At some level, your wife knows that she doesn't look good in the outfit. She may even have known that in the shop but felt obliged to follow through with the 'helpful' assistant who was lying through her teeth in order to make the sale. If so, your wife is really asking you to make the situation okay. If you say she looks good and leave it at that, you are cheating her just like the sales assistant did. When she wears the outfit to a function and hates the way she looks in it, where does that leave you?

So, before this can happen, it's better to have *authenticity conversations* with your family, friends, and work colleagues, during which you tell them that you're focusing on how to be more confident and powerful in the world and what this means about saying what you mean and meaning what you say. Ask them to help you by being equally honest with you and keeping you true to your word. You may be surprised how your public repositioning in this way changes the dynamics of your relationships and gives them much more integrity.

And if you really want to take on the full restoration of your integrity, you can also go back to friends and colleagues from your past where your relationships suffered through lack of integrity on your part and acknowledge it. Don't get into the blame game, even if the other person wants to. Just a simple acknowledgement will do: 'I just want you to know that I enjoyed most of our time together and, even though it ended badly, those good times were important to me.' Try this and you'll be amazed by how it makes you feel. You can stand taller and be more present in the world directly as a result.

Recognising that the Message Is More than Words

It is well known on the speaking circuit that the words the speaker uses are responsible for only 7 per cent of the impact of the communication. Voice and delivery add a further 38 per cent and body posture and movement add the rest – an amazing 55 per cent. So although word and voice are critical (without them communication does not exist), bringing your body into play adds massively to your impact.

Even though many speakers know the facts, they often fail dismally to do anything with them and either remain stuck behind the podium or, worse, begin to strut around the stage and wave their hands, generally getting in their own way and detracting from the impact of the message.

In the following sections, you will find ways to present your message in a congruent fashion.

Experiencing the natural school

Two schools of thought exist on body language: The theatrical school and the natural school. You are already an expert natural communicator as you have been practising it for so long you've achieved unconscious competence.

So, when you're excited you gesture, when you're intense you point and fix your subject with your eyes, when you're playful you throw back your head and raise your eyes to the sky.

Problems arise only when you become self-conscious or uncomfortable. A tight-fitting shirt at an interview can do this to you, or an audience that looks blank or hostile. Sometimes you become intimidated simply by the size or seniority of your audience. Whatever the cause, the minute you lose your natural groove, you can begin to struggle. You're not sure what to do with your hands, you jiggle the coins in your pocket, you stand in front of your visuals, and you generally feel and act like a clown.

Acting out the theatrical school

The theatrical school, the other hand, has little confidence in your ability to communicate with natural power to an audience and so advocates tried and tested gestures that you learn like drills until they become hard-wired. The problem with this approach is that speakers too often betray their drilling and never look natural or comfortable. This can set the audience on edge and greatly detract from the power of the message.

Finding your authentic approach

The best solution is usually the most authentic, and the authentic you is the one to develop. Rather than memorise a performance on stage, discover how to be yourself even when you are under pressure.

The techniques for this are not so different from one-to-one communication. As you gain in confidence and power from your increased understanding of who you are and what you want, you will be able to influence groups quite naturally.

Look at the people you are speaking to, be prepared to let them see how you feel about your message, be attentive and curious as to how they are receiving it. If you proceed in this way you are much more likely deliver a powerful, natural performance.

 Like most other things in life, if you have good technique, you can improve your public speaking with practise. Speaking clubs such as Toastmasters International provide a supportive environment in which you have the opportunity to develop communication and leadership skills, which in turn foster self-confidence and personal growth. Check them out at www.toastmasters.org.

Chapter 13

Looking the Part

● ●

In This Chapter

▶ Making the best impression

▶ Connecting with others according to how you dress

▶ Developing the style that's right for you

● ●

*H*ow you look has a two-way impact on your confidence. The image you portray to the world communicates a message to others about you and makes a statement of what you stand for. How you look also affects the way you feel about yourself. Notice, for example, how you feel when you dress up for an important occasion compared to how you feel when doing chores in an old pair of jeans.

A key element in building your confidence to take action in the world is to raise your awareness of the image you choose to present to others. How do you think you come across and how would you like to come across? This chapter is all about helping you to look the best you can be in a way that's most appropriate for you.

Being Judged by Appearances

Appearances can be deceptive. They are based on your perceptions more often than reality. By this we mean that you filter information about people based on other people you have met in the past and your own personal prejudices.

When you meet someone for the first time, you are likely to make a judgement in the first 15 to 20 seconds as to whether you like or dislike, approve or disapprove of them. And you may do this based on one aspect of their physical characteristics, dress, and grooming. For example, studies show that people consider men with beards to be less professional than men without.

Your confidence in selecting friends, employees, and partners can be based on your subjective experience rather than objective information. When you get to know the real person beyond the initial façade, your opinion may change.

Confess now. You've probably formed an opinion about people without ever having met them. You see a photo and say 'She's a kind person' or 'She's a smart cookie' or even 'She's a pain in the butt' without having anything more to go on. Consider for a moment what opinions you form of celebrities and members of royalty based on a magazine feature or a brief TV appearance.

The visual impact a person makes provides the strongest data for judging that person.

Appearing confident

A TV advertisement pictured a woman walking down the street. Her blonde hair was perfectly groomed, she had a spring in her step, a smile on her face, and attracted the admiration of on-lookeres who would whisper 'Is she wearing Harmony hairspray?' It was a memorable campaign for a low cost way to build self-confidence.

People appear confident if they are dressed in smart or fashionable clothes, if their hair is well cut and managed, if they move with energy, and if they survey the world around them with bright-eyed interest. A person who appears confident may have a voice that's loud and clear or a manner that's warm and engaging. Or they may have expensive accessories or a desirable new car. Perhaps they are the focus of attention or stand out as the leader in a group of people.

Taking a people-watching snapshot is a positive way to help you build your confidence based on your judgements about other people:

1. **Go to a crowded place.**

   Choose a place like a station or airport, a shopping centre, the doctor's waiting room, a gym, or a school playground.

2. **Look around until you spot someone who appears confident to you.**

3. **Analyse what it is that makes you think they're confident.**

   Determine what it is about the way they look, carry themselves, and speak that makes you perceive them as confident. Write down three or four things.

Crowning glory

In 1795, William Pitt put a tax on hair powder, expecting to raise loads of tax because every man and woman with pretensions to style put powder in their hair. He was hoping for around 210,000 guineas in revenue. Unfortunately for the exchequer, the tax raised only 46,000 guineas. Whig leaders opposed to the tax cut off their pigtails in defiance and agreed to abandon the use of hair powder, and the public followed suit.

Today, we still pay tax on hair products – it's a massive international industry with all those shampoos, conditioners, sprays, gels, and mousse, let alone the cost of cuts and colours. Our favourite family hairdresser, Rosy, will vouch for the confidence factor of a new haircut as her customers leave the salon. 'People look and feel ten years younger or older simply according to their haircut. It's not just the ladies, this goes for the men too – shaving off a beard or moustache or going for a new cut with a few coloured highlights can make a guy have much more impact. I know I'm biased, but it's a terrific boost!'

It's easy to get into a habit of repeating the same haircut and style for year after year. For a confidence boost within one hour, find a good hairdresser and go for a new look.

4. **Consider how you can imitate or incorporate these qualities in your own behaviour.**

   Now go out and try out your new behaviours and notice the difference.

Making the best first impression

As a struggling young butcher, Tony went off at the crack of dawn to the cattle market in a neighbouring town. To his wife's surprise, he was dressed in his finest suit. His respose to her raised eyebrows was: 'We may be very short of money, but we don't have to look it.'

Like all astute business people, Tony knew that first impressions count. He stood more chance of cutting a better deal if he looked well heeled than if he was hard up. Why else do the most successful companies put smart, enthusiastic, and well-groomed people on the reception desk? They inspire confidence in the organisation. These first impressions are what the marketing folks call 'moments of truth'. If you walk into a shop, an office, or a garage and it looks in disarray or the people are unwelcoming, then all the investment in branding and clever advertising is completely wasted, because customers avoid doing business with an organisation that gives a bad first impression.

So what impression do you create when you meet someone for the first time? Do you arrive in a flustered state of disarray with papers flying, or are you neat, organised, and well prepared? Some subtle changes in your image might make you look more confident or inspire others to feel confident about you.

For example, the most basic grooming requires that your face, hair and teeth are neatly brushed and you have no marks of food on yourself or clothing. Check yourself in a full length mirror before leaving home.

Any tears or threads in your clothes need to be fixed. But you can do better than this. Build time into your schedule to choose clothes appropriate to who you are meeting and where (making sure they are clean and well pressed), to polish your shoes, and for ladies, to apply your make-up.

If you have a very busy week, decide on Sunday night what you're going to wear each day and save the last-minute morning rush.

For business, organise your briefcase so that notes are managed in separate folders for the day ahead instead of in a heap. Arrive at your meetings early enough to tidy your appearance before you meet a client. If you're travelling on business, aim for discreet, smart luggage with compartments so you never need to display your personal belongings as you retrieve your notes or laptop.

Conveying the right attitude with your dress

The style of the well-dressed man about London in the eighteenth century was defined by the Regency dandy Beau Brummell, a chap with 'attitude'. He wore exquisitely cut dark coats over white linen shirts and well-starched neckcloths. Only the waistcoat would display lavish embroidery and design.

Dress codes change with time and place. It pays to notice what those around you are wearing, whether you choose to fit in or stand out with confidence. If you're updating your image, make sure of its appeal to the people you want to mix with. Your smile, sparkly chat, and tidy appearance may do you more favours than designer labels.

You are likely to build stronger rapport with people if you match their dress code than if you look completely different.

A client in the TV world assesses potential newsreaders and presenters by what he calls 'the girl/boy next door' test. He looks for the candidate with a face, dress, and manner that his customers, the viewing public, would invite into their living rooms for a chat. He pays attention to whether candidates convey warmth, friendliness, and an honest sense of humour. These characteristics are much more appealing to the majority of the population than slick, cool, and glamorous.

Dress at work as if you have a more senior role in the organisation. The chances are that you set the unconscious expectation that you are worthy of promotion.

When Sunita went to live in Moscow, she found the move from the UK to support her husband in his job very stressful. 'Life felt out of control because I didn't speak the language and hadn't a clue where I was going.' One thing she did that gave her more confidence that she belonged there was to dress more like the Russian women rather than as a member of the ex-pat community. She bought a long dark coat and boots and wrapped a huge scarf around her head before leaving the apartment. 'I wanted to be able to blend in with the Russians and roam inconspicuously around the city, rather than stand out as a foreigner abroad.' Dressing to suit the environment in which you are living or working helps you build rapport faster, and is especially helpful during times when your confidence is under threat.

Beware invitations that say 'dress informal'. If you're invited to an event or meeting, contact the organisers for advice about the dress code. If you have any doubts, dress 'up' rather than 'down'. It's easier to adapt your look by removing a jacket or scarf than to smarten up when you're the only one who has arrived in jeans and trainers.

If you dress down for work, still dress in clean, smart outfits so you're welcome to a meeting in the boardroom.

Finding Your Own Style

The key to dressing for success is finding a style that works for you and the way you spend your life. It's hardly sensible to invest all your clothing budget in expensive designer suits if you're spending most of your time at home with young children.

Pacing, leading, and reframing

For many years, Brinley wore a tie, white shirt, and dark suit to work, like many men in the office. There were few actual 'rules' about the dress code, but a strong sense that it was the convention, and it was expected.

Towards the millennium, this enduring convention broke down quickly. Many otherwise staid and solid organisations introduced 'dress-down' days when suits were out; a few businesses banned suits altogether in pursuit of a cool, hip new image to echo the post-millennium new economy. Mature businessmen like Brinley were thrown into sartorial crisis. They shopped for chinos and designer shirts and called in the image consultants to redress the management team.

After a period of wardrobe clearing, Brinley came to enjoy going to the office in brown loafers and no tie, confident that his new look supported his new position of executive coach and business consultant. After the bursting of the dot.com bubble, however, the new dress-down look became linked with flaky, irresponsible management.

Brinley faced a classic dilemma: He was unwilling to give up his freedom when organisations reverted to suits and ties. He wanted to be 'true' to his new position and style of presenting himself to his clients, but he also knew that some people in business consider not wearing a tie to be showing disrespect. A coaching colleague came to his rescue by pointing out that although what he wore to do his work was irrelevant to its value, it could get in the way of his audience's ability or willingness to take fully on board the important knowledge he would be delivering to them.

Thus, in order to lead his clients to a better world, Brinley first had to pace them by showing them that he could be an empathetic and valid member of the world they inhabited currently.

This change of view, or 'reframe', has completely resolved Brinley's dilemma. By far the most important aspect of his work is the personal transformation he helps his clients to achieve; everything else is secondary. He now wears ties frequently and suffers the jokes of his colleagues asking whether he is attending job interviews.

Image consultants can be worth their weight in gold by helping you find the clothes that work hardest for you. Don't be put off, thinking that consultants are just for the rich and famous or only for business people. An independent, professional eye can save you making costly mistakes.

We don't subscribe to the view that the only way to feel confident in how you look is to lose loads of weight or go under the cosmetic surgeon's knife. No one we know is perfectly slim, trim, and beautiful all the time. The art, as any image consultant worth their fee will tell you, is to show off your best assets and minimise those you're less proud of.

So our advice is to get style savvy. Work out what suits you best, and buy clothes to fit your lifestyle and body shape as it is right now – today – not some future image of yourself. You probably already know yourself what you feel best in, but it also helps to have a second opinion to stop you getting too set in your ways. A new look is a great confidence booster. So engage the services of a style consultant or invite your most honest and stylish friend to do a kind and objective review with you. You could make a party of swapping clothes amongst friends and selling those that no longer work for you for profit or charity.

According to the 80/20 principle we explain in Chapter 9, you wear 20 per cent of your clothes 80 per cent of the time. Think how much easier it would be if you only owned what is right for you just now.

Dress so that you feel comfortable in styles that flatter your body rather than fight it. Find out which colours suit your skin colouring by talking to a colour consultant and stick to a restricted palette – then you'll find that colours mix and match easily.

If you diet to become leaner, remember that when you hit your target weight you're in a perfect position to go out and treat yourself to a new wardrobe, giving away the baggier stuff to a friend or charity shop with a smug expression on your face.

Limit the amount of patterned fabric in your wardrobe, especially if you bought it in a chain store – people will just remember you wearing it again and you'll get fed up with it.

Assessing your wardrobe

Make sure you have the right clothes for your lifestyle by doing a regular check on how you spend your time and how your wardrobe matches up. Table 13-1 gives you an opportunity to review your closet and lifestyle by assigning a percentage to the amount of time you spend in each aspect of your life and evaluating the percentage of clothing you have for each role.

Table 13-1 Comparing Your Wardrobe to Your Lifestyle

Lifestyle Role/ Clothing Need	Percentage of Time Spent in this Role	Percentage of Wardrobe Useful for this Role
Formal business person/Professional attire or uniform		
Casual business person or home worker/Dress-down attire, dressy casual		
Parent, playmate, cook/Casual, at-home clothes		
Party goer, socialiser/Fancy dress, fun and stylish clothes		
Sports person/ Active wear		
DIY, cleaner, gardener/ Knock-around clothes		

Use this table once or twice a year and make adjustments to your wardrobe accordingly.

Shopping smart

Actually choosing clothes you can feel confident in isn't very difficult once you know what suits you. Use these tips to ensure smart wardrobe shopping:

- ✔ Be prepared to buy the size that fits well rather than buying an outfit to slim into.

- ✔ Take account of your body type. Some of us are curvy and some are angular. (This is true of both sexes.) If you're more curvy, choose shirts with rounded collars and jackets with rounded edges in softer fabrics. Those with a more angular shape look great in sharper cuts, stripes, and firmer fabrics.

Saluting the power of uniforms

Soldiers, sailors, airmen, vicars. It's said that girls find men in uniform irresistibly attractive. The same is true for other folks. One hospital in the south of England has a military medical team working alongside the civilian one. The service team members wear a very distinctive uniform, and among the patients, there's an awesome respect for the military team. Patients seem to feel that perhaps the military doctors have seen live action in the field and dealt with complex injuries that are different than stitching up regular accidents in the Accident and Emergency department.

Uniforms embody the wearers with attributes beyond the cut of the cloth – power, brand identity, authority, knowledge, competence, a sense of discipline and order that extends beyond that of the individual – all of which inspire confidence. In airlines, hospitals, banks, and schools the world over, smart uniforms convey a feeling of confidence in representing the values of an organisation.

Smart is important, because the minute your uniform becomes scruffy or too informal the impact is negative. Take as an example Wendy, who has been a well-respected physiotherapist for nearly 30 years. Wendy takes pride in how she looks and is always immaculately turned out. In the private practice where she works, she was dismayed when the new business owners decided on an informal dress policy with no consultation with the professional team. The team was presented with new uniforms in place of their crisp clinical white jackets and navy trousers. The quality of the new tracksuit-style garments was shoddy and the fit unflattering to even the trimmest of figures. Morale and motivation speedily took a nose dive among the professional staff, with many considering changing jobs rather than dressing in uniforms they wouldn't wear for cleaning their cars, let alone treating patients. Fortunately, after a battle of wills, the management team had the confidence to listen, back down, and admit their mistake, and the uniform reverted to the professional gear loved by staff and patients alike.

✔ Avoid buying clothes in haste. Look when you are not in a hurry to buy and can try on a range of clothes and experiment to refine your choice.

✔ Invest your money in the clothes you wear the most. Unless you're a serious partygoer, save the big money for coats rather than evening clothes.

✔ Good-quality coats, bags, and shoes are the best approach to looking great. The rest can be simple.

✔ Invest in smart accessories including belts, watches, and ties/scarves that ring the changes.

✔ Check your wardrobe before you go shopping, so you fill the gaps rather than getting wooed by another impulse outfit.

✔ Choose outfits that work for you. Versatility is the key. Check whether an outfit will be suitable for five different occasions.

Buy clothes that can take you anywhere looking good, and you'll feel confident to accept any invitation at a minute's notice.

Chapter 14

Acting with Confidence in Your Daily Life

In This Chapter

▶ Overcoming resistance from your nearest and dearest

▶ Staying the course

▶ Using your power

A key element in incorporating any new skill is making practical use of it. You have a clear sense of where you want to get to, you know what needs to be done, but you need to build your capabilities and devise strategies for doing it consistently.

You have to test your confidence in the 'real' world of daily life, to hold onto it and maintain it. In this chapter, we share more tips on gripping tight when the pressure starts to build as when you meet other people with different needs and agendas to your own, and let you know how to dovetail differing agendas and get to the win–win results you want. This means you may need to make difficult choices at times and can't always please those around you. This chapter is like a diet maintenance plan for your confidence – the information here helps you stay the course for the long term.

Dealing with Resistance to the New, Confident You

So you've broken through your comfort zone – stretched yourself, taken some risks, and know that you can do and be so much more than you originally believed to be true. And then, guess what? Reality hits. You go out in the world and find that not everyone wants you to change; they were happy with the way you were before.

In this section, we take a look at how you can sharpen up your resolve in the face of resistance.

Being firm with loved ones who want the old you

So, what if some of your nearest and dearest aren't too happy with the new, confident you? This may be your boss, your colleagues, friends, or family. You get the feeling that they'd really like the old you back, the one that didn't challenge, the one that raced around doing what they wanted first. They're used to taking the old you for granted like a favourite sweater or a comfy pair of slippers. Perhaps they feel threatened or undermined by the change, perhaps they're worried that you no longer need them and will walk off into the sunset with a new job or a new life and leave them behind.

How do you recognise the discomfort in the people around your? Well, they're not likely to be really honest with you and tell you outright what they think. It's likely to be more of a subtle undermining

ANECDOTE

Helping handle change

For some years Yema worked hard as a nurse in her local hospital. The years took their toll: early-morning and late-night shifts left her exhausted trying to be flexible around the family. With her 40th birthday approaching fast, she realised that her own health was suffering and it was time for a change.

Noticing a recruitment advertisement in her local paper, she took the plunge and applied for a job managing drug trials for a pharmaceutical company in her area. She got the job, and her career took off. Her salary increased to the point that she became the main breadwinner in the family, and due to her travel schedule, roles reversed and her husband had to be the one who was at home more for the family.

Yema knew that her change in role might have a practical downside. She also knew that her family and marriage were precious to her. When her family began to complain that their favourite foods in the fridge had run out or they didn't have clean shirts, she called a family get together where they looked objectively at all the pros and cons of her working life.

She invited everyone to say exactly what they thought, making no judgement on any comment. Her husband and children all agreed that they liked having the foreign holidays and luxuries her pay packet afforded them, and in return could divide up the chores between them, rather than asking her to give up her career to look after them on a day-to-day basis. That meant that she could return from a trip and have fun time with the family rather than catching up on the housework at weekends.

of your new interests. Perhaps they'll make occasional sarcastic comments, come up with some criticism, change the subject, or go quiet when you mention your achievements.

Hold firm. Have you heard the saying: Use it or lose it? Well, if you don't use your confidence, you lose it. You return to those old back-seat patterns and habits that don't serve you well.

In order to stand firm with your loved ones:

- ✔ Listen with respect to their viewpoint and connect with the feelings that underlie their words.
- ✔ Acknowledge the change that is happening for them and what they feel they have lost.
- ✔ Provide lots of reassurance that although you may behave differently, you still love and care about them.
- ✔ Come up with ideas together to make the change easier.

It's okay to stick to your guns – you function more healthily if you are as generous to yourself as you are to other people. Stress that you're still you, but you've grown and developed and won't go back now.

Your change can act as a catalyst, spurring changes in those around you. Look to help your friends, family, and associates change if they want to while accepting them as they are without any pressure on them to change.

Finding the confidence to rise above

Once you put yourself on the line, you may find people are envious of the choices you have created for yourself. When I (Kate) wrote my first book and sent it off to the publishers, I made a conscious decision to let go of it knowing that I had done my best with my current knowledge and time constraints. Thus, I was better prepared for any negative reviews or comments. They still hurt a bit, but I aimed to take them as useful feedback for the next edition or the next book.

It's important to rise above any negative criticism, stay true to yourself, and hold onto your own choices. You can't please all the people all the time, however hard you try.

This exercise helps you take a broader perspective on the whole of your life. It's particularly useful when you are struggling through a tough patch. In your mind's eye:

1. **Picture a line that represents your life – past, present, and future.**

   Allow it to take any shape, colour, and form that feels right for you.

2. **Step into a helicopter, a plane, or onto the wings of a bird so that you can rise above the line and look down comfortably from this distance on where you are now.**

3. **Ask yourself: What's important right now? And wait for the answer to come.**

4. **Take that answer, hold onto it, and drop back down into the moment knowing that any time you can take yourself back up when you need to.**

Reinforcing the Assertive You

Many people mistake being assertive with being aggressive. When you acknowledge, trust, and value your own thoughts and feelings, you're on the way to being *assertive*. When you exaggerate and generalise, judge and attack, you're heading down the *aggressive* route. Aggressive statements are judgemental and don't own the speaker's feelings. Assertive behaviour means you own your feelings. Table 14-2 gives you some examples.

Table 14-2	Assertive versus Aggressive Statements
Aggressive	*Assertive*
This homework is rubbish, you never get it right.	This piece of work needs some refinement to make the key points stand out clearly, please look at the structure again.
You really ought to sort this mess out.	I really want to see this area tidied up.
You are an angry person and you make me feel angry.	I feel angry when you shout and stop listening to me.

Assertiveness training focuses on helping people to develop assertive behaviours as building blocks to self-confidence. One of the key tips and tricks is to use 'I' statements to enable people to speak up and own their feelings rather than projecting them on others.

Coping with external pressures

Contrary to the glossy magazines and TV celebrity images, everything in the world doesn't run like clockwork. You face tough times in the real world. You meet people who don't work in harmony with others, you face competitive pressures, you get ill, your bank balance takes an unexpected battering.

When life feels out of control, your confidence gets stretched to the limits. Most of the time, you can cope with what comes at you, but at other times, too much comes at once when you're already feeling vulnerable. This is when you need to gather all the resources you have or can muster.

Support often comes from an unexpected person or direction. When you have the opportunity to help others, do so. You find it comes back to you when you most need it.

Have you considered what resources you can draw on when the going gets tough? It helps to draw up a list of the people you know – friends, family, members of your hobby, sports, or church groups, people at work, including colleagues, your manager, and an HR person if you have one. You can also draw on support services

---

Getting group support

Johann's confidence was badly knocked when he was made redundant from his job in the media. He was already going through the break-up of his relationship while doing major building work himself to convert his house. He felt as if all his energy was drained out of him and he completely lost any sense of direction, let alone any motivation to look for another job.

When talking about how he got back on his feet, Johann cites the two things that made the most difference as joining a group of other executives in a weekly session of job searching, and poetry from an ex-colleague. 'Somehow the group support was really valuable – it gave me the structure and focus I needed just to pick myself up once more. The other thing that made such a difference was that an ex-colleague sent me a couple of poems that I printed out and put on the wall. It was a surprisingly small and simple gesture, but I looked at them every morning and that's what helped me to remember what life was really all about. I suppose also that I felt there was somebody from the old company who actually cared about me personally rather than just the cut and thrust of delivering the work I'd been doing.'

Preparing for change

Anita works in the computer industry as a Personal Assistant (PA) to a board director. She loves the fact that it's a fast-paced, buzzing business. She expects change
to happen at regular intervals though, so whenever her boss is travelling and she
has more flexibility in her work day, Anita works through e-learning packages to
update her skills and knowledge of various systems, so that she can be flexible in
the role she takes on when the next wave of change happens.

where you live. Your doctor's surgery and the local community
noticeboards are a good starting point. You may benefit from some
professional counselling help, someone to talk things through with,
or some practical help with housework or gardening until you are
back on your feet. Your library and the Internet are also good
sources of useful information. In the Appendix at the back of this
book, you can find some useful addresses and Web sites.

Staying on top of your confidence game

Anticipation is a great quality in maintaining your confidence. This
is about looking and noticing what's coming ahead of you so that
you can prepare for it or neatly sidestep out of the way and avoid
getting knocked over in the blast.

It's useful to take regular stock of some of the challenges you know
lie ahead of you. Review with a friend or coach how you can prepare. Part of this preparation may be to meditate or practice Yoga
or Tai Chi – anything that helps you to get centred and hold your
energy for when life gets rocky.

However, there will be times when you get hit by the unexpected –
a family member falls ill, you lose your job, your marriage falls
apart, or you suffer ill – health yourself. All of these can take you
by surprise and force you to react in the moment.

Some pointers to help you:

- ✔ Take each day as it comes. Taking one day at a time is easier
  than worrying about what will happen next week or next month.

- ✔ Surround yourself with supportive people. In times of crisis,
  you have no energy to waste with people who are not helpful
  or who undermine your confidence.

✔ Let go of any non-essential responsibilities and activities. This is 'batten down the hatches' time when you need to concentrate on what really matters.

✔ Hold on tight to the bigger picture. Remind yourself of everything you have achieved, all the things you are good at and picture the time when the present situation has been resolved.

✔ Tell yourself as often as you need to that things will always work out in the end. Develop some affirmations to say to yourself every day. Chapter 20 can help you.

✔ Reward yourself with small treats and luxuries. These don't have to be expensive, especially as you may be short of cash just now. It could be a candle-lit bath or an evening in front of a log fire, time out for a walk in the country, or a phone chat with an old friend.

Living Powerfully

Living your own life and living it powerfully is about lining up all parts of yourself, making sure that you are standing up for your own life and for the values that are important to you, and taking action to make things happen. Then you are unstoppable on your journey.

Some people have great clarity about what living powerfully means to them in practical, day-to-day activities. For others this is more general, and more a state of mind than of action – words like 'living with harmony and peace' come to mind.

When you live your life with passion, you bring an exceptional level of energy and vitality into your everyday experience.

Here are some ideas to start you considering how you can live more powerfully and where specifically you want to make a difference in the world.

Look into the future. See yourself at the age of 90, sitting in your rocking chair on the veranda. Ask yourself what kind of life you want to have lived. What are the words that the younger generation use to describe you, what has your life been about, and what have you done? How have you been socially – what kind of people have you encountered and mixed with on your journey? How have you been physically – your health, energy, and body, what exercise have you done? How have you been emotionally – what have you felt and reacted to in your life?

What do you notice about what you see? Is it powerful enough for you? What do you want to change or develop in order to have bigger dreams for yourself?

Now go back to today and make a list of some of the things that drive you nuts – the injustices, inequalities, and bad behaviours. These provide the clues as to where you want to put your energy to create change for the better in the world around you.

Notice some of the tough experiences you have had and survived. What lessons have you learnt that can help others?

To really make a difference in this world, what is your legacy? Now, what is the first step to move you towards that legacy?

Part V
Engaging Others

The 5th Wave   By Rich Tennant

@RICHTENNANT

Now don't be nervous. I heard this guy has a huge ego, but don't let him intimidate you.

In this part...

You're coached on how to flex your increased personal power at work and in your private life so you stand tall and strong. Specifically, we look at what you can do at work and suggest a new take on romance, even getting the impossible date of your dreams. You see how you can encourage children to grow up with a natural awareness of what it is to be and act confidently as they face their new challenges every day – creating a great legacy.

Chapter 15

Demonstrating Confidence in the Workplace

In This Chapter

▶ Finding your confident work self

▶ Asserting yourself

▶ Dealing with everyday work situations

▶ Coping confidently with your boss

▶ Promoting yourself

▶ Tackling big changes with confidence

*T*he most confident version of you will be immediately recognisable in the workplace. You will be at ease with yourself and others, straightforward and generous in your dealings with your fellow workers, cooperative and pleasant to work with, ready to laugh at the odd joke, and *very* effective in getting your job done.

So, now it's time to consider how you are in your place of work, and to apply your confidence in your job. This chapter helps you explore your relation to your work and the impact this has on your confidence. You find many ways to increase your confidence and be able to use this to your advantage both in your work and in other parts of your life.

Developing Confidence in Your Professional Life

When you're introduced to someone new, and they ask you the age-old question, 'And what do you do?' how do you answer? So much of your sense of who you are is bound up in your work that the description you offer is a powerful indicator of the meaning that work has in your life and the degree of success you can expect.

A work-based sense of self

Some people hold onto a role-based sense of self in the face of an enormous weight of contrary evidence. Nicky is an actress who has spent only two or three years out of the last 10 working in this role. In between times, she has spent many years doing temporary office jobs, waiting on tables in restaurants, or having no job and no income at all. And yet she feels and acts the part of 'actress', albeit one who is temporarily doing something else. The 'actress' part of her self-image is her role identity; the temporary work is what she has to do to pay her bills.

When she goes to parties, as she does often, how do you think she answers the question 'what do you do? 'Does she tell people that she does 'pretty much anything to make ends meet'? Of course not: she tells people she is an actress, and if we haven't seen her recently on television, we know that this includes periods of enforced idleness and probably temporary jobs. Neither she nor we are particularly concerned about her other jobs (even though she spends 75 percent of her time doing them) because they express little or nothing about who she is as a person and what her life is about.

Your workplace gives you a constant bombardment of influences, both positive and negative, from the physical environment, the people in it, the tempo and nature of the work, and how closely you identify with what is getting done.

 Keep in mind that it is your own responsibility to maintain an attitude that helps you to get everything you need from your work: including a confident sense of pride and well being from doing your job well.

Realising that your job isn't you

Although you may protest that your job doesn't bear any direct relation to who you really are, what is important to you, or what you want to achieve in your life, it nonetheless exerts a powerful influence on your sense of identity. It is possible to hold down a job that seems at odds with your true sense of self in the world, but this is unusual and takes a lot of confidence and self-belief.

If you hate your job, or your employer, this can become a drag on your deeper beliefs about yourself and your value in the world. It is very difficult to take action with confidence from this position, because you have so little affinity with who you are being when you are working and where this is leading you.

But your *work* isn't the same thing as your *job.* Your work can be a much fuller expression of your values and beliefs about yourself than any single job can be, even a good job that suits you. Your work in the world can be something very close to your spirit, something almost sacred. But to find your true work you have to be prepared to think beyond the job you are doing.

The place to start is with you. This book can help you to think out your true sense of who you are, perhaps at a deeper level than you have ever thought about it before. As you increase your self-knowledge, you're in a far better position to decide upon the work you want to do in the world. Then, as you make the changes you find necessary, you become far more confident and better able to live powerfully a life that is balanced and fulfilling.

Defining your professional identity

If you're a medical doctor, in the absence of any other information about you, people can reasonably accurately assume a whole lot of things about your ethics, values, social standing, and so on. This is because your identity in society is defined by the work you do. For members of the professions, the magic is in the job title; it defines them to themselves and to others.

If you're not a member of a recognised profession, you don't have all the accoutrements of a professional identity. But it's still essential for you to recognise that you do a professional job that people need and value. In order to feel and act with total confidence, you must get clear about the contribution of the work you do and how it fits into the wider value chain in your organisation and beyond into society.

Try drawing a diagram of your job in its broadest context; like Figure 15-1 filling in the details. No job operates independently of everything else, so how does your role at work fit into the greater scheme of things in your business? Does your company make something, or provide a service that enables others to do their work? Perhaps you help to maintain the home or work environment that enables others to do their work. All of these things are essential for the economy to be successful.

Include think about everything you could take pride in around your work. Do you work alone or in a team? (Both need special qualities.) Do you supervise others, do you work remotely from the main office, do you work in the home providing care for your family to allow them to engage fully in the world? All of these are essential for a healthy society.

Figure 15-1: The broader context of your work.

Uncovering what you want to do

Of course, it is unlikely that you can step straight into the work of your dreams. You need to build up your skills and experience, make the contacts, gain the profile, and earn the opportunity to make the break. This is quite normal; but if you have no sense of these things, if you cannot see your way ever to getting the work you want, then you have a problem that you need to deal with.

At its highest, your *work* in the world is an expression of your being; something powerful and close to your core. But your job doesn't automatically give you the opportunity to do your chosen work. You need to manage this: take steps to acquire the skills you need and balance your life with voluntary work closer to your ideal as you take the time to develop your career.

Answer the following questions to get a clearer vision of your ideal work:

- ✔ **What do you absolutely love about working?** This is an unusual question and you may, like many people when asked it, find it easier to come up with an immediate list of what you don't like about working. Persevere, you will find there are many things you love about working, from a reason to go to town, to the great friends you work with, from the interesting people you meet, to the problems you get to solve, and so on.

Don't stop thinking until you have written down four or five things, even if they're not available in your current job role.

✔ **What aspects of your work are you really good at, or have other people told you that you're really good at?** Wow! Include all the things that you know you're good at even if nobody else does. Perhaps you are a good timekeeper, or maybe you are sensitive and caring when your co-workers are feeling down. Perhaps you are good at dealing with the boss, or the customers, or maybe you are excellent at getting on with the job without being distracted.

Stretch your thinking and go for four or five things.

✔ **What is absolutely essential for you to have available in your work?** This is a great question whether or not you believe your current role gives you what you need. You may include things like meeting people, good money, being part of a team, or the opportunity to learn new things, or the chance to make a real difference.

Think about what *you* need. How much of it would be available in your current role if you came at it a little differently?

✔ **What do you feel you really ought or would like to be doing?** Many people who want to change jobs lack clarity in their ideas about the work they wish they were doing. So, what is it for you? How much more of the things you really need would be available in the job you would prefer to be doing?

✔ **Finally, what is the truth that your answers whisper to you?** Bring all your other answers to mind. Should you be doing something else? Would it make any difference? Other than giving you more money, do you have clear insight into how you will ensure that your next role supports you better?

After answering all these questions, you have a clearer idea than ever before of how you see your work in the world and what about it is most important to you. Now you need to look at the kind of jobs you have been doing. Have they given you what you need? Will they ever? When your work aligns with your values, you can be fully confident and fully empowered in your job. What do you need to change to make it so?

This powerful exercise can help you get in touch with your deeper need for work. You are most powerful and confident in your work when you are able to find jobs and roles that match your developing sense of vocation and purpose.

Finding value in what you do

Uncovering the hidden the value in your work is important for your self-respect and contributes to your confidence.

Whether what you do is something you simply fell into, or whether it was a planned and conscious choice, your job defines you in the world more than almost anything else. You should always ask yourself what is valuable about the work you do in the larger scheme of things, and be sure you bring to mind all the hidden value.

If you work for a large company or a well-known branded business, you can take pride in that. Maybe you work for the government, or the local authority. Take a pride in that. If you work with children, or with sick people, or people with special needs, you may also have some sense of vocation and you can take pride in that.

Whatever you do, take pride in your professionalism. *Professionalism* is about knowing what needs to be done and going about it competently. When you adopt a professional approach to your work, you demonstrate your confidence to others that you know what you are doing, which in turn inspires others to be confident in you.

Eleanor Roosevelt said that the future belongs to those who believe in the beauty of their dreams. A key to confidence is having dreams. Connecting your work with your growing sense of your life's purpose and your dreams is a very powerful means to having that work sing to your soul.

Becoming Assertive

The key to effective communication and relationships with most colleagues in your organisation (including your boss) is a set of personal skills that are usually lumped together and called assertiveness. Assertiveness is one of those acquired skills you need training and practice to acquire.

Assertiveness specialist coaches claim that this skills set is more powerful than any other in business. It can protect and boost your self-esteem, build your confidence, and reduce your stress levels.

Assertive people are generally liked and respected, they respond well in tight spots, and they are not afraid to say 'no'. You know where you are with an assertive person; they don't get put upon.

So what is this miracle skills set called assertiveness? At its core, *assertiveness* is the conviction that every person is equal to every other and that each person has the responsibility to take care of his or her personal needs and rights. There is an implicit acceptance that this applies to all of us, so in claiming it for yourself you also claim it on behalf of all your colleagues.

The fundamentals of assertiveness are:

✔ You value yourself and others as equals.

✔ You have the ability to say 'yes' or 'no' to anyone when you choose, and you do not always choose to offer a reason for it.

✔ You embrace and protect your human rights. You stand up for yourself and this is something that you are unafraid to be known for doing.

✔ You take responsibility for your own needs and ensure you have them met.

✔ You take responsibility for your own contribution and the value you create. You are not afraid to admit to mistakes nor to ask for help when you need it.

✔ You express your thoughts and feelings honestly, whether positive or negative, and with due respect for others.

✔ You are able to handle conflict when it arises. You are prepared to confront difficult people when necessary or appropriate.

✔ You give and receive feedback honestly and in a straightforward manner. You take the trouble to do this effectively and completely.

✔ You respect these rights in others and understand that they have the same rights as you.

Don't worry if you don't feel you match up to all these points yet. It is important first that you know what they are. As you grow in confidence from working with this book, you will naturally become more assertive and powerful.

Showing Confidence in Specific Work Situations

Several common work situations may test your confidence. This section offers advice on how to manage your confidence in meetings and during presentations.

You can develop new skills, or *competencies* as they are often called in business, through training and practice. Nothing in business is impossible to master (certainly nothing is as difficult as learning to walk and talk, and most of us manage that). If your employer is asking you to do something for which you do not yet have the requisite skill, you should insist on the training. And if you find yourself struggling with any task at work your first question should always be: How can I acquire the skill to do this better or faster? This will take you forward into growth and confidence, rather than shrinking backward into fear and avoidance.

Demonstrating power and presence in meetings

Have you ever sat in a meeting just bursting to make a telling point only to find that the discussion has moved on before you are able to get it in? Or have you come up with a brilliant idea after the meeting is over and felt if only you could go back in time and make the point everyone would acknowledge you for solving the problem or pointing up the unnoticed flaw in the argument? If you have, then congratulations, you are a fully functioning, normal human being. We've all done it.

The main cause of such missed opportunities is the lack of balance between the *two* conversations that are going on in the meeting: the one in the room and the one in your head. When you are fully present and engaged in the meeting conversation, the conversation in your head fades into the background where it belongs most of the time. When you are feeling nervous or self-conscious, the dialogue in your head becomes predominant and prevents you from being fully engaged in the meeting.

 You may feel self-conscious just because you're in unfamiliar territory. Take a few deep breaths (from your abdomen as we explain in Chapter 10) to ease the tension, focus on who is in the room, what they're wearing, and so on just to bring yourself fully present.

Understand that this is normal, and ease up on yourself. Accept that the more natural you can be in the meeting situation the more balance you will achieve between your inner and outer dialogues.

If you can become curious about how the external conversation is developing and how the meeting will turn out, you will find yourself naturally focused on the outer discussion. From this position your own ideas and comments come up more naturally and more appropriately, it will be easier for you to make your points and you will grow in confidence.

Above all, relax. Whether the meeting is highly formal and large, or small and routine, the more engaged you become in the business of the meeting, the more effective your contribution becomes.

Shining during presentations

A whole chapter of this book, Chapter 11, is dedicated to helping you find your voice in the world and expressing yourself in the most powerful ways possible. Here you can look at some of the skills you need to make powerful work presentations.

Making effective presentations, like most other things in your professional life, is an acquired skill. Nobody is a born orator, just as no one grows up being able to read a balance sheet or create a budget. In order to give effective presentations, you need to get proper instruction from a training course, books, or tapes. There's no shortage of material to help you. And while the subject is too big to go into much detail here, we offer a few of the key things you need to bear in mind.

- ✔ Basic as it sounds, the very first thing to ask yourself is 'what is my point?' Many beginners and even many experienced speakers forget that if their talk has no point it is quite literally pointless. It's difficult to give a pointless talk with confidence and conviction. So determine your point of view and what you want your audience to do as a result of hearing what you have to say.

- ✔ Next, who are you talking to? You need to know the composition of your audience before you can start to think about how to pitch your talk. Are they knowledgeable or novices in your subject? Will you have to spell things out for them or can you assume they will know what you are talking about, jargon included?

After you consider the basics, turn yourself to the vexed question of whether you need slides. Just because a projector is available, or even habitual, consider whether slides would really add anything to your message (getting the audience's attention off you and giving yourself a crib-sheet to read off are not good enough reasons). If you decide to use a projector follow these top guidelines:

- ✔ Your slides are there for your audience. Make sure that they are legible from the back of the room and that the information on them is crisp and to the point.

- ✔ Assume your audience can read and don't treat your slides as cue cards. If you want your audience to take in what is written on the slide, shut up and let them read it.

✔ Unless you're a graphic artist, don't be tempted by fancy fonts or colour schemes, any kind of animation, or even clip art. And use slide-builds sparingly. What looks great on your office screen when you are preparing all too often looks awful when projected onto a big screen.

✔ Always test your presentation on the actual equipment you will be using. Never, ever attempt to use external links to the Internet or to some kind of live demonstration unless you are a specialist, and even then only with caution.

✔ Have a contingency plan in case your equipment fails or won't behave itself. Have copies of the slides to hand out, but don't do this before you speak unless you don't mind people flicking through the packet while you're talking.

✔ Rehearse, rehearse, and rehearse. Time yourself and get your script down onto a few cue cards. This will ensure you are confident in what you are going to say, and in your timings.

Always bear in mind the golden rules of technology when making any kind of presentation involving projection or sound equipment: *what can go wrong will go wrong* sooner or later, and *less is more* in the balance of complexity versus clarity. Keep things simple and allow yourself the chance to connect with your audience.

You will improve your skills most effectively through practice and feedback. So seek out opportunities in non-work situations to hone your developing skills. Adult education classes in local colleges, women's groups, and your local church are always on the lookout for speakers. Offer yourself up for the experience and do your learning where you won't have to live with the consequences.

Rejecting manipulation and bullying

Bullying is all too common in the workplace. Surveys show that millions of people in the UK feel bullied every day at work, which takes a heavy toll on confidence. If you feel you are a victim of serious bullying at work, seek professional help from your HR or union representative, or perhaps your functional director. Bullying is never acceptable, by anyone, in any circumstances.

Whilst the unacceptability of bullying is perfectly clear in cases of physical intimidation or sexual and racial harassment, the less dramatic, lower-intensity form of bullying by shouting, verbal abuse, and manipulation can sap your self-esteem just as surely as a flagrant assault.

The manipulative bully's techniques include sarcasm, unjustified criticism, trivial faultfinding and humiliation, especially in front of others. It can also include your being overruled, isolated, and otherwise excluded from team activities. All this is calculated to sap your self-confidence to make you more of a target.

You protect yourself best by refusing to play the victim. Recognise that it is the bully who is inadequate and needs fixing, not you. Don't be taken in by criticism, even though it may have a grain of truth in it. No amount of improvement in your performance will satisfy your bully; a bully isn't interested in improving you, only in having control over you.

If you seem to attract such people either into your professional or your private life, it may be because you exhibit certain personality traits that mark you as a target for someone with a bullying personality. *This is not your fault.* Table 15-1 contains practical tips on how to offset tendencies that make you easy prey for bully boys (and girls).

Table 15-1	Personality Traits and Being Bullied
Tendency	*Counter Behaviours*
You want to please.	Accept that you will never be able to please everyone, especially a bully.
You take on more and more to gain approval.	Set yourself sensible limits.
You find it hard to say "no".	Learn how to be more assertive.
You have a strong desire to think well of others.	Be more objective; ask others' opinions.
You want things to be perfect.	Realize that perfection isn't possible and turn to Chapter 9.
You have a strong need to feel valued.	Learn to value yourself (see Chapter 5).
You tend to discount your own contributions.	Ask yourself whether what you're expected to do is fair and reasonable.

Your first step in dealing successfully with a bully is to take control. Acknowledge your need to be more assertive, and look at that section in this chapter. There is almost certainly something you can do to stop yourself being victimised. Consider the following actions. Don't think for too long though, you need to take decisive action quickly:

- ✔ Let your union or staff representative know about the problem. Take any advice they offer you, and if this is inadequate check out any help-lines or consult your local Citizen's Advice Bureau.

- ✔ Talk about the situation to your colleagues (if they will discuss it). Find out if anyone else is suffering and if others are aware of what is happening to you. Others may be suffering in silence.

- ✔ Start a diary and keep a written record of all incidents. You may need this detailed evidence later if things come to a head but more likely it will act as a strong disincentive on your bully.

- ✔ Confront your bully in person if you feel you can, otherwise do it by e-mail or memo. In firm but non-aggressive language, make it clear what you are objecting to in their behaviour. Keep a copy and any reply. This may end their bullying.

- ✔ If you decide to make a formal complaint take advice first from HR or your union and follow your company's procedures. Ask your representatives to help you; this will cut down greatly on the stress on you.

  If you have made a formal complaint, be aware that your bully's job could now be in jeopardy. You need to be able to substantiate your allegations through witnesses or written records, and you may have to confront your bully in an investigation.

If you are not satisfied by the outcome of the internal investigation, take advice on your legal rights. If you leave your job and subsequently make a claim to an employment tribunal, they will expect you to have first tried to resolve the situation using the internal procedures. Any records you have will be heard when the tribunal hears your claim.

Managing Your Boss

Complaints about the boss are commonplace in work life and pretty much inevitable. It will help your confidence to remember that however big and scary your boss may appear to you now, she got that way by having to cope with difficult situations on her own and that underneath she is as vulnerable as you are.

The bottom line with bosses is that they need to get the job done and meet their performance targets. They need their team members to perform effectively and they have strategies for getting the required performance out of their subordinates.

When the pressure is on, bosses become anxious and scared just like anyone else, and that is when problems often show up most.

Anyone who is persistently out of sorts or bad tempered is almost certainly stressed and needs help whether they know it or not. There may be nothing you feel you can do to help your boss with her issues, but you can certainly manage your own.

Dealing with feedback

It is important for your self-confidence that you learn how to manage feedback. If you can receive and give feedback effectively, and especially turn even poorly delivered feedback to your advantage, you will grow massively in confidence and effectiveness at work.

Figure 15-2 shows an example of ineffective feedback to a secretary who fails to use the spell checker in her word processor.

Joan, you've left typos in the weekly review again.

Sorry Mrs Farrell.

Why do you think you have a spell checker? All you have to do is use it and it will find most of them for you?

Sorry Mrs Farrell.

The problem is it makes us all look slip-shod. The work you put out damages the image of the whole department; it reflects badly on me.

Sorry Mrs Farrell.

Yes, well you say you're sorry every time we have this conversation and nothing ever changes. It simply isn't good enough and you are going to have to change. If you don't mend your ways my girl this is going to end in tears, yours. Is that clear?

Yes Mrs Farrell.

Well let this be the last time, or else. I mean it.

Sorry Mrs Farrell.

Figure 15-2: How *not* to give feedback.

Figure 15-3 offers a more professional and effective way of giving feedback that might actually result in a change for the better.

Joan, thank you very much for the weekly review. Once again you have turned it around very quickly and efficiently.

Thank you Mrs Farrell.

I know we have talked about this before but there are still some typos. Are you having problems using the spell-checker?

Err, yes, I keep forgetting.

Why don't you put a sticky label on the side of the computer to remind you about spell-checking your work and then it will stop happening. It is so easy to use.

Okay Mrs Farrell, I'll definitely do that.

Good Joan; if you need any further training on the system, let me know and I can organise it.

Thank you, I will do.

Once again Joan, thank you for this.

Figure 15-3: Giving effective feedback.

The next sections offer tips for giving and getting feedback.

Giving effective feedback

When giving feedback, whether positive or negative, things gener-ally go most smoothly if you follow a few simple rules:

- ✔ **Be very clear about the information you are imparting and own the responsibility of making the point.** You don't want any grey areas at the end, and you want to make sure that your receiver knows this clear information is coming from you.

- ✔ **Focus on the action you want to take place.** Describe the facts of the situation and how you want them to change. Do not judge or offer opinions about why the problem is arising, you might get it wrong.

- ✔ **Be as specific as possible.** Take a keyhole or laser surgery approach to your intervention. Deal as precisely as possible with the situation and avoid generalisations like *always* and *never*. If your feedback deals with some aspect of behaviour, ensure that it is the behaviour you address and not the char-acter of the person.

- ✔ **Emphasise the positive aspects of the situation.** This helps the person receiving your input to keep her receiving chan-nels open. If you're correcting an error or making another point that she may receive as criticism, it can be helpful to the receiver if you sandwich the negative point between something positive, both before and after. This is not manipulative if you do it honestly; it is helpful to the person who has to take your point on board.

Turning negative feedback around

Input from your boss that you receive as criticism, nit-picking, or nagging is just an inadequate form of feedback. The information it contains may be valuable to you though, and important to your organisation, so it is worth understanding what your boss is trying to communicate.

If you can see that your boss's criticism of you is just her inadequate way of giving you information, you retain more power in the relationship. You can do two things that may surprise her and turn things around:

✔ Take on board any feedback that may be useful to you in improving your performance and let your boss know what this is.

✔ Ask permission to give your boss feedback on how she can communicate with *you* more effectively. If you do this, follow all the rules on being specific, focusing on the action, and so on from the preceding 'Giving effective feedback' section. Remember, you both share the goal of improving performance.

Getting your boss to keep her promises

The frustration of being offered some benefit or reward but not receiving it can corrupt your relationship with your employer and erode your confidence.

Unfulfilled promises generally fall into one of two cases:

✔ **Case 1:** You believe your boss has promised you something that she doesn't. She may be surprised that you feel a promise has been made.

✔ **Case 2:** You both know full well that the promise has been made and yet it is being delayed for reasons that have not been made clear to you.

In both cases, you feel maligned or abused and your self-esteem and self-confidence will suffer unless you do something about it.

At the root of both cases is a problem with communication. In Case 1, you may have unintentionally translated a good intention by your boss into a promise. In Case 2, the ambiguity may be deliberate. Your boss may simply have made the promise to keep you quiet without intending to fulfil it any time soon. Fortunately, the remedy for both is simple and it is the same action.

What you do, as a professional person of integrity, is put down in writing in the form of an email or memo any important exchanges. In clear and straightforward language, write down what you believe has been agreed. Figure 15-4 gives an example.

Dear Boss

Thanks for seeing me yesterday to discuss my pay rise. I'm obviously delighted that you have agreed to my request and I'm looking forward to receiving it. When will this be by the way? (This is the first question my wife will ask me). Do please confirm a date and let me know if there is going to be any delay.

Thanks and regards

Figure 15-4: Putting an understanding in writing.

Of course, if you have the presence of mind in the discussion to ask when the reward will take effect, you will already know the promised date and you can include it in your note.

How will your boss react to this written input? In the majority of cases, your note simply confirms what your boss agreed to do, and your confirmation acts as a reminder. If you send it as an email, your boss can forward it to her PA, HR, or payroll with a confirmation that she has agreed to your note and a request for action. Then it will be done – easy for everyone.

But what happens when your boss doesn't agree or doesn't take action? In the case of a misunderstanding, your note is likely to evoke an immediate response from your boss pointing up the mismatch. Will she be annoyed? Maybe, a little bit, since the issue has returned so quickly, but it is far better to identify her mistake in communication immediately and give her the chance to rectify it. You can apologise if necessary to maintain rapport, and immediately ask when you can expect the reward. If she can't give you any indication, then you are probably being fobbed off, which is Case 2.

So what will be your boss's reaction to your note if she is using delaying tactics? You will catch her out and force her hand. If she continues to be evasive, then you know she is simply stringing you along. You won't have your reward, but you will have your integrity restored. You may be annoyed, but it will not be directed at yourself. You may use your annoyance to give you the motivation to do something about changing your dishonest boss by changing your job.

Telling your boss she's wrong

At the heart of confidence is trust: Trust in yourself, trust in others, and trust that things will turn out okay. Telling your boss that she's wrong requires that you feel all three, so let's take a look at the structure and dynamics of the situation.

First, bear in mind that neither you nor your boss is infallible. Everyone makes mistakes from time to time; everyone makes errors of fact and judgement. This is perfectly human. What matters most in business is what you do to remedy the immediate problem and what you can then do to stop the situation occurring again.

If you are sure that you are correct about your boss's error or misjudgement, then you owe it to her to point it out before the damage gets worse. Here is where you need trust in yourself. No matter what gap there may be in age, prestige, salary, experience, or levels in the hierarchy, you are just as valuable a human being as your boss and you owe it to her, person to person, to point out her error. If you do this with respect and a little care (for example, not in front of your colleagues or in the middle of a meeting), your boss will remember and respect you for your honesty and tact.

 If you have some evidence ready to support your judgement that she has made an error, use it discreetly. It can help your boss to come to terms with her error more quickly but spare her blushes with others. If you point out your boss's errors in public, she won't thank you for it.

If you have an honest and straightforward remedy, offer it to help fix her mistake quickly. Don't become wedded to your solution, though, as she may choose another.

Fundamentally, being assertive and acting to inform your boss of the error is what counts. You will grow in confidence from your taking the action and so, if she is any good as a leader at all, will your boss.

Casting Off Your Cloak of Invisibility

More often than not, the reason nobody is acknowledging the great job you are doing is because your superiors and colleagues are too busy worrying about their own performances. Don't be afraid to seize the opportunity to take powerful action to bring your excellent work to the attention of your boss and colleagues.

The following formula creates a winning situation for everyone. If you use it, you set yourself apart as the one in a thousand employees who cares enough about performance to take it on.

Follow these steps:

1. **Ask your boss to define exactly what she wants from you in order for you to get a five-star annual appraisal.**

   The more detailed this is the better. Get her to spell out, from her point of view, what *good* looks like, then play it back: 'So if I do this, this, and this, and avoid that and that, you will think I'm doing an excellent job, right?' Once you have agreement, write it down (but don't send it anywhere just yet).

2. **Ask the same question of others who depend on you or are affected by your performance.**

   These may be customers or a group of colleagues who use your output in some significant way. Find out, from their perspective, what good looks like, play it back, get their agreement, and write it down for your own use later.

3. **Pull it all together into job objectives that you can realistically achieve.**

   You have a lot of detailed input on how other people depend on you and what they need you to do well in order to be happy with your performance.

4. **Spell out what you feel you can reliably deliver to your boss, colleagues, and customers.**

   Present them with a document that outlines the objectives you're committed to achieving (perhaps with training or some other assistance) and get their agreement to it (you may need to negotiate and compromise).

Doing the work to put together an action plan helps you achieve a number of really important objectives:

- ✔ Composing a job specification that is relevant, detailed, achievable, and creates value.

- ✔ Letting your boss and colleagues know what to expect from you and that they can rely on you to deliver.

- ✔ Laying a solid basis for renegotiating expectations and outcomes should anything change.

You have a perfect right, a duty even, to check in with your colleagues periodically to ensure they are happy with your performance. And each time you do so it will remind them of what a good and dependable job you do.

Dealing Confidently with Corporate Change

As change managers know, change tends to trigger a cycle of reactions and feelings. These fall into a sequence of predictable stages, irrespective of whether the change is planned or unplanned. Figure 15-5 shows a simple change curve.

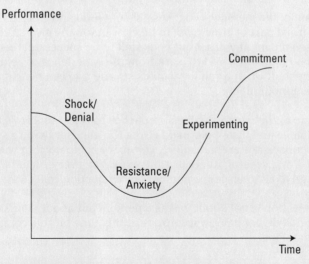

Figure 15-5: Changing with the change curve.

The time you spend at each stage and the intensity of your reaction depends on your personality and the nature of the change. To make a successful transition, however, you have to work through all the stages. The stages are

- ✔ **Shock or Denial:** At this initial response, your natural response may be to minimise the impact of the change by trivialising it or denying that it exists.

- ✔ **Resistance and Anxiety:** This stage is characterised by your strong emotions and also feelings of flatness, accompanied often by a loss of confidence. You may have difficulties in coping with the new circumstances, which makes it hard to accept the changes.

- ✔ **Experimenting:** Activity now increases as you test new ways and approaches towards the change. You may have firm ideas of how things should be in relation to the new situation and feel frustration as the inevitable mistakes are made.

- ✔ **Commitment:** By this stage, you will have adopted new behaviour and accepted the change. You're working well and confidently with the new situation. You may reflect on how and why things are different, and attempt to understand all the emotion and activity of the previous stages.

Getting through rejection

One of the messages coaches give out loud and clear is that it's a normal part of growth *not* to be chosen for any given role or assignment. If you set out your stall to be successful then you need to be prepared to learn from the experience of being rejected. Often a valid reason exists and you can benefit from the disappointment.

One of the most valuable approaches to rejection is to embrace change and disappointments from the mindset that it's simply feedback rather than failure. For every company that wins a piece of work, several others lost the work. For every successful candidate at an interview, a number got a rejection call.

Rejection is not about you as a person, but about your skills and style not being appropriate at this time for this company or customer.

Winners stay professional and persist for the long term. Confident people welcome feedback and continue to learn.

Taking on tips for job interviews

In any situation in life, you will be more confident if you know what to expect and you feel well prepared.

A job interview isn't something you experience all that often, so take advantage of the many books and any training you are offered to help you interview well.

Even the most mundane of jobs often attract many more applications than the employer can easily handle. In the initial sifting phase, almost any excuse is used to disqualify a CV from the pile of applications, so if you're called for interview, congratulate yourself for being one of the few to get through the sift.

The interview itself is structured in simple stages:

✔ The first few minutes are all about establishing the channel of communication, or *rapport*.

✔ You need to listen actively as the interviewer outlines key information about the organisation and the job.

✔ The attention turns to you next as you and the interviewer investigate how your particular mix of capability, experience, and aspiration can generate value in the job.

✔ A short closing-down phase enables you to ask any remaining questions.

This is the ideal with a trained HR professional. The interviewer's task is to eliminate candidates who won't help to create the value the company is looking to generate.

Above all, make sure you are *never* guilty of these top confidence-related reasons for rejection at interview stage:

✔ **Lack of planning:** Being unable to express clear purpose and goals.

✔ **Passive and indifferent behaviour:** Failing to express interest and enthusiasm, lack of vitality, poor eye contact.

✔ **Poor confidence and poise:** Appearing ill at ease and unduly nervous.

You have one further task as an interviewee that sets you apart from the pack. Within 24 hours, drop your interviewer a personal note thanking them for their time, and for being so helpful and informative. Confirm whether or not you remain interested in the post and, if you are, tell them you are looking forward to the next stage in the process. Don't revisit any of your answers or ask a further question at this stage. Your note is by way of a simple thank-you and confirmation to your interviewer, and doesn't require a reply. Not one in a hundred candidates shows this simple courtesy.

Taming the threat of redundancy

Since it is jobs or roles that get made redundant, and not people, you can only be made redundant if you see yourself as your job. You may find yourself out of work for a while, and it certainly won't be of your choosing, but you will avoid the quite ridiculous and yet soul-destroying label of being redundant yourself.

Fully embrace the notion of work being something you choose to do for yourself and sometimes – often – you pursue this through a job role. Now you have a clear distinction between the work you have taken on in the world and the medium through which you are currently engaged in your work. This is a far healthier relationship to your job and one that allows you to have much more personal power.

The way forward is to hold on to who you are and your true purpose and find the work or lifestyle that fits for you right now. Hold on to the idea that this is merely a transition in your life. Confidence is about accepting and embracing the energy of the change and finding the positive lesson for you. Ask someone who has been made redundant six months after the event, and many will tell you that it was the best thing that happened to them – it gave them freedom to move on and was a catalyst for change.

As a good example: When the British heavy industries of coal mining and shipbuilding were closed down over a 20-year period, hundreds of thousands of workers lost their jobs. Many of these workers had been miners or shipbuilders all their lives, and their fathers before them. Their identity was bound up in being a miner, and since the government had no more use for miners it had no further use for them. They were literally without use and useless; they were finished. Many of them reached retirement age without ever working again.

In stark contrast, thousands of others took their redundancy pay and used it to build new lives, either starting their own businesses or moving away to parts of the country where there were more and different jobs.

The ones who moved on saw the problem for what it was: Their heavy-industry jobs were gone forever and they needed to find different kinds of jobs. The rest embraced prolonged unemployment with their proud industrial identities intact.

Chapter 16

Approaching Romantic Relationships with Confidence

In This Chapter

▶ Understanding your beliefs and expectations about romance

▶ Uncovering the core of romantic relationships

▶ Considering some aspects of relationships

▶ Working through your issues in romance

A leading brand of chocolate confectionery has used a single storyline in its advertising for over 25 years. Usually at night, a handsome action man, rugged but fashionable in black, is dropped from a helicopter into a raging torrent where he has to navigate the rapids before climbing 500 feet up a sheer cliff face, in through the window of a magnificent chateau and into the bedroom of a beautiful woman. He deposits a box of chocolates by her bedside and immediately departs; and all because the lady loves the chocolates. He's been doing this for 25 years!

For your average man this is tough competition, and romance tests even the bravest hearts. On the one hand, romance seems to contain every ingredient of a fiendish confidence test: Strong desire, fear of failure and humiliation, the despair of never succeeding. But on the other hand, when things just seem to 'click', romance seems the most natural thing in the world, an effortless joyride into relationship.

Doesn't it strike you as odd that nature takes such a chance with something so important as survival of the species? The truth is that society invented the rituals of romantic relationship and you will feel much more confident about negotiating them when you know how they work, and how they work on you.

Relating with Romance

So what does romance mean to you? Originally a romance was a mediaeval tale, in song or verse, told about some chivalrous hero (like St George rescuing damsels about to be consumed by fire-breathing dragons). Key characteristics of such tales were that they were fantastic, removed from everyday life, strange, and yet moving. Nobody cared about whether they were really true – that wasn't their point. What was important was that they transported their listeners to a better, higher realm of human nature and put them in touch with the heroic in their own lives.

Several hundred years later, you seek exactly the same thing when you go to the movies or watch something romantic on TV. Human nature doesn't seem to have changed very much in that time: What has changed is the fashion in which you get your innate need for romance satisfied.

Checking in on cultural notions of romance

The influences and trends in society that shape beliefs and expectations are popularly known as *culture*. A good working definition of culture is 'the way we do things around here'. Or rather, the way we are *supposed* to do things, because the conventions and fashions embedded within culture are powerful.

Whilst it is perfectly true that you are free to accept or reject the conventions your culture offers up to you, they remain very influential in shaping how you think about things. And living comfortably outside cultural norms requires above-average power and confidence.

You don't have to settle for less than you want in matters of romance, provided what you want is achievable and supports you in building the life you want. Your starting point is an examination of your current, perhaps unconscious views of what romance means to you.

As a two-minute test, go through the scenarios in the following list and ask yourself which of them you feel are romantic:

> ✔ Coming from rival dynasties, the couple is star-crossed from the start. They rail against their families, their friends, and society to be together. Reality catches up with them when they both die in a tragic accident whilst being pursued by their families.

✔ She is assigned as a live-in nanny to work with the widower's difficult children. She becomes the children's surrogate mother, and despite the widower's initial standoffishness, their shared love of the children eventually brings them together.

✔ She is beautiful and destined for an arranged marriage to an eligible socialite when she meets the man who introduces her to raw, real life for the first time. Desperately in love, he dies tragically, giving up his own life so that she may live on.

✔ A couple overcomes radically different religious and family backgrounds to forge a passionate and loving relationship based upon who they are as individuals. Eventually, though, their cultural differences prove overwhelming and they are forced apart.

✔ This couple is best friends for many years, helping each other through difficult times with other partners before they realise that they truly love each other and were meant to be together all along.

How many of these scenarios strike chords in you? The result doesn't matter so much as your awareness of some of the stereotypes that shape your expectations. If you didn't already spot them you might enjoy revisiting them looking for the lovers from *Romeo and Juliet*, *The Sound of Music*, *Titanic*, *The Way We Were*, and *When Harry Met Sally*.

Popular culture's representation of romantic love dictates that it be hard won, occur only after trials or near-fatal mistakes, and eventually flower against all the odds. It either ends happily or, more frequently, gets snuffed out tragically and prematurely. Would any sane person choose this way to conduct an important personal relationship? And yet this is the raw material you used to shape your concept of romantic relationships.

 You can easily create your own list of favourite films, plays, and novels. It is worth doing, as it will tell you a lot about how your culture has shaped your notions of romance. Then ask yourself, how does this compare with your real life?

Choosing your own view of romance

Despite being removed from real life, these fantastic, romantic stories exert a powerful influence on you through the media of film, TV, and novels. So, unless misery and pain are in your values hierarchy, you are going to benefit from taking control of what romance means for you from now on. This section helps you to do that and renders you better able to take those scary first steps.

Take a few minutes right now to identify the things you most want in a romantic, loving relationship, and make yourself a list of the top half-dozen.

It doesn't matter whether you were together for one evening or have been married for 20 years. Think about your romantic relationships right now and summarise one or two, in one paragraph, in totally dispassionate language, as in the following examples:

> When we got together, our respective friends were amazed. We were so different from each other and so different from our partners in previous relationships. Few people, if any, thought it would last with a 16-year age difference, and although it hasn't been easy for us, 10 years later we are still happy and have two beautiful daughters.

> We grew up in the same neighbourhood with similar family backgrounds. In public I appear to be the sociable and impulsive one while my partner provides the counterbalance of quiet rationality. We felt a strong bond from our first date and have been inseparable for over 30 years.

You shouldn't need to do this more than a couple relationships before you realise that when you strip out the drama from a real-life romantic relationship, what you end up with is people rubbing along together in a perfectly natural and predictable way for better or worse much like all human relationships in all walks of life. The point is, you know how to do this; you've been doing it all your life.

Never confuse *romance* with *drama*. Be aware that the destructive, all-consuming passions and downright bad behaviour of Scarlett O'Hara and Rhett Butler are not what long-term romantic relationships are about.

Realising What Really Matters

In preparation for this chapter, we spoke to many men and women about what really matters most in a romantic relationship. People have their own views and preferences, of course, but when it comes down to the few things that really matter, most people's top three are:

- ✔ **Trust:** Everyone wants to be able to trust and wants to be trusted. This doesn't simply mean avoiding cheating and barefaced lying. It includes subtler forms of not being straightforward such as withholding and avoidance. White lies are acceptable to some people and not to others. What matters most is that you establish the parameters of trust specific to your relationship and stick to them.

✔ **Communication:** You want to be able to say anything you feel the need to say and expect your partner to feel the same freedom. In addition, you need to be willing to share your important feelings and expect your partner to do the same.

Women don't see bottling up things that should be communicated as manly; rather, they see it as a form of withholding or lying.

✔ **Acceptance:** Deep inside, everyone harbours a little neurosis. If you're like most people, you don't quite match up to the image you hold of yourself, try as you might, so you worry about not being good enough. Couples in great relationships accept each other, warts and all.

Where are *passion* and *drama* in this list of priorities? It turns out that although most people like a little excitement now and again, intense situations are such a double-edged sword that they don't usually make it onto the must-have list. It's a bit like the farmer's description of New York City: 'nice place to visit; wouldn't want to live there'.

In this case, perhaps there is a different, lighter form of romantic relating – one that can be uplifting and fun but that avoids the deep pitfalls that so often trap the traditional romantic heroes and heroines. If you like the idea of this 'romance-lite', you can build it on the top three must-haves and by adding the following factors necessary for an uplifting and fun-filled, romantic relationship:

✔ **A sense of humour:** It may surprise you to know that being funny is very sexy, especially when accompanied by self-confidence. Women find a funny, confident man just as irresistible as a drop-dead gorgeous guy who takes himself too seriously. Likewise, men enjoy women who are funny and enjoy a good laugh.

✔ **Thoughtfulness and caring:** A partner who is aware of your needs and takes the trouble to make sure they are being met is a partner who is very reassuring – as long as the care isn't taken to extremes. Good partners are also aware of their own needs and ensure that these are being met as well. Being thoughtful goes along with acceptance and includes caring about anything that is important to the loved one, including parents, siblings, children, the environment – even the 1957 Cadillac awaiting restoration in the garage.

✔ **The possibility of a compelling future:** In many ways, this quality is the most important of all. It is the true reason that Scarlett couldn't live without her Rhett and its absence probably explains why so many great romantic attachments end in ruins. Belief in a compelling future together (with whatever degree of excitement works for you) is the final magical ingredient that makes all the difference. If you have the trust, the communication, the acceptance, the humour, and the caring, then a compelling future together ensures that you never become bored with each other and never take each other for granted.

Looking at Relationships with Open Eyes

As a human being, you're born into networks of relationships and can't help but accumulate more and more as you progress through school, jobs, and the expanding relationships your family members and friends embark on. So take on board that you have many relationships already, that being 'in a relationship' is perfectly natural to you, and that many, if not most, of your relationships are extremely effective.

Making that first move

What about *the* relationship, the one real relationship with your one true love? What about that one? The stakes do seem a little higher, don't they?

Imagine yourself for a minute on a high wire between two tall buildings. You are crossing to meet your one true love, difficult enough, but in the middle is a fire-breathing dragon of the mediaeval romance kind, and you have to get past it in order to reach your love. As luck would have it, a friendly enchantress advised you in a dream before you set out that you could placate this fiery dragon by repeating a certain magic phrase. Unfortunately, when you woke up you couldn't remember what this magic phrase is. And now here you are, just a short walk from love and fulfilment, facing the probability of certain destruction if you say the wrong thing. How confident do you feel right now? How able are you to take that next step and engage this scary dragon in the make-or-break conversation?

Dating, the killing fields of confidence

In the western world, *dating* has become the killing fields of the confidence of young men and women. Asking a girl out on a first date is a daunting prospect for a man and if she happens to be the woman of your dreams, it can become paralysing. How do you get yourself to make that move? You can send your friend to ask her, but this is rarely effective much beyond puberty. You can hang around being nice and risk a braver chap stealing your true love if you take too long. The best way, the confident way, is to be authentic and act decisively. But how do you get yourself to pick up the phone or look her straight in the eye and speak out your request?

This is such a universal challenge for men that Anthony Robbins, the personal power guru, gives a dating lesson on his weekend seminar. The lesson is both brutal and funny to make the point. It culminates in Simon, a wimpish chap from the audience, up on stage asking Sarah, a beautiful, fashionably dressed young woman, to go out for a drink with him. Tough enough, but Robbins has instructed Sarah to refuse vehemently and, each time she is asked again, to pile on the agony even further.

Simon is instructed to keep on asking, regardless of the answer; he is committed to the course of action regardless of the outcome. The result is predictably hilarious and after three or four refusals Sarah is running out of insults. At this point, Simon is beginning to enjoy the game and varies his approach a little, shooting sidelong glances and making gestures to the audience. He is no longer making her refusal mean anything and he is not made wrong or damaged by her response. This is a training drill, of course; in the real world he could be guilty of harassment since by now he could go on asking her out all night with impunity.

But the amazing thing is that Sarah is also beginning to realise that her refusal has nothing to do with Simon whom she knows nothing about, she is merely responding to her programming. His refusal to be daunted by the situation is even attractive to her and she becomes a little curious about him despite his ordinary appearance. He is no longer just a face chosen at random from the audience but has become an emerging personality and despite the set-up, and the worst imaginable circumstances, a relationship is forming between them. This is life, this is how human beings function, and later Sarah and Simon can be seen chatting about their shared experience over a coffee.

The point of all this is to illustrate how taking committed action and remaining unattached to the outcome is a very powerful strategy that can empower you in the most difficult of circumstances. I (Brinley) tried it out on the woman of my dreams as recommended and it took me six months to achieve that first date. It was worth it though, as we have just had our second child and will soon be celebrating our seventh wedding anniversary.

Suddenly you snap to your senses. You are not on a high wire at all, you are at the photocopier standing beside the man or woman of your dreams. Your eyes meet, and in that instant you get a shot at finding that magical, enchanting sentence. You're just as scared, aren't you? Just as certain to end up crashed and burned.

Paradoxically, the person of your dreams is both your love *and* the dragon – what you love the most and what you fear the most. None of it is real in the objective sense; it is raging around inside your head, swamping your brain and body with extreme neurochemicals. Do you run away, or do you stay to slay the dragon and earn your prize? This is an old dilemma as Robbie Burns points out in the line: 'faint heart ne'er won a lady fair'. Except these days it applies to women too.

So, what can you do? You can prepare; you can guess that you will, sooner or later, be in this position, and you can work out some scenarios. You can work on what is likely to happen. Don't worry if this doesn't sound too romantic, you can work on that later when you are together. This first step is more about survival.

If confidence is about having the power to take the action no matter how you're feeling, then asking for a date is for many people the ultimate test. Everything you've done until now to increase your power and expand your comfort zone comes into play. Your motivation is high, you have thought through all the possible responses, and you realize that no matter what happens you're unlikely to die from it. There's nothing more to do but jump in!

Filling your partner's needs without running dry yourself

In any mutually dependent relationship, each partner shares in the responsibility for both getting what they need. This means that each first has to understand their own needs and then communicate these to their partner.

This isn't a once-and-for-all arrangement, as in a business contract, but a lifetime commitment to understand and communicate your needs and to be sensitive to the developing needs of your partner. How you stay in touch with your own needs and your partner's needs is one of the most important things you can know about relationships.

So what happens when one side of the relationship is unwilling or, more likely, unable to understand and communicate their needs? A lack in this area can damage the relationship to the point of failure and make it impossible to salvage. If you find yourself in this situation, what can you do about it?

First, make sure that your partner's need, whatever it is, doesn't become your need but realise that it creates a new need in you. If your partner is sad or depressed, never try to feel sad and depressed too. You may very well feel confused, perplexed, and perhaps angry and frustrated that your partner is locking you out by not communicating. Unless you accept your feelings as a natural consequence, you may also come to feel guilty and resentful.

So what do you do? In a serious case, you may want to seek professional counselling or some form of medical intervention, but most situations aren't that serious.

In all cases, stick to the spirit of your responsibility: Understand your own needs in this situation and communicate them as honestly as you can. Do your best to explain your feelings in a way that doesn't blame your partner (these are your feelings, after all, and your partner has enough to worry about already), reassure your partner that you are ready and willing to receive their communication whenever they are ready, and that you are prepared to help them resolve their current problems in whatever way you can, on their terms.

That's really about as much as you can do. Monitor your own feelings carefully as they develop. Eventually your partner will feel better able to communicate or you may reach a point where you need to seek help. Whatever you do, you can resolve your own feelings most quickly by maintaining full ownership of your end of the problem. These feelings are yours and they derive from your reaction to the current situation. Your response may be based on experiences you had a long time before you met your current partner.

By taking full ownership of your feelings, whatever they are, you will be in a more resourceful state from which you can help your partner more surely.

Getting by with some help from your friends

A good friend or confidant can help you to see your situation more dispassionately than you can alone. If you're having rows and fights with your partner, it may help you to try to step outside (dis-associate from) the situation and try to see it as a third party might. Remember, every human relationship involves at least two people, two histories, and two sets of strategies – some of which may be helpful and others not.

Be prepared to learn from your current experience, not just what to do for your partner but core facts about yourself: How you operate, what pushes your buttons, and so on. Just because you feel hurt or abused right now doesn't mean that you will necessarily always feel this way. You can take learning from your own life and from others. Knowing that you managed to accommodate such problems before or that you know someone who has successfully dealt with a similar situation can give you hope in the darkest times.

Above all, remember that you and your partner are both doing your best at some level. All human interaction is a kind of miracle and building a romantic, long-term relationship is an art that can take a lifetime to perfect.

In a relationship, the journey is much more important than the destination. Like Greek tragedies even the very best romantic relationships are all destined to end someday, usually with one partner feeling abandoned and in tears. This is the price you pay for romantic love; if you're smart, you make sure it is a price worth paying by extracting as much joy and fulfilment from your romantic union as possible.

Eliciting Your Love Strategy

How useful would it be to be able to reach out with love to your partner when she or he needs it the most? And how wonderful would it be if your partner had a sure-fire way of making you feel totally loved in those precise moments when you feel alone against the world? You can learn to do this, and it isn't that difficult.

You're a creature of habit; you have to be or you'd find it extremely difficult to operate efficiently in this highly complex world. Once you find a way to get somewhere, or have a need met, you tend to stick to that method for the rest of your life. You like the same foods at 50 that you liked at 25 (despite complaining they may not like you as much), you listen to the same styles of music and support the same football teams.

More subtly, you have habitual strategies for doing almost anything, such as deciding what to eat off a menu, getting yourself motivated (or in the mood), even feeling emotions. Strangest of all, you have a time- and experience-honoured method for feeling loved: this is your *love strategy*.

Allowing yourself to feel loved by another person is an essential ingredient of a romantic relationship, and something you do quite naturally. But unless you know how you do this, your partner can never achieve it at will, and may feel shut-out by you when you are feeling unlovable. And, you may be at your least resourceful when you need reassurance of your lovableness the most.

So how do you find out how you allow yourself to feel loved? Unless you're familiar with the methods of neuro-linguistic programming or have participated in a personal development programme on strategy elicitation, you probably haven't a clue. Rest assured, it's an easy thing to work out if you follow some simple steps.

The following steps are easier to run through with an intimate friend or someone else you trust who can work with you to guide you through the stages.

1. **Associate.**

   Eliciting your strategy isn't something you can do in the abstract, so the very first thing you need to do is think of a specific time when you had strong feelings of being loved by someone, it doesn't matter who, and let the memory and its associated feelings flood over you. Let this happen over a few minutes, re-live the moment and intensify your feelings as far as you are able.

   When you feel fully associated with that specific time, you are ready for Step 2.

2. **Answer questions.**

   Staying in your associated state, answer the following questions. (This step is easier if you have someone else to ask you the questions and note down your answers.)

   In order for you to feel loved is it *absolutely necessary* for the other person to show you he/she loves you by:

   - Taking you someplace? If so, where? (To your favourite restaurant for example, or out to meet your loved one's family?)

   - Buying you something? If so, what sort of thing? (An expensive gift perhaps, or some token chosen with care?)

   - Looking at you in some specific way?

   - Telling you that you are loved in a certain way (voice tonality, volume, closeness)?

   - Touching you in a certain way (place, pressure, duration)? Demonstrate exactly how.

3. Test.

Take your loved one through your list of answers, demonstrating exactly how you need to be spoken to, looked at,
and touched, and then have them speak, look, and touch in
exactly the way you describe. Don't be surprised when you
melt into feeling totally loved. After all, this is your strategy
for feeling love and you can't help but react in this way.

Knowing the specifics of your own love strategy and helping your
partners discover theirs is tremendously enlightening and removes
the strong element of chance from this important area. If you know
how to make a person feel loved by you, you know how to reach
out to them when they need it the most, and your friends or partners will know how to reach out to you.

Facing Up to Changing
Relationships

To build a relationship that gives you what you need, you really
have to take on board that you are *always* responsible for what you
are getting out of it, no matter what is happening to you. This may
seem harsh, even cruel if you are in an abusive relationship, but it
is the only basis for taking powerful action.

Making decisions

If you're suffering physical or mental abuse, you need to seek help
immediately (your abusive partner needs help too, of course, but
this is not your responsibility nor is it your immediate priority).

If your challenge is less dangerous, though perhaps equally painful
as in the case of infidelity, you need to feel your feelings and decide
as honestly as you can whether or not you are prepared to work to
restore the trust, communication, and acceptance that may have
been lost. Be prepared to share all this with your partner and perhaps a professional counsellor. You can never go back to the way
things were before, but with work you may arrive at a new and
more honest place in your relationship.

In the end, you always get to decide what happens in your life and
relationships based on the options you have available. People
change, circumstances change, and relationships change too.
Change is inherent in living; it is a necessary condition for life.
Your free choice is to grow forward into love or to shrink backward into fear. It's your life; it's your decision.

Redesigning the way you are together

Whether a troubling situation seems redeemable or irreconcilable, eventually you need to make the decision about re-committing or ending the relationship based on what you feel is best for you. Your partner must do likewise. This includes relationships involving children; you factor them into your judgement about what is best and their wellbeing often motivates you to try as hard as you can to resolve issues as amicably as possible.

If you decide to give the relationship another go, you have the opportunity to enter into a curious state of grace where you can once again consider and redesign as necessary any and all aspects of your relationship together. Leave blame behind at this point – what's done is done. What's more important now is to understand what was lacking in the relationship that allowed the situation to develop. It was probably some of the things on the list in the 'Realising What Really Matters' section earlier in this chapter. Start by looking at whether you have a compelling future and work your way through the other items until you return again to trust. Only by restoring all the elements of a fulfilling relationship can you truly face a better future.

But don't wait for trouble before working on your compelling future. You can start in small ways and not too far out; Rome wasn't built in a day. And remember, a compelling future has to be compelling to both of you. The more you talk and share your inner, deeper desires and longings, the more you have to work with.

Chapter 17

Raising Confident Children

● ●

In This Chapter

▶ Giving children the best start

▶ Encouraging natural curiosity

▶ Being a great guide and champion

● ●

*R*aising confident children begins with your confidence in your-self. Because, as you well know by now, confidence is conta-gious. The way you are with the children in your care determines how they are.

Unfortunately, babies don't arrive with a manual telling you how to look after them and fix them if things go wrong. Definitely no stan-dard model exists and parenting is a continuous process during which you and your child continue to learn from each other.

This chapter will resonate if you have a role as parent, guardian, grandparent, aunt or uncle, caregiver, or any close relationship with a little person. As you support the younger generation, you know that you're making a difference in this world and you can leave a legacy beyond your life that can continue on through generations. So a very rewarding alignment exists with your own sense of purpose too.

In this chapter, you find out what you can do to build a child's con-fidence to go out in the world and be the best they can be.

Securing the Foundations

The definition of confident children is the junior version of adult confidence. Back in Chapter 1, we define confidence as 'your abil-ity to take appropriate and effective action no matter how you are feeling right now'. Confident kids have what it takes to get up and do something they find a challenge. They're willing to have a go and make a stance. They're motivated by learning and discovery.

They may be quietly confident as well as out on the stage perform-ing to an audience with panache.

With a child's life ahead of them, you have the chance to help create the conditions and support systems around them that lay the foundations for fulfilling their potential later in life.

The first thing to realise is that every parent brings up their chil-dren differently – and that's okay. No one model is perfect and fits all scenarios. Seeking perfection in child rearing is a definite 'no go'.

You have the opportunity to lay the foundations for confidence with your children every day. And even if you don't have daily con-tact with children, you can support your friends and family in this important role. Here's how:

In Chapter 1 we introduced you to the confidence indicators, the various dimensions that are important in developing confidence. By taking on board some of the suggestions in Table 17-1, you can play a part in helping children to build these skills from a young age. When you do that, you set them on the road with a foundation that will serve them well into their adult lives. The table has sug-gestions as to what you can say and do to boost each confidence indicator. As this becomes a habitual way of behaving with your children, you strengthen their skills day by day.

Table 17-1	Encouraging Confidence
Confidence Indicator	What You Can Say and Do to Boost This Indicator
Direction and values	Talk about future possibilities and encourage bold dreams. Keep their expectations high about what is possible.
Motivation	Acknowledge all the things they do well. Celebrate successes as they work towards a target.
Emotional stability	Encourage them to get in touch with their emotions from a young age, and to tell you what makes them happy or not at the end of each day.
Positive mind-set	Help them to find the good in a difficult situation and in other people. Make sure they know how to smile!
Self-awareness	Encourage them to be proud of what they are good at and at the same time notice the impact they have on people around them.

Confidence Indicator	What You Can Say and Do to Boost This Indicator
Flexibility in behaviour	Show them how to break habits and patterns by being spontaneous, rather than always doing things in the same way. Announce a surprise trip to an exhibition or picnic in a garden.
Eagerness to discover and develop	Invite them to be inquisitive about how everyday things work, such as the car or vacuum cleaner. Encourage them to notice the natural world around them, from the cloud formation to steam from the kettle. Ask them what they have found out about a situation and what they will do to keep discovering.
Health and energy	Teach good eating and exercise habits from a young age. Set an example yourself by walking or cycling rather than always going by car or bus. Help them to make healthy food choices and avoid junk food rewards.
Willingness to take risks	Encourage them to have a go at things they are fearful of, such as speaking or performing to a group. Allow them to experience a new sport or go on a trip without you.
A sense of purpose	Talk about the world beyond their own home or family, share stories of inspiring people who have made a contribution and difference in the world – whether famous explorers, discoverers, humanitarians. Invite them to consider what they can contribute in their lives.

Being fast to praise

Why is praise important? In our society, the tendency is to be fast to criticise and slow to praise. In certain cultures, it is normal to undersell your talents, and be exceptionally humble and modest about what you are good at. Yet in the bigger picture, thinking small does not do you or the world at large any favours.

Confident children thrive on praise. So get into the habit of celebrating success, for simply having a go as well as amazing results, so they can bask in the warmth of your encouragement at every step they take. This spurs them to carry on with what they do best. When you praise kids (and this applies to adults too) for their strengths, just notice how the faults naturally fall away and become less of a problem.

Power of praise

As a reluctant swimmer, Gupti struggled through her weekly swimming lessons. Tears and terrified screams pierced the air of the local swimming pool. At the end of her first term of lessons, she was presented with a certificate for being the bravest and most improved swimmer. This praise clicked her into action. Next term she ran along happily to her lessons, and from there, no one could restrain her enthusiasm. Today she's part of a synchronised swimming team.

Make your praise very specific. If you say 'you were great', the statement is too general and does not help your child repeat a useful behaviour.

School parents' evenings give parents a very brief synopsis of a child's progress over a year, and the enthusiastic parent who wants their child to do well can come home late in the evening and unintentionally demolish their child's confidence after a year of hard work with speedy comments like: 'You've fallen behind this year. Time to pull your socks up and concentrate more in class.' Instead, try nourishing your child with a *feedback sandwich*. To build such a sandwich, follow these steps:

1. **Tell your son or daughter two specific things that they are doing well.**

2. **Suggest two specific things that they can do even better.**

3. **Finish on a high with a positive overall comment.**

So a fly on the wall listening to your conversation might overhear something like:

> 'First of all, we heard that you've done exceptionally well in your Shakespeare criticism, and worked hard to get your Spanish coursework complete. Secondly, in order to get more fluent, you need to make absolutely sure you've learnt the vocabulary thoroughly and you practise your oral test with Señora Jerez every Monday. Overall, we're really pleased with the way you've volunteered to mentor the younger girls this year with such enthusiasm.'

Setting safe boundaries

We live in a world with both dangers and exciting opportunities. Sometimes these present choices that are confusing for your child and for you.

Having a certain structure of boundaries and family rules help children feel safe to explore healthily. This doesn't mean that you need to run your home with the discipline of a Victorian housekeeper. It's more about a consistently safe approach that everyone understands. Think about boundaries as a safety harness on a trapeze artist. You wouldn't want to fly until you knew your capability, and as you get more competent you can relax certain safety aspects.

 Your inability to say 'no' to your child doesn't do anyone any favours. 'No' can be the kindest and most important word your child hears from you. Sometimes your child really wants to hear you say 'no', because they don't want to be the one to say it to their friends.

Know what's really important and when you want to be flexible. The standards you set need to be right for you and your family. Don't try to measure up against everyone else.

 You can't protect children from all the risks and dangers in the world, and you will not be around forever. Your best tactic is to give children the tools they can use to protect themselves.

 We list some ideas that can help you to ride the 'ups and downs' of family battles. Your aim should be to give children the freedom to explore and develop their own sense of responsibility while the adults enjoy peace of mind.

- ✔ **Design a family charter.** Talk to your children about safety rules – where they can go, with whom and when, and how they should let you know – and draw up a simple sheet together about what is acceptable. You can post this on the fridge and get everyone to sign up to it.

- ✔ **Anticipate what is coming up and buy yourself time to make decisions.** Set the expectation that you will not make snap decisions for permission for a particular trip or activity until you have sufficient safety information.

- ✔ **Present a united adult front.** If one parent is known to be easy going and the other strict, have an agreement between the adults to have a consistent policy where your child is concerned so that your child knows where they stand.

- ✔ **Acknowledge your own fears.** Some adults are compulsive worriers. Check that you are basing your decisions on facts, not fantasy, to avoid instilling unnecessary fears in your child.

Helping Children Develop Curiosity

The best lessons you learn in life, the ones you take on board, are through your own experience rather than through accepting somebody else's word for it. Einstein said: 'I never teach my pupils; I only attempt to provide the conditions in which they can learn.'

Developing curiosity in your children is the key to unlocking discovery, one of ten key indicators of confidence.

Providing a helpful environment

Socrates said: 'Education is the kindling of a flame, not the filling of a vessel.' Some years later in the early twentieth century, the Italian Maria Montessori pioneered an educational movement that continues to inform educationalists today. Her system is all about providing the right learning environment for each child rather than forcing the standard 'chalk and talk' teaching, telling, and learning by rote on all children. Montessori's system is on the theme of 'Help me to do it by myself'.

Find ways to encourage the children in your life to be inquisitive and independent. For example, let the little ones polish shoes and mirrors with real polish. You can find toys with buttons and button holes and laces to tie so that their early learning relates to the real skills of doing up buttons on clothing and tying shoe laces.

The curious tale of the hairbrush in the mornings

Brinley has had the good fortune to have two bites at the child-rearing cherry: first with his older, grown-up son and daughter and now with two younger little girls.

What lessons does he have to offer after all these years? As a more mature, laid-back father, his approach is to stay calm and curious as his young daughter emerges, hair unbrushed, and not ready for school as the clock ticks away.

He says: 'The approach I've learnt over the years is to ask rather than tell. So I could tell (or even yell at) her: "Just go and brush your hair", which is the first gut reaction. However, I aim to stop and ask instead: "So how is it you've got to 8.30 again today and you're not ready?" I've found that by posing questions in place of answers to my children, they come up with their own solutions, which are often far better than any I can think of for them.'

In the Montessori way, children are encouraged to take one activity from a cupboard, place it on a mat and concentrate on that activity until they have completed it. Part of the game is to put it away when they finish and before they get something else out – certainly a skill many untidy adults could master!

Remember – scale is important. Try setting up low shelves and hooks where your child can have their own miniature version of adult equipment. They will gain a sense of pride and responsibility for looking after their belongings, which is an important confidence booster, rather than always having to be dependent on an adult to do things for them.

Encouraging a space to play

What will your children remember most about their childhood? Hopefully, their memories will be full of happy and carefree days. Ideally childhood is the time that you can look back on nostalgically as a time when you had space to play.

Notice what comes to mind when you think of 'play'. For example, is it about creativity, experimenting, fun and laughter, fooling around, games, freedom, choices, making a mess, following rules, and sometimes breaking the rules?

Rousseau said, 'The world of reality has its limits: The world of imagination is boundless.' Play develops the imagination within a powerful learning space. One of the most important gifts to your child's confidence is providing the space and encouraging them to use it. Through play your child develops a number of skills, from self-expression, problem solving, and communication with others through to mastering rules and relaxation. Play allows the space to experiment, stretch, and gain mastery over overwhelming emotions – to act out aggression and fear as well as to express feelings of joy and concern for others.

Many affluent kids miss out on the opportunity to play for play's sake because they are constantly ferried from one organised activity to the next. Make sure you allow time for your kids to play actively rather than them just lolling in front of the telly or film. Invite them to cook and play in the kitchen rather than throwing in a pizza because it seems easier.

To keep play alive in your life, use these tips:

✔ Set aside times each week for playing games and doing creative activities as a family. Make time when you ban work for everyone.

✔ Allow each child a play space of their own, and as soon as they are old enough, make them responsible for looking after it.

✔ Build up a creative cupboard indoors stocked with pens, papers, glue, paint, fabrics, wools and threads, scissors, and so on.

✔ If you have outdoor space, allocate areas for games and messy activities with soil, sand, and water.

✔ Make all the cleaning up part of the game and everyone who plays takes part.

You can play this game as a family, or with a group of children. (It also works well in business for brainstorming workshops.) First, save all your glossy magazines with pictures. To play the game, have everyone grab a pile of magazines and give them five minutes to tear out any picture that appeals to them. Now pick a theme, such as 'In my wildest dreams' or 'When I grow up'. Each person then glues their pictures onto a large sheet of newspaper to form a story collage to share with the rest of the group.

Championing Your Children

An old proverb says: 'Parents hold their children's hands a while and their hearts forever.' When you champion a child, you hold all aspects of them dear to you. You see and sponsor them as people, in their own names, and in their own right. Championing allows your children to change, to develop, and to grow. Children need and deserve your sponsorship.

Seven ways to champion a child:

1. **Tell them that they are unique, important, and special.**

2. **Provide any experiences you can for them that bring out the best in them, that help them develop their sense of purpose.**

3. **Find out what they really want to have happen so that they can express themselves and their dreams, knowing that these will not be the same as your dreams.**

4. **Support them and their needs in any way you can. The more support they have, the bigger the challenges they can face.**

5. **Listen at a deeper level to get beneath the surface statements they make to find out what is really going on for them.**

6. **Tell them how much you believe in them and their potential, especially when they have trouble seeing it for themselves.**

7. **Give them the encouragement to keep going when they feel like giving up.**

Championing is not about fighting their battles for them, or taking the responsibility. It's about being there in a support role for them through good and bad times. You're there when they're frustrated little two year olds learning how to share toys with a playmate as much as when they face up to failing a driving test or rejection from their first girl- or boyfriend.

Accepting the Differences Between You

An international management guru spoke on a radio show about his daughter's new business and bemoaned the fact that she wouldn't take his professional advice even though he could spot some serious errors in her plan. It was a good lesson that no matter who you are, how famous or experienced, your kids don't always want your advice.

Your children aren't mini versions of you. From the moment a child is born, they have a mind of their own that you will never be able to control. The art is to recognise that they will almost certainly take the core values and principles that you instil in them over the years – of honesty, generosity, respect for others, and so on – but they will test out those principles and live them in their own way.

What do you do if your child hits a time when they don't want to join in with the family? Give them space and an open door to come back. Make sure they are safe and know the homeward journey. Ride the tricky moments with the most flexibility you can muster – it pays off in the long term. However tough it seems at the time, keep the lines of communication open. Use regular get-togethers, phone calls, notes, emails, cards, or whatever it takes to keep talking as they get older.

Every family has its introverts and extraverts. And being an extravert is not the same as having confidence. Introverts need more quiet time to reflect and recharge their batteries, while extraverts draw their energy from being out and about with others. Honour your child's preferred style.

Respect their hobbies and interests. Not every child wants to be dragged onto the football pitch when they want to read or paint model soldiers. Nor does another child want to stay in with you quietly when they could join a boisterous game or bike ride outside.

As they go through life, aim to find out what your child needs to do their best – and support them to learn in that way, rather than the way you do it, recognising that methods are not the same as when you were at school.

Finally, remember a time will come later in life when your roles reverse as you become elderly and they are the responsible adults. Then you can grow old disgracefully, leaving the younger generation to top up your pension! So above all, enjoy raising your confident children knowing that you are doing the most worthwhile job you'll ever have.

Part VI
The Part of Tens

ATTEMPTING TO REDUCE THE ANXIETY IN HIS LIFE, WALDO "WHIP" GUNSCHOTT GOES FROM BEING A WILD ANIMAL TRAINER, TO A WILD BALLOON ANIMAL TRAINER.

In this part...

Stop by here whenever you want a quick fix of confidence inspiration. These chapters offer a set of questions to ask yourself when you need to get up and going; reminders of what you can do day by day to build your confidence; and affirmations to plant deep in your unconscious.

Chapter 18

Ten Great Questions to Spur You into Action

In This Chapter
▶ Being your own best critic
▶ Releasing your inner dreamer
▶ Noticing the tensions in your way

Confidence is about taking the action to realise your dreams. These questions are meant to get you up and out there being your most confident self.

How Does Your Inner Voice Speak to You?

An inner dialogue goes on inside you all the time. Even as you read this question, you may be asking yourself: 'What does this mean? How does my voice speak to me?' Your inner voice tries to make sense of the question.

What kind of voice do you have inside – a nurturing and pleasant one, or a miserable and grumpy critic who's too hard to please? Do you hear: 'Well done, me. That was a good conversation I had there. Things are going well and I'm on track.' Or is it more: 'There I go again, putting my foot in it, what a silly oaf. What did I do that for? I'll never be any good at this, will I?'

Remember that the quality of your thoughts dictates the quality of your confident action. If you look after yourself from the inside, you're on track for confident action on the outside.

Start tuning into the inner dialogue in your head. If you hear it running you down and being highly critical, then practice replying with some positive phrases like: 'I did my best there' or 'I can learn from this' or even 'Hey ho, it's time to let that one go.'

Are You Proud of Your Name?

Have you ever received a call that goes like this: 'Sorry to bother you, but . . . I've been asked to talk to you about X, Y, Z.' When no name is used, no sense of identity occurs.

Always lead with your name before you state your business: 'Hello, I'm . . . and I'd like to talk to you about X, Y, Z.' Volunteer your name, look directly at the person, and state your name with a smile whenever you introduce yourself. Even when you're speaking on the phone and can't see the other person, stay smiling and imagining their face, and the energy will come through – you really can 'hear' a smile over the telephone.

When you're proud of who you are, others value you more. Set the expectation that you are a person of worth who it is worth connecting with.

Who Do You Hang Out With?

Choose your friends wisely. Do the people you spend time with pull you up or push you down? First make sure you fire toxic friends – those who drain your energy and enthusiasm, leaving you wilting and exhausted.

In their place, find people who are good role models for you – who demonstrate a quality that you'd like more of. Discover all you can about how they got to where they are. Tap into their sense of confidence and share it – they have plenty to go round. When you find someone who has conquered the fears you want to let go of, use them as a role model of success.

What's Your Confident Thought for the Day?

For many years now, the British BBC Radio 4 *Today* programme has offered a Thought for the Day slot. During this three-minute slot, unedited by the programme's producers, an eminent thinker or theologian has the chance to air their words of wisdom. The speakers pose moral questions to the listener on a theme that links to a topical item in current affairs.

It's your turn now. Imagine you have a three-minute slot on the radio to give your confident thought for the day. If you had a chance to share your wisdom with the nation on how it should act with confidence, what would your message be?

Where Are the Tensions in Your Life?

Every day you make choices and decisions on how to spend your time. There are things you say 'yes' to and things you say 'no' to. All of this creates fundamental tension, balancing and getting the balance adjusted in the best way for you. You may be juggling challenges such as:

- ✔ **Your health versus your wealth:** Perhaps you're working very hard to earn money, but that's not leaving you time to look after your health.

- ✔ **Your family and work life:** Perhaps family commitments are preventing you from doing the kind of work you want, or you have a job where you are travelling and not able to be with your family as much as you wish.

- ✔ **Time for yourself and time for other people:** Maybe you spend so much time looking after others you have no time for yourself, or vice versa.

- ✔ **Spontaneity today or planning for tomorrow:** You want to enjoy the moment and also plan for the future.

Look at the tensions you face up to every day in your life. By exploring the pluses and minuses you face, you can then ask yourself: 'What is the right answer – even if it's not easy to carry out?' Make changes so that you go with what you consider is *right* rather than what you feel is the *easiest* option. Chapter 5 helps you identify your core values.

What's Your Sticking Point?

One area in your life may keep cropping up as something to sort out, but you never quite get round to it. You know it's important, but it never quite happens. Maybe it's making time to nurture a significant relationship, to get your weight to a healthy figure on the scales, or your bank balance or home in order.

Allow yourself to uncover all the positive benefits you will enjoy when you've cracked this one. Consider all the other things in your life where you'll feel happier and more confident as a result.

Once you crack this one, you will release energy for other things in your life to take off. What are you waiting for? What's the first step? Just get on with it . . . today.

Who Are You Going to Be When You Grow Up?

When you were young, you may have had thoughts of who you were going to be when you grew up. Most people don't manage to make it as a ballet dancer, film star, or astronaut. Today you may have a more regular kind of job or life – a builder, a banker, or a bakery assistant. By facing reality and responsibility, you stop considering who you are and what you can become. You may be selling yourself short and limiting yourself by a lack of imagination and willingness to be open to new possibilities.

Allow yourself to consider who you really want to be for a while, and notice as you do so what symbol or image comes to you. Holding that symbol in front of you, follow it and see where it leads you. Then figure out how to take some of the first steps on the way to becoming who you really want to be. (Turn to Chapter 15 for tips on discovering your life's work.)

How Do You Experience Failures and Mistakes?

Confident people regard failures and mistakes as necessary stepping stones on the journey through life. Rejection is just another hoop to get through on the way onward and upward. Like the character of Tigger in the Winnie the Pooh stories, these people bounce back for more whenever they get brushed off.

As great inventors and scientists know, it takes persistence to succeed. Each time experiment doesn't work out, they take another look at the painstaking records of every detail of their experiments, make adjustments, and try again.

Winners toughen up their skin and succeed by viewing failure as a temporary inconvenience and a step in the direction of achieving their goals.

After any rejection, take stock and remind yourself of your VAT factor – V is for Values, the things important to you that help guide your choices and decisions; A is for Aims, your goals, the things you want to achieve, and T is for talents, all those qualities of excellence you have. Chapter 15 has a section on dealing with rejection confidently.

How Do You Balance Time Alone and Time with Others?

A mark of a confident person is that they are at ease in the company of others, but equally content with their own company. In particular, they can spend time alone without constantly seeking to have people buzzing around them. Time alone is necessary to replenish your sense of calmness, centring, and comfort in being who you are.

If you feel that your confidence is waning, check that you have had space for yourself to regain your personal balance, and you are not overwhelmed with the demands and distractions of being with other people. You need to get centred in order to take effective action.

What's Your 120 per cent Dream?

How often do you allow yourself to dream about what you can become or what your life can really, really be like? Maybe you had ambitious dreams for yourself when you were young and then life got in the way? But what about having a 120 per cent dream – a dream beyond the dream, something that's so exciting and so enticing that you can't fail to want it and move towards it?

Make it a big dream, a goal that really motivates you. Write it down in as much detail as you can, really getting into how it will look and feel when you've achieved it. Every day go and review it and take one action, implement one daily habit, however tiny, that takes you closer to your 120 per cent dream. At the same time, let go of one negative action or thought that gets in the way of your success.

Chapter 19

Ten Daily Habits to Raise Your Confidence

● ●

In This Chapter

▶ Finding easy ways to build your confidence muscles

▶ Starting the day in the best way

▶ Getting in tune with yourself

▶ Working out what's best for you

● ●

*B*uilding your confidence doesn't happen overnight, it's more of a drip-feed activity that starts with the things you do every day. Habits have a way of repeating themselves, so get into good habits and you'll be off to a flying start.

Start Each Day Alert and Ready for Action

'Early to bed and early to rise, makes a man healthy, wealthy, and wise' according to Benjamin Franklin. You have 168 hours in a week, and you're likely to spend about a third of those hours in bed. It's your choice as to how you create the quality of the remaining two-thirds of each day.

Do you ever have those days when the alarm goes off, you put it on the snooze feature, it goes off again, and again, and you eventually turn it off or hide it under the pillow? How does your day pan out when you get up late and head out of the door in a manic rush? Just notice, though, what happens when you have a calm and relaxed start to the day, when you have got out of bed at a reasonable hour and then take things in your stride.

Confident people love life so much that they don't want to waste a minute of it. Start your day 'on the front foot', that is, ready and prepared to proactively engage with the day and you won't waste the rest of it trying to catch up with yourself.

Concentrate Your Mind on the Page

Studies in the workplace show that it takes up to 15 minutes to get your concentration back after a phone call. Just a few interruptions and your day drifts aimlessly away. You may not be a Zen meditator, but any drill that teaches you to stop your thoughts wandering and to arrive in the 'here and now' pays dividends.

Writing pages is a useful concentration habit to develop. This is all you need to do:

Take three sides of paper – A4 size or smaller if you prefer. Write whatever comes into your head. There is no right or wrong way to write, you don't need to feel inspired by great creative verses. Just write anything, it's strictly stream of consciousness stuff: 'Hello blank pages, I haven't a clue what to write, but I'm writing anyway.' Continue until you have filled the pages. As if by magic, something useful emerges from the page. Some people write such pages every day; others write them as and when they feel the need.

The discipline of writing your thoughts on a blank page acts as an invaluable brain dump in the morning to quieten the busy and logical part of your mind and get you centred and creative.

Put Your Best Sunglasses On

Imagine if you had got up this morning and put on a pair of rose-coloured sunglasses. You'd be travelling through your day armed with a warm, healthy glow. Everybody and everything you see would take on a pinky hue. In a way, every day you do put on a pair of sunglasses. They act as a filter through which you perceive the world. It's just that you may not be aware of what type of filter you have chosen.

By choosing your sunglasses for the day, you decide how to frame your experiences that day. You decide if it is going to be a day that is rich and precious, full of interesting experiences, or one of constant battles to be fought. Your experience begins in your own head. As you start each day, decide which sort of glasses you're wearing.

As examples, here are some to try on for size: My glasses for today will be . . . savour each moment to the full . . . look for the best in the situation . . . find the humour in unlikely situations and people . . . enjoy the sounds/aromas/tastes around me.

Track Your Moods and Emotions

How are you today emotionally? Do you know how you feel and how you feel it? Emotionally intelligent people have a high level of awareness – they stay in tune with how they're feeling and the effect they have on other people.

Do a stock check during the day and begin to notice what's going on inside you. When do you feel confident and when not? How do you know what you're feeling – what are the telltale signals in your body? How do other people around you know what you're thinking – is it written on your face or conveyed by the tone of your voice or your behaviour? By tracking your moods, you have a measure of where you are at in case you need to refine the direction. (Chapter 6 shows you how to make friends with your emotions.)

Exercise Your Body

Strange as it seems, you can go to the gym feeling tired, exercise, and come away feeling energised. Your brain loves exercise. In the past few years, researchers have contradicted the commonly held belief that you're born with a fixed number of neurons and produce no more during your lifetime. Even adults can grow new brain cells, and exercise is one of the best ways to achieve this.

The good news is that exercise doesn't have to be too vigorous. Just walking sedately for half an hour a day improves your scores on abilities such as learning, concentration, and abstract reasoning. Senior citizens who walk regularly perform better on memory tests than their counterparts who sit around more. Likewise it's been found that schoolchildren aged 10 and 11 who exercise three or four times a week get higher than average exam grades.

Find a form of exercise that you enjoy and do it regularly.

Take Quiet Moments Alone

How are you with the power of silence? If you're used to rushing around and being with people non-stop, then taking ten minutes to sit quietly alone may be an enlightening experience.

So try this every single day: Switch off your phone, your door bell, your computer, your TV, and your radio. Go to a place where no one and nothing will disturb you. Sit there quietly without talking or interruption for ten minutes. Allow yourself to dream while you are free of internal chatter and noise. Just empty your mind, experience the space, and let the creativity unfold.

Go Outside and Wonder at the Beauty of the Sky

Remember, a whole world lies outside your door. Take time each day to get out there and stop to notice the natural world, the passing of the seasons, the changing patterns in the sky.

Notice how you are part of something so much bigger than you and your immediate environment and enjoy the beauty of it all. Even if you live in a big city, it's free and fun to go barefoot in the park.

Operate from a Position of Generosity

What goes round comes round. Whatever you give out has a habit of coming back to you in some way or another. Confident people act from a position of generosity and abundance. They give what they can, when they can – whether it's their time, talent, money, energy, or love.

Aim to give to others and remember to give to yourself too. Generous thoughts nurture your mind and attract generous people to you.

Review Today and Create Your Tomorrow

At the end of each day, mentally review what happened and how you experienced it. Perhaps the day worked out pretty much as planned but you didn't get as much done as you thought you would. You can learn from this; perhaps you habitually give yourself too much to do.

Every night before you turn out the light, write down the five most important things you want to do tomorrow. They can be anything at all, but make sure they are the important things and the ones that fit with your values. While you sleep your unconscious mind will be working out for you how you can achieve them most easily.

In the morning, before you get out of bed, take your list and decide how you to fit the tasks and activities into your day. If it looks a tight fit, start with the most important and leave out the least important.

You now have a day's schedule that should ensure you stay focused.

Connect with Your Life Purpose

If you were to ask yourself right now 'Why am I alive? What's my life about?' you may not have an instant answer. With a little probing, you would soon arrive at something along the lines of: 'I want to make a difference. I want to make the world a better place. I want to create love, joy, magic, harmony, peace, and so on. I want to be an example to others. I want to live a good life.' (Chapter 5 guides you toward uncovering your values.)

Your confident action is based on the meaning you make of what happens for you day by day, year by year. This is why the way you experience confidence is so different from the person next to you. No one can give you the magic confidence pill to take and make everything wonderful for you. You need to find the confidence for yourself.

As you accept that you are responsible for your own journey, you find more clarity and freedom, and thus confidence to be yourself and do what is right for you. As you travel through each day, hold the bigger picture of your life and make sure that what you are doing now fits well with the bigger picture. Then you can simply enjoy being alive, knowing that you are being your most confident self.

Chapter 20

Ten Keys to Effective Affirmations

. . . .

In This Chapter

▶ Understanding the place of affirmations

▶ Creating your personal set

▶ Using them every day

. . . .

*Y*ou cannot control everything that happens to you, but you can influence the meaning you make of life's events and create a world that better suits and supports you. Your experience of life does not simply impose itself on you without your consent.

Every chapter in this book offers you insights and tools to help you reform and recreate the reality of your life. Chapter 5 leads you to create a series of affirmations out of your rules for experiencing your values. In this chapter, you will find some of our favourite general affirmations, and simple instructions for creating your own.

An *affirmation* is a strong, positive statement about the world, *as you want to experience it*. An affirmation can strengthen your newborn sense of reality while it is still weak and tender and help prevent you from slipping back into your old patterns of thinking. You can use affirmations as a memory aid to your preferred new reality.

Building from the Right Structure

The structure of a good affirmation maximises its power and influence. You can create affirmations that meet these structural criteria by following ten simple rules:

1. **Describe the world as you *want* to experience it, not as you are experiencing it.**

   Examples: I have a wonderful new job. I have my ideal partner.

2. **Use the most positive way you can to express the affirmation; never use a negative construction.**

   Example: Rather than the negative 'I am no longer tired in the mornings' use the positive alternative, 'I wake up early every morning bursting with life and energy'.

3. **Always state an affirmation in the present tense, never in the future.**

   Example: I look wonderful and feel great (rather than I *will* look wonderful).

4. **Reinforce those feelings that you want to strengthen, don't use affirmations to destroy feelings that you don't want.**

   Example: 'I love the world and the world loves me' is far better than 'I couldn't care less about those negative ingrates who give me such a hard time'.

5. **Say or think the affirmations with emotional intensity, whether you really believe them yet or not.**

   Example: 'I am surrounded by abundance; nature is supporting me in every way'.

6. **Have the courage to create an alternative and new sense of reality. You don't have to deny your current reality.**

   Example: 'I have a full and rich life' works better than 'I have a million dollars in the bank'.

7. **Keep in mind that the shorter and more specific affirmations are, the more effective they are and the faster they become effective.**

   Example: "I'm a money-making machine" is more effective in getting you out and earning what you are worth than 'I am worthy of so much more, and I am finding the people and the projects that will enable me to earn much more money'.

8. **Always choose or invent affirmations that feel totally right for the way you want to experience reality.**

   Example: 'I can handle anything life throws at me'.

9. **Remember that your affirmations are about the way *you* want to perceive and experience the world. No one else has to approve or agree.**

   Example: 'Everyone I meet loves me just as much as they are able'.

10. **Use an affirmation as long as it suits you. Affirmations are for now, not forever. You can change your affirmations whenever and as often as you want.**

    Example: 'I have the best role in this company'.

Ten of Brinley's favourite affirmations:

1. I feel the magic in life every day.
2. I am brave and confident.
3. I trust myself and others trust me.
4. I will risk making mistakes.
5. I know my mind and will always stand up for my beliefs.
6. I can handle the situations in my life.
7. I live a charmed life.
8. I'm in charge and I decide.
9. My life is an adventure.
10. I am surrounded by love and abundance.

Ten of Kate's favourite affirmations:

1. My life is rich and precious.
2. I begin the day with free-flowing energy and health.
3. I am following the 120 per cent dream.
4. I create joy, harmony, and understanding by my actions.
5. I can risk without knowing the result.
6. Change comes from my heart.
7. I can fly when I take things lightly.
8. I have a powerful impact on those around me.
9. I can find the magic in the most difficult moments.
10. I'm the best I can be and that's enough.

Using Affirmations Every Day

The traditional way of using affirmations is to repeat each of them aloud 10 to 20 times in a continuous session. The shower is a great place to do this, or in front of a mirror, or driving to work (bus or train is not quite so good). Also jogging, where the physical exercise and rhythm help to induce a trance-like state.

You can also write them out two or three times each, longhand is best, and as you write them notice if you are meeting any resistance to a particular word or if the phraseology seems to want to change. If it does, experiment with the new wording but go back to the old words if the new form doesn't stick to the rules outlined earlier in the chapter.

You can use affirmations with a partner, a friend, or colleagues who also want to practise their affirmations in public. When you say your affirmations to someone else, also have that person speak your affirmation back to you – 'Your life is an adventure, Brinley' – or have them confirm back to you that you are what you say – 'Yes, it is'.

The great thing about affirmations is they are quick and flexible and remarkably powerful in helping you to experience the world in a new way. Try them, and enjoy them.

Appendix

Resource List

● ●

*1*n this appendix, we put together a selection of resources to help you on your confident travels. This is not an exhaustive list, and you will find many other worthy people and organisations as your interest in your own development deepens.

Contact the Authors

Kate Burton, Creativity in Communication, phone (00 44) 01189 734590; e-mail:kate@kateburton.co.uk; Web site: www.kate burton.co.uk.

Brinley Platts, Networks in Harmony, phone (00 44) 07973 745640; e-mail: brinley.platts@btinternet.com; Web site www. networksinharmony.com

Books

When you've finished reading through this book (and reading through a second time, to get your money's worth!), we recommend hunting down the following books to help build your confidence even further.

Meditation For Dummies by Stephan Bodian (Wiley)

Energy and Well Being Pocketbook by Gillian Burn (Management Pocketbooks)

Neuro-Linguistic Programming For Dummies by Romilla Ready and Kate Burton (Wiley)

Test Your Emotional Intelligence by Jill Dann (Hodder and Stoughton)

Sedona Method by Hale Dwoskin (Element Books)

You'll See It When You Believe It by Wayne Dyer (Arrow)

The Art of Loving by Eric Fromm (Thorsons)

The Inner Game of Tennis by Tim Gallwey (Pan)

Emotional Intelligence by Daniel Goleman (Bloomsbury)

In Praise of Slow by Carl Honore (Orion)

Time to Think by Nancy Kline (Ward Lock)

The Farther Reaches of Human Nature by A.H. Maslow (Penguin)

Unlimited Power by Anthony Robbins (Ballantine Books)

The Book of Luck by Heather Summers and Anne Watson (Capstone)

The Naked Leader by David Taylor (Capstone)

The Power of Now by Eckart Tolle (Hodder and Stoughton)

Training and Coaching Web Sites

The following organisations may be helpful if you're interested in receiving training or coaching on building your confidence and related areas. Either contact the authors directly or take a look at the following Web sites.

The Art of Intuition www.artofintuition.co.uk: Offering workshops for developing your intuition.

Bring Yourself to Work www.bringyourselftowork.com: This campaign is working to transform attitudes towards work. The site offers encouragement and personal development designed to help you become your authentic, confident self at work.

International Coaching Partnership www.international-coaching.com: An international group of trained professional coaches who offer one to one coaching by phone and in person.

Luck Seminars www.switchtosuccess.com: Workshops for making your own luck.

Ready Solutions www.readysolutionsgroup.com: Find information on stress-management and relationship-management workshops here.

Yoga www.samraoyoga.com: Provides information on yoga retreats and holidays plus corporate mind/body balancing awaydays here.

Your Most Confident Self www.yourmostconfidentself.com: The authors' Web site that offers a continually developing range of confidence-building events, one-to-one coaching, CDs, and additional confidence analytics and tools.

Watercress www.watercress.uk.com: Watercress offers custombuilt training in confident communication skills for business groups.

Professional Bodies

If you decide to hire a coach or therapist to work with you on a one-to-one basis, always check out their professional qualifications, experience, and code of ethics. The following organisations can help you.

British Association for Counselling and Psychotherapy (BACP) BACP House, 35-37 Albert Street, Rugby, Warks CV21 2SG; phone: 0870 443 5252; Web site: bacp.co.uk

The General Hypnotherapy Register (GHR) (the administrating agency for The General Hypnotherapy Standards Council) PO Box 204, Lymington, SO41 6WP; phone/fax: 01590 683770; Web site: www.general-hypnotherapy-register.com

International Coach Federation at www.coachfederation.org

UK Council for Pyschotherapy 167-169 Great Portland St., London, W1W 5PF; phone: 020 7436 3002; Web site: ukcp.org.uk

Index

• A •

accent, 154–155
acceptance
  identity development, 73
  romantic relationships, 209
accessories, 171
achievement
  acknowledgment, 114–115
  confidence benefits, 11
  generosity to self, 113–114
  motivation at work, 56, 61
  perfection expectations, 112
  work, 200–201
action
  acknowledgment of risk, 24
  complaint versus criticism, 83–84
  daily habit, 237–238
  fear, 108
  feedback guidelines, 196
  flow state, 106
  guaranteed success formula, 43–44
  intention setting, 23–24
  karma, 139
  negative memories, 77
  passion, 95–99
  power, 140–142
  preparation, 23
  SMART model, 41–43
  time requirements, 12
  to–do list, 33
  work achievements, 201
advancement, work, 56, 61–62
affirmation
  definition, 243
  examples, 243–246
  values experiences, 69
  values in daily life, 70
aggression
  versus assertiveness, 176–177
  workplace bullies, 192–194
aging, 149, 234

Alcoholics Anonymous (support
    group), 43
alone time, 235, 240
anger, 83–84
animal, 84
annual appraisal, 200
anticipation, 178
anxiety
  authentic living, 74
  confidence benefits, 11
  cure, 130
  danger signs, 81
  definition, 130
  disorder, 130–131
  distortion of reality, 26
  flow state, 106
  health effects, 81
  hierarchy of needs, 53
  life-work balance, 32–33
  social situations, 53–55
  versus apprehension, 130
  workplace change, 202
appearance
  first impression, 165–166
  judgements, 163–165
  overview, 163
  style, 167–172
apprehension, 130
Armstrong, Lance (athlete), 45
aroma, 147
aromatherapy, 133
art, 147
Art of Intuition (self-improvement
    organisation), 82, 248
The Art of Loving (Fromm), 248
assertiveness
  daily living, 176–179
  work, 188–189
assessment
  clothing, 169–170
  confidence, 12–17, 40–41
  congruence, 91

assessment *(continued)*
daily life, 241
emotional intelligence, 76
exhaustion, 35–37
love strategy, 216
motivation, 58–60
negative emotions, 34–37
romance, 206–207
success, 136
tough times, 29–30
toxic environment, 35–37
work achievements, 200
association, 215
assumption, personal, 31
attainability, 42
attentiveness, 55
audience, 161, 191
Auschwitz (Nazi death camp), 14
authentic living
body posture, 161–162
conversations, 159–160
daily life, 71–74
autobiography, 44, 45

• B •

baseline state, 80
basic need, 52
beard, 163
behaviour
blame exercise, 27
characteristics of confidence, 11
childhood patterns, 27–28
emotional drive, 65
guaranteed success formula, 43–44
hierarchy of needs, 53
indicators of confidence, 13
neurological levels, 90
social situations, 55
standards of perfection, 122–124
beliefs
definition, 90
health, 149–150
neurological levels, 90
in others, 10

Bennis, Warren (authority on
character-based leadership), 99
Bible (religious text), 139
bitterness, 84
blame, 27
blood sugar, 149
Bodian, Stephan (*Meditation For
Dummies*), 247
body clock, 143
body posture, 160–162, 203
body type, 170
book, 247–248
The Book of Luck (Summers and
Watson), 248
boss. *See also* work
feedback, 195–197
mistakes, 199
motivation at work, 56, 57–58
overview, 194–195
promise, 197–199
brain
mind–body connection, 144–145
research, 78
bread, 149
breathing
characteristics of confidence, 11
mind–body connection, 144–145
public speaking, 155–157
relaxation techniques, 132–133
Bring Yourself to Work (Web site),
248
British Association for Counselling
and Psychotherapy, 249
broadcasting, 154
brown rice, 149
Browning, Robert (poet), 111
bullying, 192–194
Burn, Gillian
body clock, 143
Energy and Well Being Pocketbook,
247
Burton, Kate (*Neuro-Linguistic
Programming For Dummies*), 247
business leader, 27, 99
business meeting. *See* meeting

busyness
  life-work balance, 32–33
  relaxation time, 119–122

• *C* •

cabbage, 149
calling, 96–97
capability, 90
carbon dioxide, 155
caring, 209
Cass Model, 72–74
Castaway: A Story of Survival (Irvine),
    137
celebration, 147
certainty, sense of, 68
championing, 226–227
change
  acknowledgment of risk, 24
  fear, 23
  flexibility, 178
  guaranteed success formula, 43–44
  others' resistance to new you,
      173–176
  romantic relationships, 216–217
  self as role model, 47–48
  SMART model, 41–43
  time requirements, 12
  work, 201–204
character-based leadership, 99
childhood
  causes of negative emotions, 26,
      27–29
  perfection, 112
  role changes, 27–29
children
  boundaries, 222–223
  confidence indicators, 220–221
  confidence level, 12
  curiosity, 224–226
  differences from parents, 227–228
  overview, 219–220
  parents as champions, 226–227
  perfection, 220
  play, 225–226

praise, 221–222
strength building, 22
chimp, 84
clarity, 155
clothing
  assessment, 169–170
  first impressions, 166–167
  judgement, 163–164
  shopping, 170–172
  style, 169
  work, 166–167, 168, 171
coach, 46, 248–249
cognitive behaviour therapy, 54
colour, 169
comfort zone
  expansion, 128–131
  limits, 127–128
  overview, 126
  price of success, 127
coming out, 72
commitment, 23–24, 202
communication. *See specific types*
company policy, 56
comparison, 73, 112
competence. *See specific types*
competition, 114
complaint, 83–84
computer, 43
concentration, 238
confidence
  assessment, 12–17, 40–41
  benefits, 9, 11, 24
  comparison exercise, 105
  definition, 1, 9–11
  loss, 25, 107
  wheel, 40–41
confusion, 72
congruence
  assessment, 91
  definition, 89
  neurological levels, 89–93
connection, 68, 69
consumerism, 95
conversation
  attentiveness, 55
  authenticity, 159–160
  integrity, 158–159

Cram, Steve (athlete), 74
creativity, 78
criminal, 85
criticism
   boss's feedback, 195–197
   others' resistance to new you, 175
   unhelpful assumptions, 31
   values in daily life, 71
   versus complaint, 83–84
   versus sponsorship, 22
   workplace bullying, 193
culture, 206–207
curiosity, 55, 224–226

• D •

daily life
   acknowledgment of achievements,
      114
   affirmations, 246
   assertiveness, 177–178
   assessment, 241
   authentic living, 71–74
   comfort zone expansion, 126–128
   confidence definition, 10–11
   flow state, 106
   necessary habits, 237–242
   others' resistance to new you,
      173–176
   passion into action, 95–99
   powerful living, 179–180
   preparedness, 178
   procrastination, 117–120
   stress effects, 146
   thought for the day, 232–233
   values, 69–71
Dann, Jill (Test Your Emotional
      Intelligence), 247
dating, 210–212
decision making, 216
delegation, 115–116
denial, 202
depression, 26, 146
description, of world, 26
dialect, 155
diaphragm, 155, 156–157

diction, 155
diet, 148–149, 169
Dilts, Robert (psychologist), 89–93
direction, life
   achievement at work, 61
   confidence wheel, 40–41
   guaranteed success formula, 43–44
   overview, 39
   self as role model, 47–48
   SMART model, 41–43
discipline, 223
dissatisfaction, 39
dissatisfier, 56–57
distraction, 32, 113, 238
doctor, 81
domestic chore
   delegation, 115–116
   procrastination, 116–120
   stress effects, 146
doubt, 94
drama, 208, 209
dream
   goal-setting preparation, 135–138
   ideal job, 186–187
   identification, 235
   passion, 94–95
   perfection expectations, 111, 112
   procrastination, 117–120
dress code, 166–167, 168
Dwoskin, Hale (Sedona Method), 247
Dyer, Wayne (You'll See It When You
      Believe It), 248

• E •

eagerness, 13
eating habits, 32–33
Edison, Thomas (inventor), 43
80/20 principle, 120–122, 169
embarrassment, 88, 128
emotional intelligence (EQ)
   assessment, 76
   book, 247
   empathy, 85
   overview, 76

Emotional Intelligence (Goleman), 76, 85, 248
emotions
  creativity, 78
  drive for behaviour, 65
  emotional intelligence, 76
  ends values, 65–66
  expression, 78, 79
  flow state, 106
  importance, 75–76
  indicators of confidence, 13
  intuition, 81–82
  mind–body connection, 144–145
  mood tracking, 79–81, 239
  romantic partner's needs, 213
  values conflicts, 66–67
  values in daily life, 70
  versus rational thoughts, 77
emotions, negative
  assessment, 34–37
  comfort zone expansion, 128
  control, 83–86
  danger signs, 81
  expulsion, 30–34
  health effects, 81
  identification, 233–234
  link to passion, 88
  passion drainers, 94
  passion into action, 97–98
  root issues, 26–30
empathy, 85–86
employment tribunal, 194
ends values, 65–66, 89
energy
  assessment, 35–37
  book, 247
  confident versus less confident
    people, 34–35
  conversion from anger, 83–84
  expulsion of negative feelings, 30
  mind–body connection, 144–145
  motivation at work, 56
  other people's needs, 37
  powerful living, 179–180
  procrastination, 116
  values conflicts, 66–67

Energy and Well Being Pocketbook (Burn), 247
entrepreneur, 27
environment
  children's curiosity, 224–225
  comfort zone, 126–131
  feel-good factors, 147
  neurological levels, 90
  toxic, 35–37
envy, 175
EQ (emotional intelligence)
  assessment, 76
  book, 247
  empathy, 85
  overview, 76
Estuary English (accent), 154
Event, Memory, Emotion, Knowledge, Action steps, 77
excellence, 113
exercise
  aging, 149
  feel-good factors, 147
  guidelines, 239
  habits, 145
  mind–body connection, 144
  necessity, 145
exhaustion
  assessment, 35–37
  confident versus less confident
    people, 34–35
exhilaration, 68
expectation
  children's boundaries, 223
  positive outcomes, 104–105
  self as role model, 46
experience, life
  cause of negative emotions, 29–30
  failures, 234–235
  flow state, 106
  good expectations, 104–105
  intensity, 87
  negative memories, 77
  neurological levels, 89–93
  optimism, 238–239
  peak times, 103–104

experimenting stage, 202
expert, 112–113
extrovert, 227–228

• F •

failure, 234–235
fairytale, 125
fake smile, 82
family
  confidence wheel, 40–41
  role change, 27–29
  rules, 223
  types of stress, 233
The Farther Reaches of Human Nature
    (Maslow), 248
fear
  action, 108
  authentic living, 74
  cause, 108–109
  change, 23
  children's boundaries, 223
  confidence benefits, 11
  link to passion, 88
  management, 106–109
  mental stretching, 129–131
  passion drainer, 94
  passion into action, 97–98
  public speaking, 153–154
  romantic relationships, 210–212
feedback
  assertiveness, 189
  boss's criticism, 195–197
  importance, 20
  praise for children, 222
  recognition of strengths and talents,
    20
  redirection of inner voices, 33–34
  self as role model, 48
feel-good factor, 147–148
feelings
  creativity, 78
  drive for behaviour, 65
  emotional intelligence, 76
  ends values, 65–66
  expression, 78, 79
  flow state, 106

importance, 75–76
indicators of confidence, 13
intuition, 81–82
mind–body connection, 144–145
mood tracking, 79–81, 239
romantic partner's needs, 213
values conflicts, 66–67
values in daily life, 70
versus rational thoughts, 77
feelings, negative
  assessment, 34–37
  comfort zone expansion, 128
  control, 83–86
  danger signs, 81
  expulsion, 30–34
  health effects, 81
  identification, 233–234
  link to passion, 88
  passion drainers, 94
  passion into action, 97–98
  root issues, 26–30
fight or flight response, 146
first impression, 165–166
flexibility
  blame exercise, 27
  discipline of children, 223
  indicators of confidence, 13
  perfection standards, 123–124
flow state, 105–106
forgiveness, 84, 85–86
Frankl, Victor E. (*Man's Search for
    Meaning*), 14
freedom, 124, 141
Freud, Sigmund (psychiatrist), 94–95
friend, 213–214, 232
Fromm, Eric (*The Art of Loving*), 248
future, 135–138

• G •

Gallwey, Tim (*The Inner Game of
    Tennis*), 248
game, 226
gay movement, 72
The General Hypnotherapy Register,
    249

generosity
  importance, 240
  to self, 113–114
gesture, 161
global social phobia, 54
goal setting
  confidence wheel, 41
  guaranteed success formula, 43–44
  perfection standards, 122–123
  preparation, 135–138
  procrastination, 117–120
  self as role model, 47–48
  SMART model, 41–43
  stress, 111
Goleman, Daniel (*Emotional
    Intelligence*), 76, 85, 248
grace, 140
greens, 149
grooming, 165–166
guaranteed success formula, 43–44,
    140–141

• *H* •

habit, 237–242
hair style, 165, 166
Halaby, Lisa (Queen Noor of Jordan),
    45
halo effect, 45
happiness, 63–64
harassment, 192
health
  beliefs, 149–150
  confidence level, 12
  definition, 145
  diet, 148–149
  effect of negative emotions, 81
  future self, 150
  indicators of confidence, 13
  life-work balance, 32–33
  panic attack, 131
  perfection effects, 113
  stress effects, 81, 145–148
  types of stress, 233
  values conflicts, 68–69
heart disease, 145

hemp seed oil, 148
hero, 46–48, 74
Herzberg, Frederick (theorist), 55–57
hierarchy of needs, 52–55
hobby, 228
holiday, 147
honesty, 160
Honore, Carl (*In Praise of Slow*), 248
human rights, 189
humiliation, 193
humour, 11, 209
hunger, 148
hypertension, 145

• *I* •

'I' statement, 177
identity
  creation, 234
  development, 72–74
  neurological levels, 90
  redundancy, 204
  work, 185–186
image. *See* appearance
image consultant, 168–169
imagination, 82, 225
In Praise of Slow (Honore), 248
informal dress, 167
The Inner Game of Tennis (Gallwey),
    248
inner voice
  intuition, 81–82
  overview, 231–232
  reason, 142
  redirection, 33–34
  self as role model, 48
integrity, 158–159, 198
intensity, 87
intention
  mood changes, 80
  redirection of inner voices, 33–34
  setting, 23–24
International Coach Federation, 249
International Coaching Partnership,
    248
interview, 203

introvert, 227–228
intuition, 81–82
Irvine, Lucy (*Castaway: A Story of Survival*), 137
The Islander (Kingsland), 137

• J •

jealousy, 84
job. *See also* boss
  achievements, 200–201
  assertiveness, 188–189
  bullying, 192–194
  change, 201–204
  clothing, 166–167, 168, 171
  comfort zone, 127, 129–131
  competencies, 189–190
  confidence wheel, 40–41
  delegation, 115–116
  energy assessment, 35–37
  expression of love, 78
  first impressions, 166–167
  hate for job, 184–185
  ideal job, 186–187
  interview, 203
  life-work balance, 32–33
  mental stretching, 129–131
  motivation, 55–62
  overview, 183–184
  price of success, 127
  procrastination, 116–120
  professional identity, 185–186
  relationship to, 61
  sense of self, 184, 185
  types of stress, 233
  unhelpful assumptions, 31
  values, 188
Joyce, James (*Ulysses*), 96
judgement, 163–165

• K •

karma, 139–140
key performance indicator (KPI), 136
Kingsland, Gerald (*The Islander*), 137

Kline, Nancy (*Time to Think*), 248
knowledge, 77

• L •

language, 46, 80
leadership role, 22, 99
left hemisphere, 78
lettuce, 149
life, daily
  acknowledgment of achievements, 114
  affirmations, 246
  assertiveness, 177–178
  assessment, 241
  authentic living, 71–74
  comfort zone expansion, 126–128
  confidence definition, 10–11
  flow state, 106
  necessary habits, 237–242
  others' resistance to new you, 173–176
  passion into action, 95–99
  powerful living, 179–180
  preparedness, 178
  procrastination, 117–120
  stress effects, 146
  thought for the day, 232–233
  values, 69–71
life direction
  achievement at work, 61
  confidence wheel, 40–41
  guaranteed success formula, 43–44
  overview, 39
  self as role model, 47–48
  SMART model, 41–43
life experience
  cause of negative emotions, 29–30
  failures, 234–235
  flow state, 106
  good expectations, 104–105
  intensity, 87
  negative memories, 77
  neurological levels, 89–93
  optimism, 238–239
  peak times, 103–104

life meaning
connection to, 241
indicators of confidence, 13
passion, 89, 94, 96–97
SMART model, 41–43
loneliness, 112
lost items, 32
love. *See also* relationship, romantic
expression, 78
generosity to self, 114
hierarchy of needs, 53
strategy, 214–216
Luck Seminars, 248

• *M* •

MacMillan, Harold (British Prime
Minister), 99
management style, 56, 57
manipulation, 192–194
Man's Search for Meaning (Frankl), 14
mantra, 144, 147
Maslow, Abraham (theorist)
*The Farther Reaches of Human
Nature*, 248
personal needs, 51–55
McGregor, Douglas (theorist), 55,
57–58
meaning, life
connection to, 241
indicators of confidence, 13
passion, 89, 94, 96–97
SMART model, 41–43
means values, 64, 65
measure, 42
meditation
book, 247
exercise, 120
mental stretching haven, 132–135
mind–body connection, 144
Meditation For Dummies (Bodian), 247
meeting
confidence benefits, 11
confidence definition, 10–11
power, 190–191

memory
emotional versus rational thought,
77
forgiveness, 86
peak experiences, 103
men, 82, 115
mental stretching
comfort zone expansion, 126–131
preparation for future, 135–138
restoration, 131–135
mercy, 140
milestone, 43
mind-set, positive
expulsion of negative emotions,
30–34
indicators of confidence, 13
karma, 139–140
perfection standards, 123
power, 140–142
redirection of inner voices, 33–34
modelling, 44
monkey breathing, 132–133
Montessori, Maria (education
leader), 224–225
mood
definition, 79
tracking tips, 79–81, 239
morale, 171
morning people, 143
motivation
assessment, 58–60
benefits, 51
hierarchy of needs, 52–55
indicators of confidence, 13
overview, 51
SMART model, 42
uniforms, 171
work, 55–62
motivator, 56–57
Murray, WH (mountaineer), 138
music, 133, 147

• *N* •

The Naked Leader (Taylor), 248
name, 232

natural school, 161
natural sound recording, 133
Nazi death camp, 14
needs, personal
    generosity to self, 113–114
    hierarchy of needs, 52–55
    romantic relationships, 209, 212
    yours versus others', 37
negative emotions
    assessment, 34–37
    comfort zone expansion, 128
    control, 83–86
    danger signs, 81
    expulsion, 30–34
    health effects, 81
    identification, 233–234
    link to passion, 88
    passion drainers, 94
    passion into action, 97–98
    root issues, 26–30
negative memory, 77
negative stress, 145–147
*Neuro-Linguistic Programming For
    Dummies* (Ready and Burton),
    247
Neuro-Linguistic Programming
    (NLP), 85
neurological levels, 89–93
neuroscience, 78
Nietzsche, Friedrich (philosopher), 94
night owl, 143
Nightingale, Earl (personal
    development guru), 139
NLP fast phobia cure, 85
NLP (Neuro-Linguistic
    Programming), 85

• O •

obesity, 145
objectivity, 213–214
oil, 148
ontology, 90
opinion, 163–164
optimism, 238–239
organisation, 119

organised activity, 225
outdoor time, 226, 240
overwhelmed feeling
    danger signs, 81
    delegation, 115–116
    health effects, 81
    recognition, 32
oxygen, 155

• P •

panic attack, 130–131
Pareto, Vilfredo (economist), 121
Pareto's law, 121–122
passion
    action, 95–99
    definition, 88
    development, 88–89, 94
    drainers, 94
    dream, 94–95
    leadership role, 99
    life purpose, 89, 94, 96–97
    link to negative emotions, 88
    people's response to, 87–88
    powerful living, 179–180
    romantic relationships, 209
patience, 118
patterned fabric, 169
pay, 56
peak experience, 103–104
perfection
    behavior standards, 122–124
    childhood, 112
    children, 220
    delegation, 115–116
    expectations, 111–113
    generosity to self, 113–114
    overview, 111
    procrastination, 116–119
    reality of life, 25, 112–113
    versus excellence, 113
persistence
    procrastination, 118
    success, 234–235
personal competence, 76

personal criticism. *See* criticism
personal growth
　authentic living, 71–72
　definition, 68
　motivation at work, 56
personal identity
　creation, 234
　development, 72–74
　neurological levels, 90
　redundancy, 204
　work, 185–186
personal needs
　generosity to self, 113–114
　hierarchy of needs, 52–55
　romantic relationships, 209, 212
　yours versus others', 37
personal profile, 17
phobia
　cure, 85
　definition, 68, 85
　fear management, 107
　mental stretching, 129–131
　social situations, 54
photograph, 147
physical appearance
　first impression, 165–166
　judgements, 163–165
　overview, 163
　style, 167–172
physical body
　mind–body connection, 144–145
　overview, 143
　physiological needs, 52
physical exercise
　aging, 149
　feel-good factors, 147
　guidelines, 239
　habits, 145
　mind–body connection, 144
　necessity, 145
physical experience, 67–68
physical health
　beliefs, 149–150
　confidence level, 12
　definition, 145
　diet, 148–149

　effect of negative emotions, 81
　future self, 150
　indicators of confidence, 13
　life-work balance, 32–33
　panic attack, 131
　perfection effects, 113
　stress effects, 81, 145–148
　types of stress, 233
　values conflicts, 68–69
physiological needs, 52
planning
　guaranteed success formula, 43–44
　self as role model, 47–48
　SMART model, 41–43
　to-do list, 33
Platts, Brinley (author), 247
play, 225–226
poise, 11
popular culture, 207
positive mind-set
　expulsion of negative emotions,
　　30–34
　indicators of confidence, 13
　karma, 139–140
　perfection standards, 123
　power, 140–142
　redirection of inner voices, 33–34
poverty, 139
power
　daily living, 179–180
　meeting, 190–191
　positive mind-set, 140–142
The Power of Now (Tolle), 248
practice, 156, 192
praise, 221–222
prayer, 144
preparedness, 135–138, 178
presentation. *See also* public
　speaking
　confidence benefits, 11
　confidence definition, 10–11
　fear management, 107
　guidelines for success, 191–192
　mental stretching, 128–129
pretending, 72

pride
  identity development, 73
  name, 232
  work values, 188
princess tale, 125
priorities
  identification, 21–22
  values conflicts, 67
  values identification, 64, 65–66
  values in daily life, 70
proactive behavior, 11
procrastination
  passion drainer, 94
  perfection, 116–119
  time, 118–122
productivity, 56, 57
professional identity, 185–186
professional organisation, 249
professionalism, 188
project, 11
projector, 191–192
promise, 197–199
promotion, 61–62, 129, 197
propaganda, 95
public speaking. *See also*
    presentation
  accent, 154–155
  body posture, 160–162
  breathing tips, 155–157
  fear, 153–154
  integrity, 158–159
  overview, 153
  practice, 156
  taped voice, 154–155
pumpkin seed, 149
purpose, sense of
  connection to, 241
  indicators of confidence, 13
  passion, 89, 94, 96–97
  SMART model, 41–43

• *Q* •

Queen Noor of Jordan (Lisa
    Halaby), 45
quiet moment, 120, 240

• *R* •

racial harassment, 192
rapport, 203
rational thought, 77
Ready, Romilla (*Neuro-Linguistic
    Programming For Dummies*), 247
Ready Solutions (Web site), 249
reason, 142
received pronunciation (RP), 154
recognition
  generosity to self, 113–114
  hierarchy of needs, 53
  motivation at work, 56
  work promotions, 56, 61
Redgrave, Steve (athlete), 45
redundancy, 204
rejection, 202, 211
relationship
  authentic conversations, 160
  confidence wheel, 40–41
  connections, 68, 69
  empathy, 85–86
  guaranteed success formula, 44
  hierarchy of needs, 53
  improvement exercise, 28–29
  motivation at work, 56, 57–58
  others' resistance to new you,
    173–176
  self as role model, 48
  to work, 61
relationship, romantic. *See also* love
  challenges, 214
  change, 216–217
  culture, 206–207
  dating, 210–212
  drama versus romance, 208
  fear, 210–212
  habits, 214
  love strategy, 214–216
  objectivity of friends, 213–214
  overview, 205–206
  partner's needs, 209, 212
  recommitment, 217
  values, 208–210
  view of romance, 207–208

relaxation
  meetings, 191
  mental stretching haven, 131–135
  perfection, 119–120
religion, 90, 139
Remen, Naomi (*The Search for Healing*), 115
resistance, 173–176, 202
resource, 137
responsibility, 56, 189
rest and recuperation (R&R), 131–135
reward
  daily life, 179
  SMART model, 42
  work achievements, 56, 61
rice, 149
right hemisphere, 78
risk taking
  acknowledgment of risk, 24
  aversion to risk, 94
  indicators of confidence, 13
Robbins, Anthony (personal power guru)
  dating, 211
  Unlimited Power, 248
Rogers, Carl (therapist), 115
role model, 44–48, 232
romantic relationship. *See* relationship, romantic
routine
  flexibility, 123–124
  generosity to self, 114
  mood tracking, 80
  procrastination, 117–120
  values in daily life, 70
RP (received pronunciation), 154
R&R (rest and recuperation), 131–135

• S •

safety needs, 52, 222–223
salary, 56
salt, 149
sarcasm, 193

schedule
  flexibility, 123–124
  generosity to self, 114
  mood tracking, 80
  procrastination, 117–120
  values in daily life, 70
The Search for Healing (Remen), 115
secrecy, 10
Sedona Method (Dwoskin), 247
seed, 149
self-actualisation, 53
self-assuredness, 10
self-awareness
  authentic living, 71–72
  blame exercise, 27
  indicators of confidence, 13
  mood tracking, 80
  self as role model, 48
self-esteem
  characteristics of confident people, 17
  definition, 17–18
  hierarchy of needs, 53
  other people's needs, 37
self-help book, 39, 247–248
self-identity. *See* identity
self-improvement, 12, 39
seratonin, 54
setting goals
  confidence wheel, 41
  guaranteed success formula, 43–44
  perfection standards, 122–123
  preparation, 135–138
  procrastination, 117–120
  self as role model, 47–48
  SMART model, 41–43
  stress, 111
sexual harassment, 192
shock, 202
shopping, clothes, 170–172
shyness, 54
The Six Million Dollar Man (TV show), 45
sixth sense, 82
skill, 189–190
sleep, 143, 237

slide, 191–192
SMART model, 41–43
smile, fake, 82
smoking, 149
social anxiety disorder, 54
social competence, 76
social situation, 53–55
speaking, public. *See also*
     presentation
  accent, 154–155
  body posture, 160–162
  breathing tips, 155–157
  fear, 153–154
  integrity, 158–159
  overview, 153
  practice, 156
  taped voice, 154–155
specificity, 41–42, 196
spinach, 149
spirit, 90
sponsorship, 22
standards, personal, 46
state, 80
strengths
  building, 17–18
  childhood accomplishments, 22
  inventory, 19
  visualisation exercise, 21
stress
  acknowledgment of achievements,
     114
  assertiveness, 177–178
  distortion of reality, 26
  goal setting, 111
  health effects, 81, 145–148
  life-work balance, 32–33
  overview, 145
  perfection expectations, 112–113
  types, 233
style, 167–172
success
  assessment, 136
  comfort zone, 127
  formula, 43–44, 140–141
  goal-setting preparation, 136

list, 114–115
  persistence, 234–235
Summers, Heather (*The Book of
     Luck*), 248
sunflower seed, 149
supervision, 56, 57–58
support group, 147, 177–178
sweets, 149
synthesis, 73

• T •

talent
  feedback from others, 20
  ideal job, 187
  inventory, 18–19
  visualisation exercise, 21
Taylor, David (*The Naked Leader*), 248
technology, 191–192
tension, 233
Test Your Emotional Intelligence
     (Dann), 247
thank-you note, 203
theatrical school, 161
Theory X, 57
Theory Y, 57–58
thoughtfulness, 209
time
  alone, 235, 240
  children's play, 226
  creativity, 78
  procrastination, 118–122
  SMART model, 42
  work-life balance, 32–33
Time to Think (Kline), 248
Toastmasters International (speaking
     club), 162
tobacco, 149
to-do list, 33, 116
tolerance, 73
Tolle, Eckart (*The Power of Now*), 248
tough times index, 29–30
toxic environment, 35–37
toxic friend, 35
training, 248–249

trapped feeling, 107
trust, 141, 208–209
truth, 48
Tynan, Ronan (recording artist), 45

• *U* •

UK Council for Psychotherapy, 249
ultimate confidence, 140
Ulysses (Joyce), 96
uniform, 171
Unlimited Power (Robbins), 248

• *V* •

values
  assertiveness, 189
  conflicts, 66–69
  daily life, 69–71
  definition, 90
  goal-setting preparation, 137–138
  identification, 63–69
  indicators of confidence, 12,
      220–221
  integrity, 158–159
  intensity of experiences, 87
  neurological levels, 90
  overview, 63
  relationship to confidence, 18
  romantic relationship, 208–210
  work, 188
victimisation, 193–194
visualisation
  milestones, 43
  overview, 21
  redirection of inner voices, 33–34
  relaxation techniques, 133–135
  translation, 46
voice
  accent, 154–155
  overview, 153
  taped, 154–155
voice, inner
  intuition, 81–82
  overview, 231–232
  reason, 142

redirection, 33–34
self as role model, 48

• *W* •

wants
  careful consideration, 138
  goal-setting preparation, 135
  ideal job, 186–187
  karma, 139–140
water, 148
Watercress (Web site), 249
Watson, Anne (*The Book of Luck*), 248
wealth, 95, 139
Web sites
  aging, 149
  confidence assessment, 17
  intuition information, 82, 248
  professional associations, 249
  public speaking, 162
  training, 248–249
wholemeal bread, 149
women, 82, 115
work. *See also* boss
  achievements, 200–201
  assertiveness, 188–189
  bullying, 192–194
  change, 201–204
  clothing, 166–167, 168, 171
  comfort zone, 127, 129–131
  competencies, 189–190
  confidence wheel, 40–41
  delegation, 115–116
  energy assessment, 35–37
  expression of love, 78
  first impressions, 166–167
  hate for job, 184–185
  ideal job, 186–187
  interview, 203
  life-work balance, 32–33
  mental stretching, 129–131
  motivation, 55–62
  overview, 183–184
  price of success, 127
  procrastination, 116–120
  professional identity, 185–186

work *(continued)*
  relationship to, 61
  sense of self, 184, 185
  types of stress, 233
  unhelpful assumptions, 31
  values, 188
working conditions, 56
writing, 238

• X •

X then Y gridlock scenario, 117–118

• Y •

yoga, 144, 146, 249
You'll See It When You Believe It
  (Dyer), 248
Your Most Confident Self (Web site),
  249

• Z •

zinc, 149

Notes

....

Notes

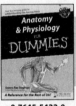

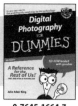
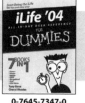